# Aspirations and Realities

**Recent Titles in**
**Contributions in Economics and Economic History**

Corporate Networks and Corporate Control: The Case of the Delaware Valley
*Ralph M. Faris*

Night Boat to New England, 1815-1900
*Edwin L. Dunbaugh*

Income and Inequality: The Role of the Service Sector in the Changing Distribution of Income
*Cathy Kassab*

Rural Change in the Third World: Pakistan and the Aga Khan Rural Support Program
*Mahmood Hasan Khan and Shoaib Sultan Khan*

Soviet Political Economy in Transition: From Lenin to Gorbachev
*A. F. Dowlah*

The Diary of Rexford G. Tugwell: The New Deal, 1932-1935
*Michael Vincent Namorato, editor*

Making Markets: An Interdisciplinary Perspective on Economic Exchange
*Robin Cantor, Stuart Henry, and Steve Rayner*

Technology and U.S. Competitiveness: An Institutional Focus
*W. Henry Lambright and Dianne Rahm, editors*

The Development of the Greek Economy, 1950-1991
*George A. Jouganatos*

Business Finance in Less Developed Capital Markets
*Klaus P. Fischer and George J. Papaioannou, editors*

Logs for Capital: The Timber Industry and Capitalist Enterprise in the Nineteenth Century
*Sing C. Chew*

The American Pulp and Paper Industry, 1900-1940: Mill Survival, Firm Structure, and Industry Relocation
*Nancy Kane Ohanian*

# Aspirations and Realities

*A Documentary History of Economic Development Policy in Ireland since 1922*

James L. Wiles
and
Richard B. Finnegan

Contributions in Economics and Economic History,
Number 137

**Greenwood Press**
Westport, Connecticut • London

**Library of Congress Cataloging-in-Publication Data**

Wiles, James L.
Aspirations and realities : a documentary history of economic development policy in Ireland since 1922 / James L. Wiles and Richard B. Finnegan.
p. cm.—(Contributions in economics and economic history, ISSN 0084-9235 ; no. 137)
Includes bibliographical references (p. ) and index.
ISBN 0-313-27440-1 (alk. paper)
1. Ireland—Economic policy—Sources. 2. Ireland—Economic conditions—Sources. I. Finnegan, Richard B. II. Title. III. Series.
HC260.5.W55 1993
338.9415'009'04—dc20 92-1123

British Library Cataloguing in Publication Data is available.



Library of Congress Catalog Card Number: 92-1123
ISBN: 0-313-27440-1
ISSN: 0084-9235

First published in 1993

Greenwood Press, 88 Post Road West, Westport, CT 06881
An imprint of Greenwood Publishing Group, Inc.

Printed in the United States of America

The paper used in this book complies with the Permanent Paper Standard issued by the National Information Standards Organization (Z39.48-1984).

10 9 8 7 6 5 4 3 2 1

# Contents


| | | |
|---|---|---|
| Preface | | vii |
| Chapter One: | Introduction: The Era of British Control, 1800-1922 | 1 |
| Chapter Two: | From Independence to the "Emergency," 1922-1945 | 15 |
| Chapter Three: | From the "Emergency" to Economic Planning, 1946-1959 | 45 |
| Chapter Four: | From the Advent of Planning to Entry into the European Community, 1959-1972 | 89 |
| Chapter Five: | From Entry to Europe to the Single European Act, 1973-1990 | 127 |
| Statistical Appendix | | 209 |
| Bibliography | | 217 |
| Index | | 225 |

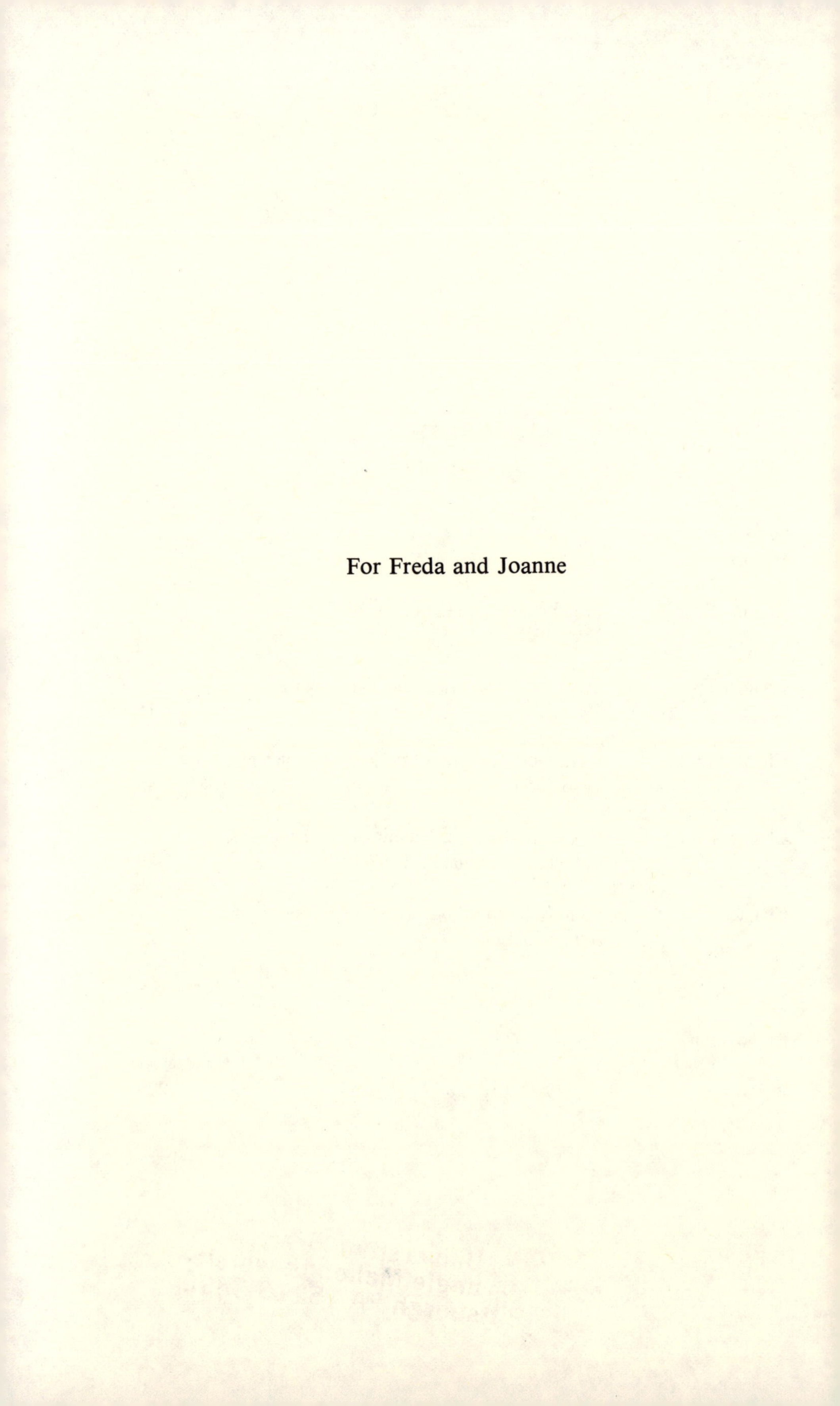

For Freda and Joanne

# Preface

The changes in the Irish economy, both historical and contemporary, are subjects of the teaching and research of both the authors. To illuminate the topic for a broader audience, we organized a lecture series in 1989 at Stonehill College. That series provoked on our part the collection of Irish Official Publications concerning economic development over the past twenty-five years. The search for the documents expanded beyond its initial role as a supplement to the lectures. Ultimately, the project evolved such as to make the documents the central focus of this book.

The purpose of this book is to present these documents, not widely available to the reader, and to provide a companion volume on economic development policy to the many works on the political and social history of modern Ireland. Through the assembled official publications, parliamentary reports, commissions and the like, the reader can explore the assumptions and perspectives on economic development held by decision makers in the Republic since 1922. The paths taken and avoided, the results expected and unexpected, the problems solved and unsolved are presented in the documents. The parties in power, the political and economic contexts of the documents are incorporated in the narrative that links them together.

We were aided in this task by a group of people on whose good will we continually transgressed. Thanks are due to Tony Eklof, Official Publications Librarian of University College Dublin, who helped us find documents unavailable to us elsewhere. We also owe thanks to Geoffry Keating, Vice Consul for Ireland in Boston, and Martin McGovern, Director of Communications at Stonehill. Cynthia Harris and Mark Kane of Greenwood Press were most helpful to us from the initial response to our proposal through to the final production of the book.

Stonehill College is a most hospitable environment in which to pursue Irish Studies. We received support from the Faculty Development Grant Fund and assistance from the Academic Dean's funds for the support of faculty research. Our thanks go to Judy Cruz for her help in typing the manuscript, and to Donna Benoit for her invaluable help both in typing the manuscript and in preparing it for publication. Joanne Scotti Finnegan and Freda MacLeod also deserve thanks for their patience with this project and Freda MacLeod also should be given special thanks for help in tracking down documents in Ireland and work on the index.

We wish to thank the Controller of the Stationary Office of the Republic of Ireland for permission to reproduce the excerpts of Irish government Official Publications included in the book.

We take responsibility for whatever errors are included in the book, as well as for responsibility for what is valuable to the readers. We hope the latter outweighs the former.

# One

# Introduction: The Era of British Control, 1800–1922

In the *Importance of Being Earnest* the governess, Miss Prism, issues the following order to her young charge: "Cecily, you will read your political economy in my absence. The chapter on the fall of the rupee you may omit. It is somewhat too sensational."

Few share with Miss Prism the judgement that the reader of economic history risks an overexcitation of the passions. Still, the question of long-term economic growth in Ireland has rarely been a matter of indifference. For two centuries it has been bound up with a number of emotional issues: the problems of jobs and emigration, the place of agriculture in the economy and society, and economic relations with Britain, to name but a few. Normally, people have not debated the desirability of economic growth for Ireland, although some have argued that it would change the country for the worse. Rather, the debates have centered on means-the policies best calculated to bring about a sustained increase in output, taking into account changes in prices and population.

It is these policies that we have focused upon in selecting documents dating from 1922 to the present. Each one addresses, directly or indirectly, two compelling questions: what are the prospects for economic growth in Ireland, and what should be done to achieve that growth? We have selected official publications of the government of Ireland, not memoirs, letters, or recollections.

Within this context the book seeks to explore assessments of the Irish economy as they were put forth by the governments of Ireland in the periods for which they were responsible. The assessments in the documents include descriptions of the economy's condition, the goals sought by the government, the policy options chosen to achieve those goals, and evaluations of the results. In retrospect, the assessments may be accurate or inaccurate, and the prescriptions may have been right or wrong from the standpoint of their goals, but our concern is on the economic conditions and possibilities as the governments saw them.

Up to the publication of the first *Programme* in 1958 these documents do not usually take the form of formal plans, rather, the various departmental reports, studies, white papers, and commission inquiries provide us with a record that we can probe for the economic aspirations of the governments of Ireland. We can also evaluate these policies in light of the realities of economic performance. After 1958 the documents take on the more formal character of plans with analysis, interpretation, projections, and goals. Planning in Ireland was, and is, more a matter of setting goals and providing incentives than close management of economic activity which adhered to a macroeconomic blueprint. Nevertheless the accumulation of plans provides an extended comprehensive portrait of government aspirations and subsequent realities. The commentary weaves together the documents in order to place them in the context of the conditions in which they were generated. The goals and means are measured against the economic performance for the period that the document covered. Successive Irish governments have stated in their official publications their vision of Irish economic conditions and their policy choices to effect change. This book presents that record.

To set down and analyze this record of goals, means, and ends in economic policy requires drawing upon the indispensible work of economic historians and political historians. They provide the contextual richness which helps to understand the personalities, conflicts, and decisions of Irish leaders. This book is designed to complement those forms of historiography by providing material for the reader who does not have ready access to Irish Official Publications.

Although the theme of economic growth in the nineteenth century is fascinating, this book concentrates on the modern era. The period of union with Britain, when economic policy was made in London, provides the backdrop and covers over 120 years. It is reviewed in this chapter. The remaining chapters are devoted to the period after independence with greater weight placed on the post-World War II years. Particular attention is given to the "planning period" which began in 1958.

While the record is not perhaps "somewhat too sensational," it nonetheless is marked by the drama of Irish governments seeking to overcome the economy's deficiencies. Often overwhelmed by the pressure of external events, government policy sought to stimulate economic growth in a small agricultural economy in order to provide a decent life for its citizens.

The general impression of Irish economic development in the past 200 years is that it was erratic at best and disappointing overall. Studies show that Ireland was poor by European standards in the years before the Famine of 1845 (Mokyr 1983). In more recent times, it appears that the country's real product per capita ranked tenth among twenty-two European nations on the eve of World War I, but had fallen to sixteenth place by 1985 (Kennedy, Giblin, and

McHugh 1988: 14). Whether better outcomes were possible has been a central question of Irish economic history. It is clear, however, that the problem of economic growth in Ireland has not been neglected. Rather, it has occupied a prominent place in official deliberations on both sides of the Irish Sea. Moreover, the quest for national autonomy and independence on the part of Irish nationalists prompted them to incorporate economic dimensions into the nationalist vision. These dimensions served as part of the goal—escape from economic subservience to the UK—and part of the means —the development of native agriculture and industry to reinforce political autonomy. While we concentrate on efforts undertaken after 1922, it is desirable to sketch events dating to the period of Britain's industrial revolution in order to show the long-standing concern about the Irish economy's performance.

Economic outcomes up to 1922 can be stated briefly. Most striking is the decline in population between 1841 and 1921: 6.5 million to 3.1 million. Over five million people emigrated during that period. This demographic phenomenon affected the labor supply and the demand for goods and services in Ireland. The gain in per capita income registered in the post-Famine decades reflects this population loss rather than a significant increase in output. But there were successes as well. Mary Daly (1981:88) cites the considerable achievements of Ulster industry. Cormac O'Grada argues that, despite its difficulies, Irish agriculture proved responsive to price changes, to the advantages of regional specialization, and to opportunities for innovation (O'Grada 1988: 146). The nineteenth century also saw improvements in transportation and communication, banking, and the civil service. Still, agriculture accounted for about fifty-four percent of the Free State's employment in the mid-1920s and the increase in nonagricultural jobs had fallen far short of the pace needed to slow emigration or employ surplus farm labor (Daly 1981:88).

Official efforts to stimulate economic growth in nineteenth-century Ireland are less easily summarized. It became clear relatively early in the century that Ireland required special attention. The overall impression was that growth was possible but not easily attained because of obstacles different from those encountered in England. There were a variety of views on the nature and significance of these obstacles to investment. Was "tranquility" in Ireland a necessary precondition for investment, or would economic development itself promote "tranquility"? Should the government undertake public works projects—roads, bridges, land reclamation and railways—in order to encourage private investment? Were population pressures in Ireland so severe that economic growth was stifled? And, particularly in the post-Famine years, did land tenure arrangements inhibit agricultural improvements?

All of these concerns were addressed in British documents of the period. In the main, they share the belief that if obstacles were removed or reduced, free market forces would ensure that investment and growth would occur. In recent years economic historians and economic theorists have offered other explanations of lagging development in Ireland. For example, Joel Mokyr provides a list of "causal factors" bearing upon that question for the nineteenth century. He suggests that geographical, social, and entrepreneurial considerations (among others) be examined (Mokyr 1983). Eoin O'Malley (1989) focuses on the continuing problems encountered by the "latecomer" to industrialization. In view of "the barriers to entry" faced by newcomers to an industry, he is particularly critical of the free market path to industrialization. Our aim, however, is not to assess the efficacy of the various recent models, but rather to emphasize approaches taken by policy makers at the time. That is, we provide a brief political and economic context for official attempts to achieve and maintain long-term growth in Ireland. Those attempts can then be examined in conjunction with more detailed interpretive works. In this chapter on the era of British control we cite (but do not reproduce) selected official publications which relate to Irish economic growth. Subsequent chapters will contain excerpts from Irish official publications.

The Act of Union which took effect on January 1, 1801 can serve as a starting point. This Act brought about a major change in the political relationship between England and Ireland. It established a single Parliament in London to legislate for the two countries. It also allowed for the gradual lowering of trade barriers and arranged for fiscal unity between the two islands. Although later generations in Ireland denounced the Act as inimical to their economic well being, the debates on the Act took place at a time when Irish economic prospects appeared bright. The Industrial Revolution had come to Ireland in the 1780s and 1790s. Changes in organization, scale, and technology were evident in such industries as flour, textiles, glass, and brewing (Cullen 1972: 190). If these developments were incomplete by English standards, they were nonetheless well enough along to pose some threat to manufacturers in England. All this combined with the wartime demand for Irish agricultural output to create a generally buoyant atmosphere.

For the most part, proponents and opponents of the Union saw the Irish economy in this light. William Pitt, the English Prime Minister, argued that the Act of Union and Catholic Relief would calm Ireland and would stimulate capital flows to that country. This process would narrow the economic disparity between the two islands (Bolton 1966: 374). British manufacturers tended to concur in this view. They believed that the Irish had several important advantages: a smaller debt and lower taxes, cheaper land and labor, and an ability to absorb English capital and skilled labor as machinery became more commonplace in industry. (Bolton 1965: 370). By 1800, English cotton manufacturers were confident enough not to oppose Union but the woolen industry was still wary of Irish prospects and argued against the Act (Bolton 1966: 200). Anti-Union spokesmen on the Irish side asserted that their country's recent progress made the Union unnecessary (Malcomson 1978: 58). Indeed, the Union would threaten that prosperity by obliging the Irish to assume some of England's growing public debt (Bolton 1966: 79). Irish cotton manufacturers, not surprisingly, employed the infant industry argument and opposed the Union. They received some concessions on the timing of tariff reduction, but all in all "the Irish opposition failed signally to make full use of this commercial disquiet" (Ibid: 194).

It appears then that, in the late 1790s, observers in both countries held optimistic expectations of Ireland's continued economic progress. A number of realities tended to deflate that optimism. In the political arena, George III rejected any movement toward Catholic emancipation, impairing the Union's assumption of a more tranquil Ireland. Economic considerations also worked against Ireland's aspirations. We might mention her lack of coal and the huge advantages of scale and external economies enjoyed by English manufacturers (Dickson 1978: 111). Agriculture, too, was beginning to show signs of weakness. "Already by 1800 competition for employment and plots of land among laborers was increasing, reducing their already minimal standard of living" (Daly 1981: 12). But, as in industry, "these ominous developments were not recognized by those living in Ireland at the time and are obviously much more apparent with hindsight" (Ibid: 12).

By the mid-1820s it was clear that the benign results expected of the Union had not materialized. In fact, the worst cases foreseen by Irish protectionists had come to pass, although most economic historians now agree that the Union had little to do with those outcomes. The government was not unaware of the situation.

> After the Napoleonic Wars the political and economic difficulties of Ireland became increasingly evident, and the "Irish Question" came to occupy the attention of Government and the time of Parliament more and more. (Black 1960: 2)

The *Report* from the Select Committee on the Employment of the Poor in Ireland catalogues the depressed conditions of the early 1820s. Some observations in their Report proved to be remarkably relevant to the Famine conditions of the 1840s: inadequate incomes and lack of recourse to markets. Other sections of the Report dealt with themes that have persisted over time: population problems and the question of a capital shortage in Ireland. Finally, the Committee recognized the difficulties of effecting long-term change and suggested, somewhat tentatively, that government should take the lead.

The overall policy goal was clear enough to observers at the time. It was and is the classic aim of economic development: to bring about "a substantial increase in the real product and real income per head of Ireland" (Black 1960: 239). No single solution to Irish poverty came to the fore. No single act, such as the Union, was put forward as the answer to the Irish question. Rather, several approaches to the situation appeared.

In contrast to the Act of Union, they addressed directly the problem of Ireland's economic underdevelopment. The Union sought economic progress through political restructuring and reform. In accordance with contemporary opinion, the proposals emerging some twenty-five years later took the opposite tack: measures that successfully promoted economic growth would also reduce political, social, and religious tensions in Ireland. The Committee on the Employment of the Poor was particularly keen on this point. The members noted that "disquiet" in Ireland inhibited the flow of English private capital, despite the profit potential. The efforts of Daniel O'Connell and Young Ireland during this period indicated that the "disquiet" had, at least, the potential of attaining Home Rule, O'Connell's goal. At most, it might lead to an independent Ireland, Young Ireland's goal. Presumably, these movements discouraged private capital flows but they also revealed the degree to which Parliament's legislation for Ireland was either unfair, such as the incorporation of the tithe into land rents, or inappropriate, such as the Poor Law. Tranquility could be restored by "encouraging industry among the people." Thus, "some (public) assistance may wisely be given by the nation to stimulate private exertions." While the "danger of public interference" is cited frequently, the scale of the "Irish Question" sometimes led Parliamentary observers to question the efficacy of the laissez-faire approach.

While there was general agreement that economic growth was a proper goal, there was some disagreement on the specific approaches needed to promote Irish economic development. Three main diagnoses and their related policy initiatives emerged in the several decades before the Famine: (1) the notion that overpopulation was stifling Ireland's chances for progress; (2) the view that Ireland suffered from underinvestment and required substantial capital accumulation to cure her ills; and (3) the sense that existing land tenure arrangements were incompatible with widespread, sustained economic growth (Solow 1971: 2). The first two, distinct but related, were deeply entrenched in classical economic theory. They formed the basis for many of the policy recommendations made in the 1820s and 1830s. The land tenure approach, although mentioned in the discussion of the time, was not yet the force it was to become after the Famine (Ibid: 2). Consequently, we will defer a consideration of that movement until later in the chapter.

The overpopulation view was perhaps the most widely accepted explanation of Irish poverty, pre-Famine. Too many people were placing too much pressure on too little land, with the result that incomes tended to fall to the subsistence level. This is, of course, the famous Malthusian problem which combines population growth and the law of diminishing returns. Joel Mokyr quotes Malthus on the subject. In a letter to David Ricardo in 1817, Malthus wrote that "the land in Ireland is infinitely more peopled than in England; and to give full effect to the natural resources of the country a great part of the population should be swept from the soil" (Mokyr 1980: 159). Mokyr comments that "the 'overpopulation' explanation became conventional wisdom in nineteenth-century England."

To turn this vicious circle into a benign sequence it is necessary to alter the labor to land ratio, first by reducing the number of workers, and secondly by increasing the amount of usable land. Here were two pillars of classical policy on which pre-Famine hopes rested. In the first instance, emigration was to reduce population pressure, in particular the more permanent transatlantic emigration to Canada and the United States. Emigration questions are dealt with in the massive *Reports and Minutes of Evidence from the Select Committee on Emigration from the United Kingdom* (1826 and 1827).

The existence of a "superabundant population" was not confined to Ireland. In fact, English and Scottish hand-loom weavers had lost their jobs when power looms came into operation in the early 1820s, and emigration was recommended as a way to alleviate their distress. Having faced this concern, the Select Committee concluded its Report with the warning that the major emigration initiative must be directed at Ireland, where distress was more widespread still. The third of these reports added that Irish emigration should be an overseas movement, lest a flood of migrants enter England and compound the problems there. Malthus himself emphasized that point in his testimony before the Committee. He went on to say that emigration was necessary to permit Ireland to realize her "very great capabilities" of becoming a rich and flourishing country.

Both the Committee on the Employment of the Poor in Ireland and the Committee on Emigration cited the need to expand employment opportunities in Ireland by increasing that country's stock of arable land and its stock of industrial capital. While emigration would reduce the (superabundant) supply of labor, these other initiatives would tend to increase the demand for labor.

Evidence before the Select Committee on Emigration as well as other documentary evidence refers more explicitly to the problem of underinvestment. Two approaches emerge from these pages: (1) the policy of land reclamation; and (2) the provision or upgrading of such public goods as roads, bridges, and navigation facilities.

Under the first heading, Commissioners had been appointed earlier in the century to "consider the practicality of draining the bogs in Ireland." The possibilities associated with this undertaking have retained their allure to the present day. The four early Reports (1810-1814) tell us something about the nature and scope of the project. In the 1820s, an expert witness, Alexander Nimmo, outlined the prospects and problems of bog reclamation in the West of Ireland for the Emigration Committee. Interestingly, his testimony alluded to land tenure arrangements as a factor in realizing gains from these projects. Specifically, Nimmo pointed out that lease holdings and common rights to bog land "prevents the appropriation of any portion of it to a great system of improvement."

The second type of policy focused on public goods, or the "infrastructure." Among the many documents dealing with this question we can cite the *Second Report of the Commissioners of Public Works, Ireland* (1835).

Each of these approaches envisioned government expenditure as a necessary prerequisite for profitable private investment. Land reclamation, of course, aimed at easing the Malthusian trap by increasing the amount of usable land in Ireland. A Report to the Devon Commission in 1845 labeled some 3.5 million acres of Irish land "improveable." It is not surprising, then, that land reclamation schemes were widely discussed and widely supported as the better alternative to emigration (Black 1960: 178-79). It was a slow process, legislatively and administratively. Nonetheless, by 1871 about one-half of the "improveable" lands had been reclaimed (Ibid: 187).

The public works approach was also consistent with the orthodox political economy of the time. Economists recognized that private capital was not likely to support such undertakings and that the government had a legitimate, if not sharply defined, role to play. The expectation was that private enterprise would then build upon the public foundation. (Ibid: 178). The record shows that much was done in the area of public works during the pre-Famine period. What were the results of these varied initiatives? A detailed survey of the pre-Famine economy is beyond the scope of this chapter. It can hardly be doubted, however, that "the Irish were abysmally poor by standard criteria" (O'Grada 1988: 15), although O'Grada and Mokyr have pointed out that the picture was not entirely bleak.

Looking at agricultural performance, it seems fair to say that the pre-Famine picture remains a bit cloudy. The traditional view that Irish agriculture was stagnant in the decades before 1845 is not altogether accurate (Ibid: 66). Somewhat tentative estimates of productivity, crop yields, and output indicate that agriculture did quite well under constraints not faced by English farmers: "less land per worker, poorer soils, lower prices" (Ibid: 54). There were other problems also. Internal communication had improved dramatically but it was still inferior to the system in England. Investment in physical and human capital remained low. All told, O'Grada holds that "our estimate of pre-Famine output (does not) deny the image of a 'ramshackle, ill-balanced agricultural system'." Moreover, whatever gains *were* registered in that period were unequally distributed. "By implication access to land was highly unequal, and inequality in pre-Famine Irish agriculture matched that found in many underdeveloped counties today" (Ibid: 66-67).

The Famine itself prompted Parliament to act further on Ireland's behalf. In this instance, of course, the problem was one of short-term relief and income maintenance. While the Famine certainly had far reaching consequences for the Irish economy, Famine-related documents take us away from our emphasis on policies calculated to effect long-term economic change. However, we can sketch briefly the events of the mid-1840s to convey some sense of the disaster's magnitude.

The relief programs' weaknesses were due partly to ideological biases and partly to a misreading of Irish economic conditions. On the one hand, free market considerations were difficult to overcome. At the same time, the absence of a retail network in much of Ireland limited the efficacy of monetary relief payments (Cullen 1972: 132). In the event, between one-half and one million people died, most from "Famine Fever" (Kennedy, Giblin, and McHugh 1988: 4). By 1851, the date ascribed to the Famine's end, Irish population had fallen to 6.6 million from a level of 8.2 million in 1841. In that period one to one-and-a-half million people emigrated (Daly 1981: 24).

By the time of the Famine, then, it appears that the structural approaches taken by policy makers had only a limited impact on Irish economic performance. Nonetheless, this overall strategy reasserted itself after the Famine. The fall in population revived hopes that a more favorable labor/land ratio would bring better results. In this context, attention focused more and more on landlord-tenant relations as the key to progress. What came to be known as the "Land Question" now rivaled population theories as an explanation for Ireland's economic backwardness.

The issue was by no means purely, or even mainly, economic. Barbara Solow wondered if by concentrating on the land question, the Irish had "sacrificed economic progress on the altar of Irish nationalism" (Solow 1971: 204). Still, reform proponents argued that if their proposals were enacted economic gains would ensue, directly or indirectly. Black separates these proposals into two categories. The first type did emphasize economic progress—maximum real product—as a goal. The second set of proposals looked "to the security of the existing rural population as a goal" (Black 1960: 70). In the latter case, it was said, security of tenure would enhance the prospects for economic growth. There were major differences in the underlying rationales of these two approaches. The first assumed that English agricultural structure and practice were most conducive to progress and that they should be adopted in Ireland. This meant cultivation on medium to large farms "held by capitalist tenants under lease from improving landlords, and worked by wage-paid labor" (Ibid: 70). The second view held that the English system was not appropriate for Ireland and could not be attained. Simply put, in England "absolute ownership of land by landlords had not proved unacceptable to the people. This was not so in Ireland" (Boylan and Foley 1984: 106). Rather, proposals in this category "sought to see established a system of peasant proprietorship or copyhold tenancy" (Black 1960: 70). As time went on, advocates of this approach frequently pointed to Continental agriculture as proof that small farming could be efficient.

In the event, the Land Act of 1870 recognized to some extent the difference between the two economies. It stipulated that landlord-tenant relations could be based "on concepts of status and custom," rather than on "free contract" (Black 1960: 69). The Act "legalized the Ulster custom (which) enabled tenants to claim compensation for improvements or eviction" (Daly 1981: 45). The 1870 law also made some provision for land purchase by tenants.

The second Land Act, that of 1881, came into being under less favorable economic circumstances. As agricultural prices fell, shorter term cyclical considerations once again took precedence over the longer term structural view. Inability to pay rent had become the pressing issue and the Act established a mechanism for determining "fair rent." In effect fair rents meant reduced rents, which "helped to tide farmers over difficult years" (Daly 1981: 48). Mary Daly states that by reducing his income the Act "marked the end of the Irish landlord." Finally, the 1881 law also provided for land purchase. The Ashbourne Act of 1885 furthered this option by allowing purchasers to borrow the full amount of the selling price (Ibid: 49).

It appears, therefore, that land legislation encompassed some of the major recommendations of the more radical classical political economy: tenure that was more secure and in accordance with Irish custom, as well as opportunities for tenants to purchase land. It reflects as well the reorganization of Irish political movements after the Famine, especially the creation of the Land League by Michael Davitt in 1879 and the Home Rule League in 1873, which coalesced under the leadership of Charles Stewart Parnell in 1879.

We should note at first that Irish farmers prospered in the twenty years or so between the Famine and the first Land Act. However, while the period 1850-1875 was one of "prosperity interrupted by temporary setback, (the years after 1879) brought stagnation occasionally disturbed by short periods of prosperity" (Vaughan 1984: 40). In the first period, land reform does not seem to have been essential to agricultural progress. Indeed, Vaughan holds that earlier granting of the three Fs (fixed tenancy, fair rents, and free sale) would have resulted in *higher* rents and *more* evictions. The crisis of 1879 ushered in a long-term decline in agriculture. In this setting, investment in land became less attractive and land purchases by tenants fell short of expectations. It was only after 1900 that most tenants purchased their farms. Nonetheless, by the time of the First World War, "one tenant in four was still paying rent" (Daly 1981: 51). Mary Daly also points out that under the land purchase schemes there was, in fact, no redistribution of the land. "The irregularities of rural Ireland" remained and "land purchase brought little benefit to the many tenants whose farms were too small to support a family" (Ibid: 51-52).

As we have seen, the aspirations and policy prescriptions of British political economy stemmed from certain assumptions about the proper structure for an agrarian economy. Nineteenth-century observers were absorbed with this approach —the focus on structure rather than performance.

> Because of the well established obsession with landlord-tenant relations, and the events of 1879-1882, the whole issue of Irish land came to be viewed exclusively in terms of ownership and occupation. The minutiae of agricultural improvement and rural organization seemed dull. (Vaughan 1984: 40)

Assessments of Irish agriculture have continued to emphasize structure up to our own time. Cormac O'Grada states that "the goals and achievements of the ordinary Irish farmer and farm worker have attracted little attention." Moreover, "work on the humdrum details of farming practice and technique has been neglected" (O'Grada 1988: 46-47). As scholars gradually provide some of these details, however, Irish farmers appear to have been responsive to price changes and to the advantages of regional specialization. They were also aware of and willing to adopt new techniques, including larger farms to realize economies of scale from innovation (Ibid: 146).

After the virtual collapse of Irish industry in the early part of the nineteenth century, hopes for economic development centered on agriculture. Industry was not ignored completely, but in the main its reemergence was anticipated only in the wake of improvements in Ireland's infrastructure and the status of its agriculture. There was also the long-standing quest for "tranquility" in Ireland as a prerequisite for private investment. The Land Acts addressed this latter point. But in a more immediate fashion, Parliament ventured into the industrial sector itself by forming a Select Committee on Irish Industries in 1885. Its charge was to "inquire into the material resources of Ireland, and into the present condition of its manufacturing and productive industries." The Committee also hoped to present recommendations on ways to improve those industries. However, because of its appointment late in the Session, the Committee prepared only a proposed draft of a preliminary report on its activities.

Once again, Ireland's industrial potential was favorably cited. And once again, this review identified structural problems which hampered development. Many of the problems were familiar: the need for adequate land drainage and the rather serious limitations inherent in public transportation and communication, railroads in this instance. Other observations were somewhat more novel. The Committee emphasized the virtues of technical education, a topic of interest in England as it faced competition from German industry. And the Committee suggested reforesting in Ireland as a means of utilizing poor land and as a way to obtain charcoal for indigenous industries. All in all, however, the report left no illusions about the state of Irish industry. Despite the country's potential, its "manufacturing and productive industries" were "in a most unsatisfactory and deplorable condition." In retrospect, it does seem that this picture was too bleakly drawn. The Committee does agree that the linen industry in the north was prospering. Engineering and ship building in the north also deserved mention. Still, for much of the country it was probably fair to state, as the Committee did, that "There is manifest in many districts of Ireland 'a total absence of life.'"

Something of this pessimism and sense of urgency was also found in the Reports of the Royal Commission on Irish Public Works in the late 1880s. There, too, emphasis was on the railways as an agent of development. The greater part of railway investment in Ireland was carried out by the private sector, but the Tramway Acts (1883-1896) subsidized the building of light "feeder" lines in remote areas. The Congested Districts Board (1891) also contributed to railway construction. However, these government initiatives had only limited success in achieving their goal: solving the special economic problems of such areas as Donegal and several counties in Connaught (Daly 1981: 53-54; Cullen 1971: 152-53).

We conclude this chapter by coming full circle to an issue joined at the time of Union: the question of the financial arrangements between the two countries. Throughout the nineteenth century, the Irish had registered frequent complaints about the tax burden imposed upon them by the Union. A number of House of Commons Committees investigated these allegations, with little practical effect. In the 1890s, however, a new consideration prompted another inquiry into the matter. This was the prospect of Home Rule for Ireland, a contentious Parliamentary issue raised initially in the previous decade and embodied anew in the Home Rule Bill of 1893. In preparing the Bill, the House of Commons requested a fresh review of these "financial arrangements." The findings are contained in the *Final Report of the Royal Commission on the Financial Relations Between Great Britain and Ireland* (1896).

The points on which the Committee agreed indicate that important changes were in the offing. In addition to acknowledging Irish fiscal grievances, the members also concluded "that Great Britain and Ireland must, for the purposes of this inquiry, be considered as separate entities." A less conceptual separation was now only a quarter-century away.

While the depth and breadth of Ireland's economic problems cannot be denied, the nineteenth-century Irish can claim some successes in industry and in agriculture. It is also true that there were notable achievements registered in the service sector, "where English competition was less of a problem" (Daly 1981: 84). Such accomplishments came in the face of an overriding problem: the proximity to England and Ireland's close economic ties to that industrial power. Fluctuations in English income had a major impact on Irish agricultural exports and, in turn, these export fluctuations affected Irish income and spending. If the outcomes fell short of aspirations, it is because the aspirations were derived in large measure from a model of economic change that glossed over economic, social, and political realities.

Although he is referring explicitly to the Land Act of 1870, it is tempting to broaden Black's assertion that "it is difficult to exempt the economists from the charge of having offered the wrong advice at the right time and the right advice at the wrong time" (Black 1960: 71). This lament is clearly in accord with Keynes' dictum about the power of economic ideas, whether they are right or whether they are wrong. We might debate their precise influence in this instance but it remains true that a considerable amount of the economists' thought did find its way into public policy —too much, in fact, for Irish tastes. The "Limerick Declaration" of 1868 "announced that 'Ireland had had enough of political economy'" (Boylan and Foley 1984: 113). If British political economy did not transform Ireland, the Irish Question did help to transform British political economy. The Irish experience moved some economists to question both laissez-faire tenets and the penchant for policies based on abstractions too removed from reality.

# *Two*

# From Independence to the "Emergency," 1922–1945

The final ten years of British rule in Ireland were tumultuous ones. Between 1912 and 1922 there occurred the acrimonious debate over and passage of Home Rule, the 1914-1918 war and the Easter Rising of 1916. At the end of the period came the Anglo-Irish War of 1920-1921. The war ended in peace negotiations and the 1922 Treaty which granted Commonwealth status as a Free State to Ireland's twenty-six southern countries. However, the clash between pro- and anti-Treaty forces in the Irish Civil War of 1922-1923 further delayed a return to normalcy.

Great expectations attended the departure of the British because their withdrawal had seemed to many a sufficient condition for economic growth in Ireland. Well established departments and institutions had been transferred to Irish control in an orderly way. As Meenan says: "It appeared to be self-evident that, once the framing of policy was regained by Irishmen, progress would be quickly made" (Meenan 1970: 272).

Whether this view placed too much emphasis on political change, and too little on unchanged economic realities, is debatable. For example, some have questioned the appropriateness to Irish conditions of two central economic institutions inherited from Britain: the joint stock banking System and trade unionism (Lee 1989: 89). In any event, much was certainly expected of the Free State government as it sought to "frame policy." As a first order of business, attention turned to an examination of the economy and its prospects for growth.

It was more difficult then than now to obtain a reasonably clear picture of an economy's overall performance. Today, National Income figures, unemployment data and the like permit the type of measurement that was not attainable in the 1920s. For that same reason it was not feasible then for policy makers to stipulate precise economic goals such as growth paths or changes in unemployment rates. Nonetheless, it was evident at the time that Ireland was in the throes of the worldwide postwar recession, with agricultural prices and incomes being particularly depressed. The implications for Ireland's balance of payments and the economy as a whole were well understood.

After the strains of the years 1916-1922 it was understandable that the new government undertook economic policy with some caution. Political stability and domestic quietude were primary aims and an orderly, businesslike approach to the economy seemed best suited to the times. It was also in keeping with the attitude prevalent in the post-World War I international economy: the attempt to return to the good old days by restoring such old familiar ways as free trade and the gold standard. Moreover, civil servants trained in the British tradition were not disposed to recommend radical departures from past policies. Nor would such departures have found much support in the economic literature of the day.

The major economic documents of the 1920s, which contain modest policy aspirations, reflect these conditions. The documents focus on agriculture as the leading sector in the economy and on dairying as the backbone of that sector. They look to private enterprise and individual initiative, rather than the government, as the key to economic progress. And they espouse a free trade position as the best way to enhance Irish prosperity.

The configuration of partisan interests also conspired to structure economic choices into a conservative neo-classical framework. The Civil War had been fought over the degree of autonomy from Great Britain and the conditions of that autonomy. Those who had accepted the Treaty of 1922 were the ones most willing to accept linkage with London. This involved the partition of Ireland, the use of Irish ports, the oath to the Crown and the payment of land annuities. This group, made up of larger farmers, businessmen, and the urban professional class, were as disposed to a conservative approach to economic policy as they were to political compromise. The political party emerging from the pro-treaty Irish Nationalists was called Cumann na nGaedheal and was a middle-class-based party. Supporters of this party were supporters of the Sinn Fein Independence movement. However, they were tired of the martial law and violence and accepted dominion status for Ireland. Major social and economic transformation was hardly their policy of choice. This party governed the Free State from 1922 to 1932. Thus it is no surprise to find in the documents modest aspirations and a hewing to economic orthodoxy that was as unshakable as it was unproductive. The political leaders responsible for the various departments reflected the interests that supported the party. The initial Minister of Finance, Ernest Blythe, and Secretary to the Department of Finance, Joseph Brennan, had in common a view that state expenditure should be cut, and a hostility to labor. Blythe reduced state expenditures from £42 million in 1923-1924 to £24 million in 1926-1927. Patrick Hogan, the Minister for Agriculture, as did others, placed the responsibility for economic growth on stimulating the amount and quality of agricultural output, which in the decade produced little more than stagnation.

As noted below, the disposition of the government was reflected in the conservative free trade position of the Fiscal Inquiry Committee in 1923 which echoed the sentiments of the government that created it.

The administration of economic policy, such as it was, was located in the Department of Finance. This department, wedded to fiscal orthodoxy, was never counterbalanced in the early years by the Department of Industry and Commerce under Gordon Campbell (Lee 1989: 121). Economic policy was based upon rigidly orthodox finance and it may not be an overstatement by J. J. Lee to say government finance policy "amounted to a virtual abdication in favor of established financial interests" (Lee 1989: 111). In the late 1920s when Campbell began to challenge the noninterventionist posture, he was frustrated by the power of the Department of Finance and the orthodoxy of the Cosgrave cabinet.

The interests that might have supported greater economic interventionist policies had been excluded from a major policy role because of the independence movement and the Civil War. To examine Labour first we must return to the rise of Sinn Fein from 1916 to 1918. After the 1916 rising, the Labour Party was thrust into a choice between contesting the 1918 election in Ireland on a class basis, that is, advocating that the working class stick together to advance radical economic reform, or uniting with the broader umbrella of the nationalist movement Sinn Fein. Labour chose the latter path and submerged their economic differences with the other sectors of Sinn Fein. Sinn Fein won a major victory in the 1918 election throughout Ireland, save Ulster. The victory of this broad front with its more conservative approach to economic policy drew Labour's claws and left them a small party never able to move radical state economic intervention onto the agenda after 1922. While the Labour Party was the principal opposition to Cumann na nGaedheal from 1922 to 1927, it was not as large as the segment of Sinn Fein which had lost the Civil War and which refused to take their seats in the Dail. It was this group that accepted a greater degree of government activism in the economy but it would not get to implement those policies until 1932.

Thus, by default, the dominant economic perspective was based upon free trade, a balanced budget, and private sector initiatives for growth. The socialist alternative rooted in a Labour party was stunted at birth. An alternative perspective rooted in Sinn Fein was excluded until 1932 by the abstention of the anti-treaty nationalists from participation in government.

In this political context, beginning in 1922 the Free State Government pursued a series of inquiries which assessed the state of the economy and examined past policies and practices in light of the new political environment. The Commission on Agriculture (1922), the Fiscal Inquiry Committee (1923), and the Banking Commission of 1926 provided a detailed sketch of the Irish economy in both its "real" and monetary aspects. Many of the issues joined in those investigations (and the aspirations voiced) were familiar: how to accelerate national output, the role of agriculture in the economy and in society as a whole, the relative merits of tillage and dairying, the prospects for industrial development and the related question of trade restrictions, balance of payments problems, and finally, the efficacy of Irish financial institutions in promoting economic development. These themes, and others dealt with in the inquiries, continue to occupy policy makers.

In keeping with its central place in Ireland, a position enhanced by the loss of Northern industry through partition, agriculture was the first area examined. The government established the Commission on Agriculture in November of 1922. The Commission was to examine the causes of the depression in agriculture and to recommend measures which would help that crucial sector of the economy achieve "future expansion and prosperity." The Commission focused on such considerations as state aid to agriculture, education and the size of holdings. It acknowledged that the question of protective duties was also of central importance, but noted that issue had been taken up by the Fiscal Inquiry Committee, appointed in June of 1923.

Drawing upon the testimony of industry representatives, these two early Free State inquiries describe in considerable detail the problems and prospects of virtually every sector in the Irish economy. Statistical information is meager and much of the evidence presented appears to be impressionistic. From time to time, the Committees note that testimony is clearly at variance with widely known fact, or is contradictory, or that a witness has committed an elementary economic blunder.

Still, several major themes emerge. All agree that agriculture is Ireland's premier industry, although in the future more balanced growth would be desirable. The majority of the Agricultural Committee holds that the State's role in agricultural development should be directed primarily at education and technical assistance in an increasingly complex international economy. In that connection, the Report stresses the need for improvements in the quality of Irish dairy products.

## *COMMISSION ON AGRICULTURE*

### *Introduction*

*1. The Commission on Agriculture which now presents its Final Report was appointed on the 2nd November, 1922, and held its first sitting on the 3rd November, 1922. It has sat fifty-six times in public and thirty-eight times in private session.*

*2. It has examined one hundred and twenty-one witnesses representing every phase of agricultural thought and activity. It has already presented Interim Reports on Tobacco Growing, The Marketing and Transit of Butter and Eggs, Agricultural Credit and the Licensing of Bulls.*

*3. The wide and comprehensive scope of the terms of reference indicates the far-reaching importance of agriculture in An Saorstat. The most convincing proof of this fact is afforded by the following estimate of the exports from An Saorstat during 1922:*

*Farm Produce .. .. .. 68 per cent.*
*Raw material .. .. .. 4 do.*
*Manufactured goods .. .. 15 do.*
*Drink and Tobacco .. .. 13 do.*

*If half the export of drink and tobacco are included with farm produce, these figures would show that between 70 and 75 per cent of the total exports from An Saorstat are farm produce. Furthermore, as something like 50 per cent of the farm produce, produced within An Saorstat is consumed within An Saorstat, it seems to be quite clear that about 75 per cent of the real wealth produced within An Saorstat is farm produce.*

*4. Agriculture is the foundation on which the commercial and business life of the country is based, and the circumstances that affect agriculture react sensibly through the entire economic life of the nation. It is for this very reason that alarm is not unnaturally felt when agriculture is depressed as it is at the present time; but dependence on a single industry has both its advantages and its disadvantages. On the one hand, it connotes a rural population, capable of supporting itself in the matter of food supplies and, therefore, not so sensitive to economic depression as a large and highly articulated urban population. On the other hand, a country which is chiefly urban and whose occupations are mainly industrial may benefit by lower food prices which agricultural depression implies; and the prosperity of these urban interests may enable the burden to be so adjusted as to relieve the rural section. In Ireland no relief can be obtained by agriculture by shifting the burden on to other industries, and agriculture must, therefore, find its salvation from within, or it must perish.*

*5. A great Irish political philosopher who lived in the 18th century, Edmund Burke, in his pamphlet—"Thoughts and Details on Scarcity, " (a suggestive title at the present time) says— "To provide for us in our necessities is not in the power of government. It would be a vain presumption in statesmen to think they can do it. The people maintain them, and not they the people. It is in the power of government to prevent much evil, and it can do very little positive good in this or perhaps anything else." While we do not commend these words in their literal meaning, we think it timely to give them publicity, because much of the evidence laid before us revealed a belief that the state possesses, or should possess, the philosopher's stone that can solve all economic and social ills. We do not accept this view; but we do believe that where the people are industrious, enlightened and alert, the state will reflect the same qualities. We feel compelled to make these observations, lest some set too high a value on the proposals we make for state assistance towards agriculture. We do not wish to belittle the power of wise state action; but we consider that the overwhelming stimulus for betterment will come from voluntary effort, collective and individual, on the part of the people themselves.*

*LIMITATIONS OF STATE ASSISTANCE*

*18. A number of proposals involving state assistance to agriculture in one form or another have been submitted to us. It therefore appears desirable to lay down the general principles which, in our opinion, should govern the policy of the government in this respect.*

*19. We consider that state funds should be mainly applied towards the promotion and attainment of better practice both in the production and marketing of agricultural produce. This much to be desired object will mainly result from a better understanding both of the theory and practice of farming, and we regard education in these matters as the main concern of the state. We firmly believe in the co-operative system, as calculated to promote better business methods, and, we consider that the state may, with advantage, spend substantial sums in the teaching of practical co-operation. This proposal is developed at more length in another portion of our report.*

*20. It has been represented to us that the development of the home market through the agency of protective duties might be of advantage to the home food producer. This involves a consideration of great complexity which is not within the terms of reference, and which has been the subject of enquiry by a special committee. We would only observe that, while the day may come when the home market will absorb the bulk of our home-grown agricultural produce at profitable rates and provide industrial products in exchange, the country must for many years rely on its export trade with which to buy the requirements that are not produced at home. While this condition lasts Ireland will be compelled to sell her exports in competition with other countries in a market that will, in all probability, be open to all comers. Any measures, therefore, which tend to increase the cost of the produce of the land will reduce our purchasing power abroad, and be prejudicial to the country's trade.*

*21. Apart from very exceptional cases, we do not favour subsidies, grants, bounties, guaranteed prices or any such measures of direct assistance. In a country like Ireland, which is mainly agricultural, the cost of such assistance will be paid, for the most part, by the agricultural community itself by passing money from one pocket to another with the added expense due to the cost of administrative services.*

*22. There are, however, certain operations of special experimental character, which it is unreasonable to expect private capital to finance in the early stages, such as the growing of tobacco, sugar beet, the manufacture of industrial alcohol, or the reclamation of boglands. In such cases the state might, with advantage, assist to a limited extent by means of direct subsidy; but even here, we counsel extreme caution, as there should be a real and genuine prospect of the venture (if the state experiment proved successful) being taken up on a general scale by private capital.*

*23. We have already in an interim report made recommendations in regard to state credit for agriculture. It has always been the policy of the state to lend money to farmers at favourable rates, repayable over long periods, for the purpose of productive expenditure, such as the erection of buildings and the drainage and fencing of lands. We are of opinion that this policy should be continued.*

*ALTERNATIVE EMPLOYMENT IN RURAL AREAS*

*125. (a) Reclamation and Drainage of Land: The question of to what extent the Irish bogs could be reclaimed and made available for agriculture is intimately bound up with the problem of the utilization of peat for fuel. If the land at present under bog could be reclaimed and turned into arable land the agricultural output of the country would be greatly increased, but this very desirable development must necessarily await the results of the experiments to be conducted on the peat fuel question. This matter has been very fully dealt with by the Peat Committee, whose recommendations appear to us not to have received the attention they deserve from the government. We are of opinion that the recommendations of the Fuel Research Board relating to experiments on the utilization of peat for fuel and the reclamation of bogs should be carried into effect.*

*126. Another matter to which we desire to draw attention is the urgent need for extensive schemes of arterial drainage. At present the catchment areas of many Irish rivers, especially of the Barrow, suffer severely from flooding, with consequent serious losses to farmers in the neighbourhood whose crops are frequently destroyed from this cause. The existing defective drainage system is moreover productive of danger to the health of the community in the affected areas. While we do not feel justified in entering in detail into this question, in view of the scanty evidence we have received in the matter, we nevertheless have come to the conclusion that the undertaking of extensive schemes of arterial drainage in the districts which at present are subject to flooding would be productive of permanent benefit to the agriculture of the country by increasing the area that could be profitably cultivated, while the draining operations themselves would provide considerable employment.*

*CONCLUSION*

*140. In concluding our Final Report we would venture to repeat some of the considerations referred to in the opening pages. The causes of the present agricultural depression in Ireland are partly world-wide and partly local. In so far as they are world-wide, no recommendations that we could make would help to remove them, but in so far as they are local it is to be hoped that our labours will not prove to have been altogether in vain. But, even assuming that the state does everything that it can be suggested that it should do, the main work of agricultural recuperation must rest with the individual farmer, whether working singly or organized in co-operation with his fellows.*

*141. The insistence which we have laid throughout this report on the need of educating and organizing the farming community must not be taken to suggest that nothing has already been done in these respects. On the contrary, the last quarter of a century has witnessed a remarkable awakening of interest in the development of Irish rural economy owing principally to the enterprise and initiative of Sir Horace Plunkett, who in assembling and presiding over the Recess Committee created a turning point in Irish agricultural history. The Department of Agriculture has established a record of valuable service and useful work, and the Irish co-operative movement has set an example to similar movements in any other countries. Nothing that we have said is intended to belittle the achievements of these bodies, or of the numerous other bodies interested in agricultural development, such, for example, as the Royal Dublin Society, or to suggest that their activities have not been fruitful. Our recommendations are all in the direction of supplementing rather than of criticizing the work of these organizations. At the same time, we feel that the degree of public assistance necessary for agriculture in the future will be greater than it has been in the past; that the problems of to-day are more complex and more pressing than the problems of yesterday; and that the twentieth century, with the advent of overseas competition of a kind heretofore unprecedented, will prove a difficult and trying time for Ireland's premier industry. The very complexity of the problem involved both emphasizes the urgency and increases the interest of attempting its solution.*

*142. While we are conscious that we have not explored some of the problems suggested in our very wide terms of reference to the utmost possible limits, we feel that we have not been guilty of neglecting or of overlooking any of the main aspects of the Irish agricultural situation. The very voluminous nature of the evidence has necessarily protracted our discussions, and the fact that two-thirds of our members are also members of the Oireachtas has prevented our meetings from being as frequent or as consecutive as we could have desired. We have, moreover, been restricted in our discussion by the exclusion from the terms of reference of the question of the relations between employers and employed, without a consideration of which it is extremely difficult to reach any satisfactory conclusion on many of the problems which it was our duty to examine.*

For its part, the Fiscal Inquiry Committee focused attention on proposals to protect Irish industry from foreign competition. Specifically, the Committee undertook to examine the existing "fiscal system" and the measures "regulating or restricting imports." The Committee was asked further to examine the effects of any measures proposed to "foster the development of industry and agriculture."

The Committee concluded that there was very little support for the protection of domestic industries. Although "the plan of small duties on certain products (in particular wheat and barley) was regarded as feasible," it was noted that "no one proposes or desires any protection for the main products of agriculture." While twenty-three of forty-one industries examined sought protection, the Committee argued that no major manufacturing sector was protectionist. A recent assessment holds that a majority of Committee members consciously favored free trade and avoided an objective debate on the issue (Lee 1989: 118-19).

Support for free trade did not necessarily reflect confidence in Ireland's ability to compete. Rather, it acknowledged that ready access to foreign markets was essential to the economy's development. Moreover, some industrialists feared that British firms would soon establish themselves behind an Irish tariff wall, to the detriment of domestic companies.

In fact, testimony before the Fiscal Inquiry Committee spelled out a long list of difficulties allegedly facing Irish industry. These ranged from such considerations as labor productivity and capital shortages, to the absence of scale economies and the lack of marketing skills. Although few witnesses said so directly, it seemed obvious to the Committee that many problems stemmed from "the recent political and social condition of the country" which had a stultifying effect on enterprise and "industrial vitality." Other problems could be ascribed to dislocations in the international economy associated with World War I and its aftermath. However, even if these "abnormal" adverse forces were to weaken over time, much of Irish industry would still have difficulty competing in a free trade environment.

### *FINAL REPORT OF THE FISCAL INQUIRY COMMITTEE*

*1. The Committee was appointed on the 15th June, 1923, by the Minister of Industry and Commerce in conjunction with the Minister of Agriculture, and with the following terms of reference:*

*"To investigate and report —*

*(a) as to the effect of the existing fiscal system, and of any measures regulating or restricting imports or exports, on industry and agriculture in the Saorstat and*

*(b) as to the effect of any changes therein intended to foster the development of industry and agriculture, with due regard to the interests of the general community and to the economic relations of the Saorstat with other countries."*

*4. In the present report the Committee accordingly confines itself to that part of its inquiry which deals with proposals made with the intention of fostering industry and agriculture in An Saorstat. In reviewing these the Committee has had to consider both the competence of these proposals to effect the object intended, and the effect which, if accepted, they are likely to have upon the interests of agriculture, other industries and the general community. In the analysis of the proposals from these points of view the Committee has confined itself strictly to the task of reviewing them in the light of ascertained facts and common experience as economic means devised to secure economic ends. The Committee has not presumed to suggest or to forecast a fiscal policy for the country: it has taken its task to be rather that of collecting and analyzing facts and presenting them to the best of its ability for the consideration of those with whom the final decision and the shaping of a national policy must rest. In adopting this course the Committee has strictly conformed to the line of conduct set forth by the President in his statement in the Dail on the 15th June, 1923, when he said:*

> *"It is facts and not policy which the committee is intended to determine. Every proposition that is advanced will be examined solely with a view to ascertain and to inform the community as to all the facts. The Committee is not expected to advocate policy. That will be a matter for the people and the Government when they have the facts before them."*

*6. It is thought that the following summary of the evidence (which does not profess to follow the order of the importance of the industries or that of the attendance of the witnesses) will be helpful as an introduction to the critical analysis which follows.*

*7. Agriculture: No official representative of the farmers appeared before the Committee, but individual witnesses of high competence stated certain aspects of the question of protective duties in relation to agriculture. Thus, the position of agriculture as "the main source of productive wealth" and that "agriculture in Ireland requires an outside market" were presented in the evidence. So was the difficulty of arranging a suitable general tariff. The plan of small duties on certain products (in particular wheat and barley) was regarded as feasible. One witness suggested a duty of one shilling per ewt, on wheat, with a bounty on export supplied by the duty. The proposed British import duty on barley of ten shillings per quarter was treated as desirable by one witness but opposed by another. The great importance of the maintenance of the export of Irish agricultural products was recognized. The agricultural witnesses believed that the farmers would not regard a small duty on flour unfavourably. The claim of agriculture to receive its share of the operation of a tariff was also put forward. That protective duties designed to aid other industries would probably raise the cost of living and compel the farmer to pay higher wages was a further point in this evidence.*

*18. Woollen manufacture: Evidence was presented on behalf of the Woollen and Worsted Manufacturers' Association. An estimate of the consumption of woollens in Ireland was put in, but without any statistical support. The condition of the industry was stated to be one of depression due to the "dumping" of English woollens at prices under cost. The remedy advocated was an ad valorem duty, perhaps temporary, of thirty-three and one-third per cent, a low duty, e.g., ten per cent, could not be of any service; one of fifty per cent, or seventy-five per cent, would be much better. Further points in the evidence were that a great increase of employment would follow, and capital would be kept in the country; that the depression in England is worse than in Ireland; that the Irish woollen industry is fairly well organized, although there are some struggling mills. Another witness, who was concerned with the export business, was opposed to any duty on woollen imports since smuggling would be encouraged and the cost of living raised and since the industry could be best aided by subsidies. The industry does not appear to be under any disadvantage from higher cost of labour. Neither witness supplied any reliable statistics of production, import or export.*

*66. This rapid survey of the evidence tendered to the Committee suggests certain general reflexions. In spite of the number of the witnesses and the great importance of some of the industries which they represented, it would appear, nevertheless, that the volume of industry which is anxious to obtain a protective tariff is small compared with that which desires no change in the existing system. Several of the most important witnesses — e.g., those who appeared on behalf of the maltsters, the biscuit industry, and the jute industry — were opposed to the application of protection to their own industries, and the Committee must assume that this view is shared by the numerous and important industries that did not offer to give evidence — e.g., the brewing and distilling industries and the industries connected with agriculture, such as bacon curing and butter making, not to speak of agriculture itself. Although these industries did not submit evidence, the Committee could not shut its eyes to their existence or their interests, and drew the conclusion that their non-appearance was tantamount to an expression of contentment with the present fiscal arrangements. Even the industries that advocated a measure of protection were not in complete accord regarding the articles for which protection was required. Many articles which some witnesses wished to have protected, other witnesses wished to have admitted free; and suggestions regarding certain articles were acceptable to some witnesses while, at the same time, they were highly objectionable to others. Nor were the witnesses agreed as to the nature or the amount of the assistance required. In several cases the amount of protection asked for would not, in view of the figures supplied by the witnesses, give the native manufacturer any appreciable competitive advantage and would in fact serve no other purpose than that of a revenue duty. In spite of this lack of unanimity, amounting in some cases to positive disagreement, among the witnesses, their evidence contained numerous points which were agreed on by all or any of them, and which may therefore be considered as forming the main basis of their proposals. These points may in general be said to amount to the assertion, from various aspects, of the inability of Irish industries to hold their own against outside competition.*

*67. The competitive disabilities of which such full statements were submitted by the various witnesses appear to be capable of division into two classes: (1) those of a normal and permanent character (2) those of an abnormal character arising out of the exceptional conditions of the last few years. The Committee proceeds to examine each of these classes in turn.*

*68. One disadvantage from which many Irish industries suffer is the difficulty of obtaining raw materials. For example, the most important raw materials of the woollen industry, the papermaking industry, the jute industry, the manufacture of fertilizers, brushes, pottery and clay pipes, the coachbuilding industry and the furniture industry are imported. The same difficulty especially applies to the wide range of industries based on iron and steel —for example, the manufacture of agricultural machinery and of bicycles. Even in the case of flour milling a very large part of the wheat milled for Irish consumption has to be imported.*

*69. The most important source of industrial power cannot be obtained as cheaply in Ireland as in most European countries. The supply of Irish coal at present available is utterly inadequate for the needs of Irish industry, and the necessary supply of imported coal can only be obtained at a higher price than it costs in its country of origin. This disability is specially serious in the case of industries situated at a distance from the ports. In some instances water power has been substituted for coal, but it is not yet certain that water power or wind power can be relied on as a substitute for coal, except in small-scale industries.*

*70. All the evidence given to the Committee points to the conclusion that transport charges in Ireland are excessive, and that Irish industry, in nearly all its branches, is hampered from this cause, especially in competition with imported commodities which have the benefit of through rates. The Committee is impressed by the serious nature of this disadvantage, and is led to the conclusion that the development of all means of transport, whether by land or water, and its organization upon economic lines, are urgently required in the interests of industrial progress.*

*71. Another serious disability under which the Irish manufacturer suffers is the lack of a supply of skilled labour specially trained for and adapted to his requirements. Industry in An Saorstat has not the advantage, enjoyed so widely in other countries, of being able to call upon a constant supply of workers endowed with a hereditary aptitude for certain forms of skilled labour. Complaints under this head have been received from representatives of the furniture, boot, cycle, pottery, jute and glass bottle industries. Certain employers have had the extra burden placed on them of having to train their own skilled workers, many of whom, especially in periods of depression in Ireland, emigrate to the great external labour markets. As soon as trade revives in Ireland the manufacturer finds himself without the supplies of skilled labour necessary to resume his operations. This difficulty might in part be met by adequate technical instruction; but, up to the present, financial and administrative difficulties, combined in some cases with a reluctance on the part of the workers to avail themselves of the instruction provided, seem to have retarded this most desirable development.*

*72. Practically every witness who appeared before the Committee to advocate the claims of a particular industry to protection, asserted that wages in An Saorstat were higher than in Great Britain or Northern Ireland and that his higher wage was a handicap upon Irish industry in competition with its British rivals. At the same time the Committee obtained little, if any, help from the witnesses in determining the approximate weight of this handicap. In the first place, very few of the witnesses were able to give exact figures even of the money wages earned in their own industries, or of the wages in corresponding industries in Great Britain and Northern Ireland, while emphatic in their assertions as to the cheaper labour to be obtained not only in Great Britain and Northern Ireland, but even in several European countries. In at least one case statements were made as to the relative rates of money wages in An Saorstat and Northern Ireland which were at variance with facts known to the Committee. Again, the witnesses who laid stress upon the amount of money wages paid in their industries were not able to give any very clear replies as to the relative efficiency of labour in An Saorstat and in Great Britain nor did they always seem to be aware of the fact that money wages and cost of labour are not the same thing. Had any scientific system of costing been in general use in the industries which these witnesses represented, this confusion of mind could not have occurred and the witnesses would have been able to produce costing figures which, showing that they understood the meaning of the phrase "cost of labour," would have given the Committee more confidence in their statements as to the relatively high cost of labour in Ireland. A higher money wage does not prove of itself that labour costs more; as efficient labour paid at a high wage may be less costly than inefficient labour paid at a low wage. The Committee has been at some pains to ascertain the money wages paid in a number of industries in An Saorstat, Northern Ireland, and Great Britain respectively; the detailed figures will be found in Appendix A. But these figures will only prove that Irish labour costs more than labour in Great Britain on the assumption that British and Irish labour are on precisely the same level of efficiency.*

*73. With regard to the efficiency of labour in Ireland, as distinguished from the money wages paid, the evidence is more conflicting. The Committee has received evidence that in many industries there is a widespread feeling of dissatisfaction on the part of the employers with the efficiency of labour in this particular industries. A satisfactory determination of the justice of their complaints is hardly possible in the absence of any scientific comparison of the average output of Irish workers in particular industries with that of English or other labour. Until figures are available upon which to base statistics of comparative efficiency it is impossible to determine the precise weight of the burden under which industry labours from any given amount of money wages. As already pointed out, high money wages do not necessarily mean a high cost of labour, which may be due to several causes, among which the inefficiency of the management is not less important than the inefficiency of labour.*

*74. Capital for the promotion of industrial enterprise is not readily obtainable in Ireland. The number of new companies which have been floated in recent years is comparatively small and in many cases these have been nothing more than conversions of private firms. The Committee is aware that the policy of Irish banks has been to afford sufficient credit facilities to well established enterprises. Indeed it seems that in this matter they have gone as far as the limits of safety will allow. It is a recognized principle of commercial banking that banks should not provide the capital for new companies; and the justice of this principle can scarcely be questioned in view of the admitted necessity for keeping a large proportion of their assets in a fluid condition. These fluid assets will naturally be placed in the nearest important money market in forms which can be ready realized On the other hand, there has been some investment of outside capital in certain Irish industries and this tendency will no doubt increase if general conditions in the country improve.*

*75. Another point to which many witnesses drew attention is the large proportion of the cost of manufactured articles represented by so-called "overhead charges." It was urged that the restricted output of Irish industries under present conditions and the relatively small size of Irish factories made this item in costs a serious handicap in comparison with the products of large-scale industries with which they were in competition. But it was difficult to determine in many cases what items in the cost of production were included in the category of "overhead charges." Some witnesses were not certain whether "overhead charges" did or did not include the costs of advertizing and marketing; one witness even included wages in his "overhead charges."*

*76. The Irish manufacturer moreover is hampered by the fact that he is called upon to produce a wide variety of articles, which prevents the development of specialized skill and machinery. Certain Irish industries which produce for the export market have succeeded in specializing to a very high degree and these industries are in a position to hold their own in the world market with all competitors. It would appear that the possibility of this degree of specialization being attained depends upon the existence of a very wide market and that it could hardly be reached by any industry which produces for the Irish market alone. This state of affairs reacts unfavourably on the supply of skilled labour.*

*77. With regard to the organization of business, the Committee has received evidence from the representatives of the trade unions, that the high cost of production in Ireland is partly to be explained by the absence of efficient management. This is partly due to the absence of a widespread system of higher commercial education; but, in the case of those industries which have to be conducted on a small scale, it would be difficult, even with efficient management, to effect the fullest economics in production. Moreover, some evidence has been tendered to the effect that the methods by which managerial staffs are sometimes recruited are not such as to lead to the highest grade of efficiency.*

*78. The evidence tends to show that the marketing organization of Irish industries leaves much to be desired. Very little effort is made to present products in an attractive form, with the result that Irish articles are passed over in favour of attractively packed foreign products. Irish industry moreover suffers from insufficient advertizing and from the failure of many firms to employ the best possible travelling agents. The Committee cannot refrain from indicating that the removal of these disabilities lies in the hands of the manufacturer's themselves.*

*79. Another great difficulty under which Irish industries suffer is their inability to market their products on the most economical terms. The absence of developed manufacturing centres necessitates the establishment of factories which are remote from any large market. This remoteness, in some cases amounting to isolation, excludes the Irish manufacturer from many benefits in connexion with marketing which are enjoyed by his competitors. Many of the smaller woollen mills and flour mills are situated very disadvantageously in this respect, as are also the boot, furniture and jute factories. The disadvantages resulting from the unfavourable location of these industries could be materially alleviated by an improvement in postal and transit facilities, and in methods of commercial intelligence.*

*80. The Committee received a large volume of evidence from a number of witnesses, representing many different industries, pointing to the existence of a strong and decided prejudice on the part of the Irish public against certain classes of Irish products. Evidence of this kind was given by representatives of the confectionery trade and of the cycle, flour milling, boot and brush industries. The Committee has been assured that the Irish trade mark in the case of one industry has been regarded by the Irish consumer as a deterrent rather than as an attraction. This would seem to point to the conclusion that the use of any national trade mark which is not accompanied by a reliable guarantee of quality is doomed to be ineffective if not injurious.*

*81. The Committee proceeds to examine those abnormal disadvantages which are partly internal and partly external. The internal difficulties are those caused by the recent political and social condition of the country; the external difficulties are due to the prevalent economic dislocation, and are illustrated by the effects of the depreciation of the currencies of several European countries and the various forms of "dumping." The recent political and social conditions in Ireland, though comparatively little was said about them in the evidence given to the Committee, cannot but have had a profoundly adverse effect upon Irish industry. From 1918 to the conclusion of the Anglo-Irish Treaty, the methods of increasing rigour adopted by the then government in the hope of enforcing its authority had the effect, among others, of discouraging enterprise, disturbing credit, dislocating economic machinery and depressing industrial vitality. The period following the Treaty was one of unrest and instability which merged finally into civil war. Under such conditions normal industrial enterprise was impossible. Capital for fresh development was increasingly difficult, and indeed in most cases impossible, to obtain. Many existing industries were carried on under such disabilities as led eventually to their cessation. Transport was insecure, owing to the destruction of bridges, roads and railways. Labour was in a state of unrest and resulting inefficiency. It is safe to say that even had Ireland no natural and permanent industrial disadvantages a state of affairs such as prevailed for the five years from 1918 to 1923 would have inflicted a deep and serious wound upon the body of her industries. It is impossible to estimate how far this is responsible for the present industrial depression. The Committee has had evidence from more than one industry of a period of comparative and even growing prosperity up to 1914 or later; though the witnesses claimed that the present position of these industries is so precarious that their extinction is threatened unless immediate measures are adopted for their protection. For these gloomy anticipations the disturbed period under review must be held, at least partly, if not largely, responsible.*

*87. Setting aside these temporary and abnormal conditions, the position of Irish industries with regard to the claim for protection is not uniform. No one proposes or desires any protection for the main products of agriculture, such as eggs, bacon and butter, or for such exports as biscuits, beer and whiskey. These are at present the main exports from An Saorstat. Agriculture is and must be for a long time the principal Irish industry, and the brewing and distilling industries (with the subsidiary industry of malting) use in their manufacture the products of agriculture. In fact, it seems probable that the strongest opposition to a proposal to protect them would come from these industries themselves. Agricultural pursuits absorb the greatest volume of Irish capital and labour, and the effect upon their interests must be considered as of paramount importance in estimating the result of any proposal to protect Irish industry.*

These documents reveal clearly the preferential status of agriculture in the new nation's aspirations for economic growth. While hardly novel, this emphasis did not reflect a unanimous opinion. In the several decades before Independence, such Irish leaders as Arthur Griffith had urged that more attention be paid to industrialization. This approach held that a growing number of industrial jobs would cut deeply into the Irish emigration figures, an important nationalist goal (Kennedy, Giblin, and McHugh 1988: 34). However, a policy of that type would require "infant industry" protection, at least in its early stages, a prospect that ran counter to the prevailing free trade view.

The primacy accorded agriculture in the early 1920s saw that sector as the "engine of growth" that would pull the rest of the economy along. With this view prevailing, it was inevitable that a general free trade policy would ensue. The majority felt that such a policy would enhance agriculture's export opportunities, both by encouraging reciprocity from Ireland's customers and by keeping import prices low. The latter consideration would tend to reduce production costs in agriculture and allow Irish exports to remain competitive in international markets.

On the whole then, despite some vigorous minority dissents, the two enquiries did not recommend an activist, interventionist role for the new Government. Rather, they espoused a cautious "framework" approach, establishing the conditions necessary for an open economy and providing some limited technical support for farms and firms competing in that setting. An exception was the passage of the Trade Loans (Guarantee) Act of 1924 which permitted the Minister for Industry and Commerce to guarantee payment of loans made to certain firms. (Meenan 1970: 148). As indicated above, some historians attribute the Free State's reluctance to break from traditional paths to the belief that political and social stability had to be attained before economic innovation could be attempted. On the protectionist issue, for example, "any radical departure on tariffs would have upset the British, worried the Irish banks and alienated the large farmers and businessmen who subscribed to national loans. Therefore, nothing dramatic could be attempted" (Daly 1981: 139). It might be said again that the specific elements in this cautious approach were consistent with economic thinking in Britain and Ireland at that time (Kennedy, Giblin, and McHugh 1988: 35; Fanning 1984: 148).

Although their view did not prevail, some did have doubts about the major policy lines taken: the primacy of agriculture, free trade, and the limited role for government. In the mid-1920s a critic denounced the free trade stand of the Fiscal Inquiry Committee, arguing that it denied Ireland the opportunity to move to a new economic direction (Lee 1989: 118). The Minister for Industry and Commerce, Gordon Campbell, became increasingly skeptical of "agriculture-led growth." He also became convinced that the government should be more active in stimulating industrial development, including efforts to attract foreign entrepreneurial skills and capital. As a political realist, however, he also noted the futility of making policy recommendations that deviated from the mainstream economics of the day (Ibid: 121-23).

We can see a blend of the prevailing and dissenting schools of thought in a further set of documents. They deal with the Shannon Scheme, an attempt to improve Ireland's "infrastructure" and thereby increase the prospects for economic growth. In that sense, it was an approach similar to a number of nineteenth-century proposals. Launched in 1925, the plan called for "the development of Electrical Power from the River Shannon and its distribution over the area of the Free State." As the largest Government undertaking in the first decade of independence, the scheme heralded a new approach. The plan was calculated to compensate for the lack of coal cited by the Fiscal Inquiry Committee as an obstacle to development. This initiative foreshadowed other government ventures which established semi-State enterprises in such fields as beet sugar (1933), turf development (1934), air transport (1936) and tourism (1939) (Kennedy, Giblin, and McHugh 1988: 44).

*PROPOSED HYDRO-ELECTRIC SCHEME AND THE RIVER SHANNON*

*Correspondence between the Ministry of Industry and Commerce and*

*Siemens-Schuckertwerke, Berlin*

---

*Abreacht Thionnscail Agus Tracheala*
*(Ministry of Industry and Commerce)*

*Sraid Mruurpetheaus Uacht.*
*26 February, 1924*

*A Chara,*

*I am directed by the Minister of Industry and Commerce to refer to your interview with the President and other Ministers on the 8th instant, when you outlined on behalf of your firm proposals for the development of Electrical Power from the River Shannon and its distribution over the area of the Free State. You represented that your examination of the existing data as in the water power available in the Shannon and your impression of the river and its lakes were such as to satisfy you, in the light of your firm's great and recent experience with hydro-electrical schemes in various parts of the continent, that electrical power in sufficient quantity and at a low price could be procured from the Shannon to meet the present and prospective needs of the whole of the Free State. You further represented that your scheme would include full consideration for navigation, irrigation and fishing interests and that it would tend to diminish flooding of the area adjacent to the river.*

*The Government is not at present in a position to judge of the merits of your proposals on their technical or economic side, but having regard to the importance of the provision of electrical power to the future of the Free State, it is ready to give your firm a full opportunity of further developing its proposals on the lines indicated in this letter of which the Executive Committee have approved. It has been explained to you that previous inquiries into the possibilities of the River Shannon for the purpose of hydro-electrical development had proved much less optimistic than those at which your firm has arrived and the Government notes that you appreciate this position and accept the responsibility of justifying the ultimate proposals of your firm from the technical and economic point of view to whatever expert examination the Government may think desirable.*

*Siemens-Schuckertwerke*

*Siemenstadt Bei Berlin, Den*

*G.m.b.H. 29th February, 1924.*
*Direktion.*

*The Minister of Industry and Commerce,*
*Government Buildings,*
*Dublin*

*Sir,*

*We are in receipt of Mr. Campbell's letter of the 26th instant addressed to our Director, Dr. Wallem, in which he deals on your behalf with our proposals for the development of electric power from the River Shannon and its distribution over the area of the Irish Free State.*

*We accept the complete contents of this letter, including all its interpretations and modifications of our proposals, as the basis for our proceeding with the scheme. We will proceed with the necessary preliminary investigations sending our engineers to the Shannon, as soon as it suits the convenience of the Government.*

*We are, Sir,*
*Your obedient Servants,*
*SIEMENS-SCHUCKERTWERKE,*
*Gesellscbaft mit besobrankter Haftung.*

*(Sgd.) Reyss.*
*H. Wallem.*

To the Secretary of Industry and Commerce, the Shannon Scheme embodied a fruitful approach to the problem of Irish economic development: the utilization of knowledgeable experts and modern technology to exploit to the full the nation's limited supply of material resources. In reality, this strategy required going beyond Ireland's borders for the necessary ingredients. The Siemens firm of Berlin was central to the Shannon project, which underwent scrutiny by a jury of foreign experts who evaluated the proposal as it developed. The Scheme was also debated in the Dail and denounced by a variety of opponents throughout the Free State. Nonetheless, the Shannon Electricity Bill became law in the Spring of 1925 and the Scheme began operation in 1929 (Meenan 1970: 172-73).

Apart from its impact on the availability of electrical power, the Shannon Scheme of the mid-1920s had an important psychological effect. "It stimulated public self-confidence when encouragement was badly needed" (Ibid: 169). The project demonstrated that the Free State government was willing to develop resources even at a time of fiscal austerity.

Foreign experts also played a major role in other inquiries pursued by the Irish government: the Banking Commissions of 1926 and 1934-1938 (Fanning 1984: 150). These Commissions examined the extent to which Irish monetary and credit arrangements were compatible with the nation's growth aspirations. The 1926 inquiry sought to maintain or restore confidence in Ireland's currency and banking system. Recommendations included adopting the pound sterling as the standard unit of value, making it identical with the British pound sterling and at parity with the latter currency. The Currency Act of 1927 and the Currency Commission established by the Act were put in place to ensure an adequate money supply. "The 1927 Act worked well from the start" (Meenan 1970: 220).

The outcome was less clear in the question of the financial sector's contribution to economic progress, that is the efficacy of credit facilities available to agriculture, industry, and commerce. Although witnesses assured the Commission that existing arrangements did not present an obstacle to growth, some found the acceptance of that conclusion "complacent" (Lee 1989: 123). For its part, in stating "The General Problem" the Commission majority argued that it was the lack of creditworthy borrowers, not the lack of capital, which hampers lending in Ireland.

On another important issue, the 1926 Commission recommended that a Central Bank *not* be established at that time. That prospect arose again in the Banking Commission of 1934-1938, this time with a different recommendation. The Central Bank was established in the war year of 1942.

*BANKING COMMISSION, 1926*

*FINAL REPORTS*
*of*
*THE BANKING COMMISSION*

*5. Our First Conclusion*

*To put our first and fundamental conclusion into plainer language therefore, we may say that, in our opinion, whatever is done here should be done in such a way as to avoid for the present any serious breach with the currency, banking and trade system of Great Britain. But this conclusion presupposes, of course, that that system is, on the whole, defensible and sound, and that the adoption of measures which harmonise with it does not commit this country to the pursuit of any policy which on more general grounds would seem to be hazardous or indefensible. In order to justify or even defend, therefore, the general opinion which we have expressed with regard to relationships with the British currency system it seems at least desirable to express a definite opinion with regard to Great Britain's current monetary and banking policy. What has that policy been? In general it has been a return to the gold standard of value, looking forward probably to an eventual restoration of absolutely free trade in, and free movement of gold. Accompanying this policy, of course, has been a recognition that such action would incidentally result in cutting prices somewhat back from the level which they had reached when the policy was initiated, although not necessarily involving any deliberate effort to drive them to a permanently lower level. There has also been recognition of the fact international trade in general is being rapidly restored to a definite gold basis, and that commerce between the chief industrialized nations of the world has already been placed upon that footing regardless of the temporary hardships that might be incident to any such policy.*

*19. Marketing Situation in the Saorstat*

*There should be no hesitation in applying these principles in the case of the Saorstat. Its markets are almost wholly found in Great Britain at the present time, due mainly to the fact that its exports are almost wholly agricultural, and until some modification of this condition is created in the future, and until some action has been taken which would develop an independent machinery of marketing, wholesaling and dealing between it and foreign countries, they are likely to continue as at present. In those circumstances, any change in currency or banking policies that would create a decided separation from, or opposition to, those of Great Britain should be carefully considered before being adopted, because of the indirect and incidental harm undoubtedly to be expected therefrom, as regards immediate incomes of the farmer the producer and the business man.*

*The lesson which is thus to be drawn from the experience of other countries may be considered first of all, in connection with the currency unit to be adopted in the Saorstat. Undoubtedly, the accounting system of Great Britain, based upon the pound sterling, with its division into twenty shillings, each of which is divided into twelve pence, is difficult in practical use. It would be far better if a decimal system could be substituted for it by introducing a complete transformation or some modification. That, however, would of course involve the introduction of unit of measurement separate from the unit of Great Britain, and, as we have already seen, the institution of a different scale of prices; different if for no reason other than that they are quoted in a currency unit which is not the basis of British trade. The effect of such a separation of the two currency systems would, for the reasons which we have already set forth, be not only unsettling and disturbing, but directly injurious to Irish agriculture and business. But what is true of the currency unit or unit of account is much more largely true of the standard of value. To adopt a standard of value different from that of Great Britain would necessarily mean a different scale of prices not only in so far as resulted from difference in the unit of measurement, but also in consequence of a difference in the basis or standard of measurement.*

*29. Summary of Recommendations*

*Summing up this entire situation, we may say that our recommendations as to standards of value and legal tender note currency are as follows:*

*(1) The adoption of the pound sterling as the standard unit of value and of accounting, such pound sterling to be identical with the British pound sterling.*

*(2) Provision for the eventual coinage of an actual Irish pound sterling, to be minted in gold of equal weight and fineness with the British pound sterling, coinage and issue thereof not to take place until return to an actual practical gold standard shall have been assured.*

*(3) Immediate provision for, and issue of, an Irish paper pound sterling which shall be legal tender and which shall be maintained at a parity of value with that of Great Britain by holding behind it a reserve of 100 per cent of the amount of such notes outstanding, carried primarily in British Government securities of varying maturities, but including also in the total such sum in current bank and other cash balances or in gold or both, as may be determined upon by qualified persons hereinafter to be designated, the object in view being the maintenance of immediate convertibility of outstanding legal tender paper at all times on demand into British sterling.*

*30. Summary of Effects and Consequences*

*It is worth while also to summarize very briefly the effects and consequences to be expected from the carrying out of these recommendations. (1) We think, as we have said, that the first and greatest result will be the maintenance of confidence and the restoration of it where it is now lacking on the part of the business community and the saving public. (2) We think further that such action will tend to maintain a parity of price level between the Saorstat and Great Britain and to bring about a freedom of interchange of commodities and remittances which could not otherwise be insured. (3) We believe that it will largely tend to stop the transfer of funds to Great Britain and to call back for investment in the Saorstat such funds as have already been transferred to British banks. (4) Finally, we believe that it will result in giving to the Saorstat its own individual currency system of unquestioned value and eventually, when as and if desired, a gold monetary base of its own.*

*The technique of the process whereby these recommendations may be carried into effect naturally calls for the most careful attention, that there may be no uncertainty at any time in the public mind, no shortage of legal tender currency, no doubt as to the proper funds for use in liquidating debts and no shock to business. We have set forth in considerable detail our views regarding these practical phases of the subject in our our First Interim Report. We, therefore, need not repeat the detailed recommendations therein contained.*

*39. A "Central Bank"*

*The question may, therefore, be asked whether the Saorstat ought not, in the reorganization of its banking and currency system, to provide for the creation of a strong central banking institution, whose duty it should be to provide for a satisfactory fiduciary note issue as well as to perform other central banking functions. That subject must now receive consideration. The creation of a central bank is a matter which has been brought forcefully to the attention of the Commission and has been carefully studied by it. The Commission has decided against recommending the establishment of any such organization at the present moment and for a variety of reasons. The foremost of these reasons is the fact that there does not exist in the Saorstat at the present moment what may be described as a capital market or money market.*

*40. Resort to London Market*

*For many years past, the Saorstat has resorted to the London market for both capital and money, and has failed to develop locally anything that might be regarded as even an approximation to such markets. A study of the portfolios of Irish banks located in the Saorstat will show how largely they have invested their funds in London. They carried in 1925 in money at call, investments, and Government debt about £95,000,000, practically all of it no doubt, in the British market. This is for reasons which we shall speak of more fully later on. The point to be borne in mind at the present moment is that they do so invest their spare funds, and that enterprises organized in the Free State do habitually resort to outside markets, usually in London, as the source of their capital or even at times their short term accommodation. In these circumstances a central bank, if organized in the Saorstat, would find it necessary, first of all, practically to create a short term market, while it would lack the support that comes from the existence of a well-defined capital market. Such a central bank should never, we think, habitually compete with existing banks for the business of the individual depositors. While there are central banks which do thus compete from day to day with other banks on more or less nearly equal terms for ordinary business at least in certain narrowly and well-defined branches of lending, it is not a wholesome state of affairs, and is one which is being gradually eliminated in practically every country of modern banking organization.*

*48. An Adequate System*

*In general, we believe the system of banking in the Saorstat is adequate, sound, and well operated, and we find that this is the prevailing view of the population. There are some standard types of complaints to which we shall presently refer but we feel that these do not affect the general opinion as to the quality of the system itself. In so saying we, of course, express no opinion as to the position, assets or strength of any given institution or even of all combined. We have made no examination of them, and had no mandate to make any. We express merely a general opinion as to the system or type of organization.*

*63. Business Capital Needs of the Saorstat*

*And yet, embarking upon its new national career, the Saorstat naturally finds itself requiring capital for various long term business purposes. In some cases such business enterprises have been cut off from their former markets through establishment of tariff and other barriers. In other cases, they have undergone changes of demand and alterations of prospect which are partly the outgrowth of political changes, and are partly the reflection of changing habits of consumption or of buying, resulting from commercial disturbances which have followed upon the close of the war. In still others, it has appeared that there was need to put capital into newly-organized enterprises which probably could not get it through direct applications to the banks, in view of the bounden duty of these institutions not to tie up their capital in long term loans beyond a certain very easily-reached point, and not to put it into such loans at all, unless quite certain that they could be liquidated within at least a moderate space of time. Believing, as we do, that this field of banking or credit operations is one which calls for a special type of institution, we should probably be disposed to recommend some means of providing such an institution or of furnishing the capital which is needed by meritorious business undertakings, pending the time when a full-fledged investment market will have been developed in the Saorstat, were it not that the Government has already found it needful to provide a means of its own for dealing with such necessities. It has, however, adopted and put into effect the Trade Loans Guarantee Act, and has renewed that measure, thus indicating its intention to maintain the policy originally contemplated by it.*

*66. The General Problem*

*While we have thus surveyed the principal branches of the banking and credit question as presented in the Saorstat at the present moment, we are well aware that there is much to be said of the situation which cannot be disposed of under any concrete or specific head. It is quite essential to real success in the establishment of an independent banking and currency system in the Saorstat that the Government possess the decided co-operation of the public at large in bringing about a condition of confidence and a disposition to support local industries and to purchase local securities which will furnish the necessary back ground for the appropriate adjustment of outstanding issues. The Irish public at large is disposed to complain of the banks for investing so much of their funds abroad, but it is itself at fault in this particular. It blames the banks for not lending more freely and generously on agricultural security, but as we have shown in our Interim Reports, it refuses (particularly in the agricultural districts) to establish that condition of security and collectibility which is needful in order that local loans may be made in the assurance that they will be repaid. It is disposed to find fault with the Government for not assisting in the development of agriculture and business, but it ignores the fact that in few or no countries has the Government done so much for the land owner. Some provision for business requirements has moreover been made under the Trades Loan Guarantee Acts, while the banks are generally admitted to have been lending to substantially large amounts both in favour of agriculture and of business for the supplying of capital needs. Greater confidence on the part of the public, greater disposition to support and maintain local industries and to buy their securities, stronger public opinion on behalf of the collection of legitimate debts, and a determination to bring about the growth of an active, vigorous, home market for capital and home money will be absolutely essential as a background for the full success of the plans which we have outlined in this Report. We are aware that the attainment of these ends is not an easy or transitory process. They cannot be attained at all without the recognition on the part of influential members of the public that they are called for, or without determination on their part to assist in the achievement. The first step toward the development of such a condition among the public at large is obviously the recording and making known our opinion concerning it, and this we have accordingly undertaken to do in the foregoing pages and in the four Interim Reports to which we have made reference.*

Changing economic circumstances and a further appraisal of the economy's performance led to significant policy alterations in the early 1930s. As the Great Depression deepened, Britain abandoned the gold standard and adopted protectionist measures to bolster its faltering economy. These actions and the prospect of Britain's "dumping" goods in Ireland would have prompted a similar response from the Irish. In addition, the movement away from free trade was reenforced by the disappointing economic record of the Free State's first decade.

Agricultural output had increased only slightly between 1924/25 and 1929/30 and remained 10 percent below the figure of 1912/13. The value of net agricultural output was actually 5 percent lower in 1929/30 than in 1924/25. The gains registered in industrial employment during the 1920s were too small to compensate for the loss of jobs in agriculture. And while heavy emigration led to a population decline between 1922 and 1931, the Depression in Britain and the United States effectively halted that movement. Immigration restriction by the United States was another factor which affected Irish mobility and as population increased, the pressure for protectionism and job creation grew apace (Kennedy, Giblin, and McHugh 1988: 37-39).

As noted below, the Fianna Fáil victory in the 1932 election ushered in a new era in Irish economic policy, an era which persisted well into the post-World War II period. The new policy initiatives repudiated the approach taken by the Free State government during the 1920s: the priority given to agricultural development and the acceptance of a free trade philosophy. Perhaps the earlier policy goals were too modest or misdirected. Perhaps, too, the policy instruments were not adequate to the tasks at hand. Certainly the economy's performance in those years did not meet the expectations which attended Independence. International economic conditions worked against the attainment of the policy aspirations. This was particularly true of the expectation that agriculture would provide the drive for Irish economic growth. Equally significant was the existence of a flawed assumption: that "the welfare of agriculture was automatically identical with the welfare of the nation" (Daly 1981: 142). Specifically, agricultural well being was associated with high food prices, low wages, low taxes, and low social services (Ibid).

Yet, it should be said that some gains were achieved in agriculture, as Ireland's reputation for quality products was restored. It is also true that the Irish could point to important political gains in that first decade. Democratic processes were consolidated, as the orderly transfer of power in 1932 attests (Kennedy, Giblin, and McHugh 1988: 37-40). This peaceful transition did not take place in quiet times. The Depression worsened, a trade dispute with Britain was in the offing and, when that problem was finally resolved, World War II began.

Sinn Fein had held to the position that the Free State was an illegitimate entity. From 1922 until 1926 Eamon deValera, the leader of Sinn Fein, held to this position and in successive elections earned the second largest number of votes after Cumann na nGaedheal. But time was passing and abstention from the Dail meant that Sinn Fein was increasingly left out as the Free State government established its writ over Ireland. Eamon deValera recognized that Sinn Fein ran the risk of becoming a marginal force as the years passed and he determined to create a party that would take its seats under certain conditions. In 1926 he founded Fianna Fáil which absorbed the bulk of the former Sinn Fein supporters. Thus Fianna Fáil came to represent the interests and doctrines of the nationalist movement. The party's support was drawn from workers (more workers supported Fianna Fáil than supported the Labour Party), small farmers and landholders, agricultural laborers in rural areas of Ireland, segments of the middle class businessmen such as pub owners, and self-employed skilled tradesmen. In terms of economic doctrine these interests were more supportive of government intervention than Cumann na nGaedheal. Though a minority held to a radical position, Peadar O'Donnell for example, the economic doctrine of Fianna Fáil was certainly more reformist than radical. Radical rearrangement of property ownership was no more contemplated in Fianna Fáil than in Cumann na nGaedheal. In 1927, Fianna Fáil deputies took their seats on the Dail and five years later won control of the government. Ready to implement the doctrines of economic self sufficiency inherited from Arthur Griffith, Fianna Fáil sought to implement policies that favored the interests that supported the party. Thus, Fianna Fáil made efforts to help small farmers with subsidies and the unemployed with government assistance. It advocated health insurance which included the poor, pensions for widows and orphans, and the improvement of safety and working conditions.

DeValera's conception of Irish self sufficiency, coupled with the views of Sean Lemass, Minister for Industry and Commerce, led to the doctrine of protectionism in order to foster industrial development. The active use of the state as a tool of development led to the creation of the semi-state bodies.

Politically, the hold of Fianna Fáil over the electorate was strengthened to the point that they ruled uninterrupted for sixteen years. Moreover the opposition parties coalesced into a single party, Fine Gael, in 1932. This left the Irish party system organized, however loosely, with classes and interests supporting Fianna Fáil, Fine Gael, and Labour in descending order of support.

The personality and abilities of Sean Lemass at Industry and Commerce are widely acknowledged to have influenced the pace of industrial growth. Sean McEntee at Finance came to adopt the traditional orthodox view of that Department, but not to the degree that paralyzed state development efforts in the 1920s.

Changes in the new government's economic policy appeared to be dramatic and far-reaching. In place of the open economy of the previous decade, policy now aimed at self-sufficiency with emphasis placed on lessening Ireland's dependence on Britain. The Finance Act of 1932 placed duties of from 15 to 75 percent on a large number of imports. This measure was calculated to increase employment both in industry and in agriculture and thereby reduce emigration. While this approach had popular support, it also entailed a probable decline in the Irish standard of living. This prospect was made more palatable as the "Economic War" with Britain stirred old animosities (Ibid: 40).

The Economic War, which began in 1932, centered on "the imposition by the British government of levies on Irish cattle exports in order to recover the value of land annuities which the Fianna Fail government decided to withhold" (Daly 1981: 148). In short order, the dispute led to increased trade barriers erected by the two governments. In Ireland's case, "most of these impositions were not retaliatory but rather in pursuance of the government's protectionist policy" (Kennedy, Giblin, and McHugh 1988: 43). The Control of Manufactures Acts (1932 and 1934) supplemented this policy by discouraging foreign investment behind the newly assembled tariff walls (Meenan 1970: 151).

Although some of its impact had been softened by agreements reached in 1935, the Economic War did not end until 1938. At that point, on the eve of the Second World War, the Depression, the Economic War, and the protectionist policies had combined to work a number of changes in Irish economic performance. Trade was particularly affected, with both the volume and value of merchandise and agricultural exports falling. "The average annual value of exports in the years between 1932 and 1938, £21.3 million, was less than half the average in the preceding seven years (1925-1931), £43.1 million" (Kennedy, Giblin, and McHugh 1988: 45). Prices of imports also fell, but less than export prices and there was a worsening in the terms of trade. This posed a problem for those Irish industries dependent upon imported materials or semifinished goods (Ibid: 45). Agricultural output changed little during the 1930s. While industrial output did increase at about 6 percent per year, the impact on total employment was slight (Ibid: 46-48).

However, employment figures for 1926 and 1938 do show some interesting outcomes associated with the events and policies of the 1930s. There are changes in the structure of the economy: agriculture's share of total employment fell from 53.5 percent in 1926 to 48 percent in 1938. The comparable figures for industry are 13.3 percent and 17.8 percent. Total employment rose slightly from 1,220,000 in 1926 to 1,224,000 in 1938, with job gains in industry and services offsetting losses in agriculture. While the overall gain appears modest, "it was the first increase in numbers employed since the famine. The rise in industrial employment of over 50,000 was the most dramatic achieved in this century" (Daly 1981: 150).

Real Gross National Product in 1938 was 10 percent above the figure for 1931. However, even though there was little population change during the decade, the deterioration in the terms of trade forestalled any gain in real income per capita (Kennedy, Giblin, and McHugh 1988: 48).

A recent survey of the Irish economy warns against overstating the radical nature of Fianna Fáil's departures from the approaches of the 1920s. Although industry was accorded greater protection, that sector was not seen as replacing agriculture as the "engine of growth." Land policy still aimed at establishing peasant proprietorships on small holdings. And the newly instituted State bodies in such areas as electricity, beet sugar, and turf development were clearly meant to satisfy needs unmet by private enterprise. In its land and industrial policies, the government manifested "the same pragmatic approach, social in outlook but definitely not socialist" (Ibid: 51).

The war years of 1939-1945 bring our period to a close. Ireland was neutral during that conflict but was hardly unaffected by the war. Imports fell off sharply, reinforcing the policy of self-sufficiency adopted in the 1930s. A shortage of British shipping services in itself would have created difficulties for Ireland. In addition, Britain's military needs led to a severe reduction in the materials available to the Irish economy: fertilizer, fuel, machinery, spare parts, and semifinished goods to be worked on by manufacturing firms.

As a result of these difficulties, industrial output fell sharply during the war years. Agriculture diversified to meet domestic needs and, where possible, to satisfy some of Britain's growing demand. Overall agricultural output was maintained with difficulty. In this setting, long-term development efforts had to await the war's end. The primary problem of those years was adapting to such straitened circumstances that a fall in living standards was inevitable. The end of the war in 1945 saw Ireland's real GNP and real per capita GNP at prewar levels, although many goods were not available to consumers and businesses. Population had held steady, despite significant emigration to Britain for work or for military service (Ibid: 51). By 1946, total employment was close to the prewar level of 1,225,000. Agriculture's share had dropped to 46.4 percent of the total, while industry accounted for 18.4 percent of those employed.

As in 1918, the end of hostilities brought the expectation of better times to come. However, the environment in post-World War II Europe was different in several important respects from that of the years following the Armistice. There was the potential for greater international cooperation and coordination than before. And in an important development that would ultimately be felt in Ireland, Britain and the United States moved towards the management of economic change. The Beveridge Report in Britain and the Employment Act of 1946 in the U.S. reflected the Keynesian view that governments could (and should) act to promote stable economic growth.

# *Three*

# From the "Emergency" to Economic Planning, 1946–1959

The effects of the war, the "Emergency" in Ireland, were felt in all sectors of the economy. In the agricultural area Irish farms could still produce an agricultural surplus but that surplus was not an adequate substitute for many foods that had been imported before the war. Thus, despite the development of new crops there were many shortages of foodstuffs. The demand for agricultural products in Britain provided a market for Irish agriculture but an increase in production was difficult due to the shortages of fuel and fertilizer (about a 90 percent loss from prewar levels). Agricultural feed was also in short supply. A serious shortage of farm machinery and parts for farm machinery hampered the ability of farmers to expand agricultural output.

Farmers also began to produce products for the home market, cut off by shortages, which diminished their capacity to increase production of crops for export. It was a credit to the Irish farmers that they maintained production at about the same level as 1938 while imports, including fuel and parts, dropped four-fifths by 1943 (Kennedy, Giblin, and McHugh 1988: 50).

In the underdeveloped industrial sector the impact was all the greater. The same fuel and parts shortages were exacerbated by a shortage of raw materials. The volume of industrial output dropped by 1943 to only 75 percent of that before the war. A corresponding drop in industrial employment of 23,000 people occurred.

Several long term characteristics of the Irish economy were amplified by the war. The traditional dependence on the United Kingdom market was intensified. Though the total volume of exports was halved, and imports dropped by two-thirds the proportion of products going to, and coming from, the U. K. increased. The outflow of population during the war was twice that of the period of the 1930s and was concentrated on the U. K. Young men left Ireland to serve in the U. K. armed forces but most went to work in the war-stoked industries in Britain. The standard of living dropped during the war.

The constraints on imports caused tea, sugar, clothes, butter, tobacco, and fruit to be virtually eliminated. No one was allowed to drive a car after 1943. The fact that at the end of the war GNP and GNP per capita were essentially the same as at the beginning of the war masked serious difficulties in the Irish economy.

After the "Emergency" there were three developments in the Irish economy. The first was a period of expansion from 1947 to 1951, the second was a period of stagnation from 1952 until 1958, and the third was the underlying accumulation from 1950 to 1958 of institutions, legislation, and policies which were to provide the foundation for rapid economic growth during the 1960s.

The importance of agriculture to the Irish economy cannot be overstated. As noted above, in 1922 agriculture accounted for one-half of the work force and one-third of the Free State's Gross National Product. The situation was no different in 1945. The attempt to formulate a postwar policy was addressed by a committee of Inquiry on Post Emergency Agricultural Policy. In a series of interim reports, and in a concluding *Reports on Agricultural Policy* issued in 1945, the Committee sought measures for "increasing the fertility of the land, promoting efficiency in the industry and making the various branches of the industry self supporting" (*Reports on Agricultural Policy* 1945: 1).

The committee recognized the need for increased exports and the degree to which agriculture was dependent upon the British market. The measures to increase productivity included soil surveys, investment in fertilizer, cultivation of grassland, and improvement in technical support. Protectionist perspectives persisted as the Committee noted that the subsidies put in place during the war should not be removed. An "Advisory Council" was recommended to assist in agricultural development.

*REPORTS*
*on*
*AGRICULTURAL POLICY*
*1945*

*157. In the post-Emergency period efficiency in the production, processing and distribution of agricultural commodities must be developed to the maximum degree and all the factors which make for efficiency must be employed. Among these are agricultural education, credit on favourable terms, availablity of suitable machinery and implements, manures, and feeding stuffs, the breeding of the best type of stock and the proper feeding thereof, reduction in losses arising from diseases of animals and crops, a machinery service for farmers, co-operative effort, and efficient marketing of agricultural produce.*

*158. The development of agriculture, the necessary increase in output, and the maintenance of people on the land through the establishment of a better balance between the income from agriculture and that from non-agricultural industries cannot be secured solely by the employment of better methods and improved technique on the part of the agricultural producer. In the past, farmers were disinclined to put capital back into the land and to adopt increased efficiency measures because of the uncertainty of the market for their produce. While we realise the necessity for increased efficiency it appears to us that mere insistence on efficiency is of little value. Efficiency will be secured only if the farmer is provided with an assured market for his products at fair prices thus enabling him to plan his production ahead and stimulating him to invest capital in his enterprise. This can be done by the adoption of a long-term policy under which the home market is reserved, as far as practicable, to our farmers and price levels maintained thereon. The basis of policy must be the exploitation of the home market to the maximum possible extent and the fixing of prices so as to secure and maintain stability in our agricultural industry.*

*159. The contention that the maintenance of price levels on the home market for certain goods would be detrimental to our export trade is without foundation and based on fallacious reasoning. On the contrary, we believe that increased production cannot be secured in the absence of price stability for certain products at least.*

*160. If the industrial worker has, as a result of a policy of fixed prices for certain agricultural products, to pay somewhat more than world prices for his food requirements he must realise that agriculturists are in many cases paying more than world prices for industrial products used in agriculture owing to the industrial protection policy.*

*161. The system of husbandry whereby land was permanently grazed has, except in a very limited area of first-class pasture, been responsible for a considerable reduction in soil fertility. The restoration of fertility is essential for efficient production. This can be achieved by bringing the deteriorated grasslands into cultivation and by the application of farmyard manure, artificial fertilisers and, where necessary, lime, and by improved husbandry methods. The renovation of deteriorated pastures by tillage will, however, be adopted only if the tillage crops grown in the process of breaking up the land yield a profit.*

*162. In the interest of improved soil fertility, of increased and efficient production, of the better winter feeding of stock, and for the purpose of increasing employment on the land, it is imperative that a certain amount of tillage be maintained on all holdings. We anticipate that a large number of our farmers would, at the termination of the Emergency and in the absence of compulsory measures, automatically revert to permanent pasture, a contingency which must be avoided.*

*163. Because of the comparatively limited amount of employment so far available in this country in non-agricultural industry, the maintenance in rural occupations of as many of our people as possible is imperative. The depopulation of the countryside should be arrested. Agriculture should be enabled to pay wages which bear a closer relationship to industrial wages, and life in the country should be made attractive. A general economic policy of employment for all citizens would, by increasing the demand of the home market for home-produced agricultural produce, benefit agriculture and give increased employment on the land.*

*164. We have aimed at producing conditions which will remove the elements of speculation connected with the production and sale of agricultural produce, call forth industrious effort on the part of the farmer and foster a prosperous and populous rural community. In the absence of an assurance of a reasonable return for the sale of agricultural produce we can see no prospect of the successful development of agriculture in the post-Emergency period. A policy which aims specifically at reducing production costs to a minimum in order to cater for a speculative export market cannot, in our opinion, be regarded as a solution of the problems of our agriculture.*

*The policy we have outlined will provide stability for agriculture and will secure to efficient producers remunerative prices for the produce of their land. The adoption of our recommendations will enable farmers to contract ahead of production, and we are confident that, following the improvement in their position which would result, producers will develop an efficient and enterprising farming technique and will from their own resources invest the capital necessary for full and economical production.*

Politically, 1948 brought a change to the Irish government. Fianna Fáil, while winning more seats than any other party, found all the other parties willing to bury their very considerable differences to form a coalition government. The leading figure of the interparty government was Sean McBride, of the new Clann na Poblachta party, who became Minister for External Affairs. The Prime Minister was John A. Costello of Fine Gael. The economic interests supporting this coalition ranged from the big farmers and bankers of Fine Gael to the unionized workers of the Labour Party. The prominence of McBride and the fact that the Marshall Plan aid from the United States came through External Affairs elevated his influence. The Plan paid for fifty percent of state expenditures during this period. The lack of a coherent strategy for use of the Marshall Plan funds reflected the strong influence of orthodox Fine Gael thinking which felt that the government should not be borrowing and spending at all. In addition, the Minister of Agriculture sought to spend the money on a major land reclamation project while McBride's own priorities included electricity, telephones, and afforestation. McBride also sought to spend some of the money on building factories and leasing them to businesses, a project requiring more consensus than was present in the coalition. The principal thrust of development policy in this period remained the European Recovery Programme discussed below, far more a product of

McBride's haste to get the U.S. aid than a coherent vision for the Irish economy.

This marked committment to protection on the part of the government to promote agriculture was evident in the comment that to "cater for a speculative export import ... cannot be in our opinion, regarded as a solution" (*Reports on Agricultural Policy* 1945). Two minority submissions to the Report, those of Mr. J. Mahoney and Professor E. J. Sheehy, and those of Dr. Henry Kennedy, advocated a greater degree of protection, proposed prohibiting imports, guaranteed prices, obliging farms to cultivate land, and suggested research institutes, direct grants for farm improvement, as well as councils to provide advice to the Department of Agriculture. This committment to government protection in both majority and minority reports was seen as increasing efficiency and increasing employment, and keeping people on the land.

The problems identified in the 1945 report were echoed in two other government reports, in 1948 and 1949, under the new government. The 1948 report was prepared by G. A. Holmes and entitled *On the Present State and Methods of Improvement of Irish Land.* Holmes was an authority on grasslands from New Zealand. He focused on the deficiencies in drainage, liming, fertilizer, seed, pasture management, and weeds. The Report stresses the potential of Irish agriculture: "First of all, there is no area of comparable size in the Northern hemisphere which has such marvelous potentialities for pasture production as Eire undoubtedly has" (*On the Present State* 1948: 8). That potential had not been exploited and, as the Report cautiously noted, could not be realized with a "magician's wand" but "perhaps a ten year plan, carefully studied, will raise production on many farms by a full 100 per cent but it is important that the expenditure to achieve this should throughout be in proportion to returns" (*On the Present State* 1948: 9). The next year, 1949, the Dail passed the Land Reclamation Act implementing some of the recommendations of the 1945 and 1948 reports on agriculture. This ten year reclamation scheme, partially funded by the Marshall Plan, improved drainage, fertilization, liming, and farm machinery.

In 1949 the Department of Agriculture reviewed the government subsidies to dairy products. The *Guaranteed Market and Prices for Dairy Produce* report reiterated the argument for subsidized prices for butter made in the 1945 report and concludes "The Government have decided that the best form of encouragement for the dairy industry is an assurance that there would be a market for creameries' total output at prices guaranteed far in advance for a number of years" (*Guaranteed Market* 1949: 8).

Another manifestation of Ireland's aspirations for agriculture (and tourist and industrial development) is *The European Recovery Programme: Ireland's Long Term Programme (1949-1953)* presented to the government by the Minister of External Affairs in 1948. The report outlined the problems that plagued agriculture due to the War, outlined the aid needed for "imports of grains, feeding stuffs, machinery, oil and other commodities from the dollar area for which, because her available dollar resources are meagre and uncertain, she is not in a position to pay in the absence of United States aid" (*European Recovery Programme* 1948: 10). The goals that the report projected for 1952-1953 were an increase in total production of 22 percent over 1947 and an increase in export volume of over 100 percent. And where was the destination of the growth in production and exports? "It is anticipated that virtually all of Ireland's exports will continue to go to the United Kingdom... the amount of $295 million to the United Kingdom out of an export total of $317 million for 1952/53" (*European Recovery Programme* 1948: 14).

Thus the aspirations for agriculture in the period from 1945 to 1953 were clear; to stimulate production, reclaim land, improve efficiency, expand exports, and increase employment. The means chosen were the Land Act of 1949 and price supports. The results were disappointing.

*THE EUROPEAN RECOVERY PROGRAMME*
*Ireland's Long Term Programme (1949-1953)*
*1948*

*III. AGRICULTURE*

*12. Agriculture is Ireland's basic industry and it is in the agricultural sphere that the country can make the most effective contribution to the success of the European Recovery Programme. By increasing the production and, thereby, the exports of the foods of high protein value on which she has traditionally concentrated and which she is particularly suited to produce — meat, eggs and dairy produce — Ireland can play an important part in meeting an urgent demand and reducing the dependence of Participating Countries (especially Great Britain) on dollar sources of supply. Ireland relies on a considerable recovery in food exports from their present depressed level for the increase in earnings necessary to put her external finances on a sound foundation. The improvement in agricultural output, upon which her own recovery and the contribution she can make to the recovery of Europe generally depend, cannot be secured without imports of grains, feeding stuffs, machinery, oil and other commodities from the dollar area for which, because her available dollar resources are meagre and uncertain, she is not in a position to pay in the absence of United States aid.*

*13. The importance of agriculture in the Irish economy is indicated by the facts that it employs almost half the working population and that it is the source of the bulk of Ireland's exports. The proportion of the population engaged in industry is low even by comparison with countries of a somewhat similar economy. The production of livestock and livestock produce is the principal branch of Irish farming. It is in this field, and not in bread grain production, that Ireland has special advantages and can economically produce valuable exportable surpluses. For countries with a suitable soil and climate or in which agriculture is a subsidiary element in the economy and provides merely an offset to import requirements of food, concentration on bread grains may be advantageous but it would entail in the circumstances of this country a waste of resources.*

*14. The effect of the war years on agricultural production in Ireland is indicated by the fact that the volume of output of livestock and livestock products in 1947 was only 84 per cent of 1938-39. It is a major aim of Ireland's long term programme to make good the losses sustained during the war years as quickly as possible. The essential conditions of recovery are the availablity of materials and the existence of satisfactory prices on the export market.*

*V. DESTINATION OF EXPORTS*

*22. It is anticipated that virtually all of Ireland's exports will continue to go to the United Kingdom and other Participating Countries, thereby reducing their dependence on dollar sources of supply. Under a Trade Agreement with Great Britain concluded last June, the basis of trade in agricultural produce has been settled for the four years from 1st July, 1948, to 30th June, 1952. On the assumption that conditions will still be favourable in 1952/53 and beyond for the expansion of exports to that market, the amount of $295 million has been allocated to the United Kingdom out of the export total of $317 million for 1952/53. Other Participating Countries are expected to take exports to the value of $14 million — principally meat in the form of cattle. In the case of North and Central America, exports are expected to reach $3 million in 1952/53, as against $1.2 million actual for 1947.*

*(iii) INDUSTRY*

*The number of persons engaged in industry is, however, still low even in comparison with countries which, like Ireland, have a predominantly agricultural economy. Less than one-fifth of the working population of about 1,250,000 is engaged in industrial production as against over one-fourth in New Zealand and one-third in Denmark. This position obtains despite the efforts which were made before the war, by the establishment and development of native industries, to absorb in productive activity at home some of the surplus population for whom the land does not provide an adequate employment or livelihood. In 1926 the total number employed in industries covered by the Census of Industrial Production and excluding, therefore, the numbers in very small concerns was only 102,500; the number had been expanded to 166,000 by 1938. Despite this increase in industrial employment, net emigration in the decade 1926/36 totalled 169,316 persons.*

*41. The drastic reduction in the volume of imports during the war years contracted the field of employment in industry, and emigration took place on a very large scale, with the result that the decade 1936/46 showed a total net emigration of 189,942 persons. The effect of emigration on this scale has been to prevent the natural increase (i.e. the excess of births over deaths) from causing any rise in the total population. The improvement in imports since 1945 has been accompanied by an increase in employment and the number now in industrial employment is about 184,000. Industrial production generally is now approximately 14 per cent above 1938. Proposals for the establishment of many new factories have been approved; these include such industries as aluminum hollow-ware; asbestos cement goods; bricks; canning of fish; concrete blocks and other concrete products; confectionery; detergents; electric transformers, motors and switch gear, and a variety of other electrical goods; fluorescent lighting equipment; furniture (metal and wooden); glassware; glue and gelatine; grass meal; grindery for boots and shoes; leather cloth; machinery for the tanning and leather dressing industry; metal wire; paints; pharmaceutical goods; plaster board and wallboard; plastic goods of various kinds; refrigeration equipment; seaweed processing; sparking plugs; starch; structural steel; tiles; timber products; tools and implements (hand); windows (metal); wireless sets and components; wool combing.*

*42. A large proportion of the country's population is centered in the Dublin area and many of the new industries naturally are attracted to this centre. Government industrial policy, however, continues to encourage industrial promoters to locate their factories in provincial towns and country districts with a view to establishing a local as well as a national balance between agricultural and industrial pursuits.*

*43. A measure of protection is recognised as necessary to enable new industries to gain a sound foothold in countries underdeveloped industrially. The proximity of a highly industrialised country with an established market in Ireland and a well organised advertising system designed to maintain the goodwill of its products is a factor which has strengthened the well-known economic justification for protection of infant industries. The Government is, however, insisting increasingly, as a condition of protection, on the highest degree of efficiency being attained in industrial production so that the products of protected industries will be competitive in quality and price with those produced in other countries.*

*44. In general, conditions in Ireland are favourable to the establishment of new industries. There is an adequate supply of labour which has in practice been found to be adaptable and quick to learn new processes. Political and economic conditions are stable; the level of taxation compares favourably with that in other countries; local authorities and local industrial development associations are prepared to welcome industrialists to their localities and to arrange for local capital participation and other facilities where required.*

On the supply side Irish agriculture had a fall in production of 13 percent between 1945 and 1947, before the Marshall Plan proposal. There was a drop of 7 percent between 1949 and 1952 and by the target date agricultural output had hardly increased by the 22 percent projected in the *Programme*. The failure in productivity was caused by a structural element, the small farm. In addition, the terms of trade in agricultural products deteriorated and there was a contraction of demand for Irish agricultural products in the United Kingdom market.

The total export projected by the *Programme* was wildly optimistic as, from the end of the war to the mid 1950s, the United Kingdom's demand for Irish agricultural output was stagnant and foreign competition stiff. Irish exports to Britain did not provide the necessary prod to increased agricultural production. From 1945 to 1960 Irish agricultural output grew only by 8 percent. Thus in the late 1950s the Irish Government recast both its aspiration and means to stimulate agricultural production.

After the war the Irish economy enjoyed a surge in tourism. Tourist revenues accounted for about one-third of Ireland's invisible exports through 1949, but the overall pattern of tourism in this period was less than spectacular as the initial boom after the war was followed by a drop in revenues. The Irish Tourist Board was created in 1939 to classify accommodations and assist in staff training. In the postwar period the Department of Industry and Commerce issued a brief report *Tourist Development Programme* (1946) which noted that the disruption of tourism on the continent was an opportunity for Ireland. The report recommended increased government loans to develop facilities and indicated that the Tourist Board itself could take responsibility for developing facilities.

The report's prediction was accurate as tourism boomed due to the availability of plentiful food in Ireland, the postwar currency restrictions, and the less than scintillating attractions of war damage on the continent. The peak year was 1948.

Ireland's *European Recovery Programme* report was as optimistic about the revenues from tourism as it was about agricultural exports to Britain. Noting that net income from tourism in 1947 was $112 million, the report states "but it would be unrealistic to expect the revenue from tourism could be maintained uninterruptedly at such a high level" (*European Recovery Programme* 1948: 23). The report goes on to point out that the United States tourist dollar component of that $112 million was $7 million, or about 6 percent of the total. The report projected the dollar component of revenues in 1952/1953 to be $13 million, which would have been a total tourist income of about $217 million dollars (*European Recovery Programme* 1948: 24).

In 1951 a series of reports summarized the results of a mission to the United States to find ways to improve Irish tourism: *Synthesis of Reports on Tourism 1950-51*. Dealing with publicity, advertising, transport, and accommodations, the report projected an increase in American tourists from 21,000 in 1949 to 70,000 in 1953. That report also recommended the consolidation of the Irish Tourist Board and Irish Tourist Association. In the event the 1952 Tourist Traffic Act transformed the earlier Board to Bord Failte and created a Tourist Publicity Organization. Along with these organizations to stimulate tourism, the government provided interest free loans for improvement of hotels and guesthouses. Access to this money was burdened by excessive legal and bureaucratic hurdles and its availability, however, did not prove to be an incentive to the hospitality industry. Two more legislative steps were taken to generate tourism; the 1955 absorption of all tourist functions by Bord Failte and the 1957 Tourist Traffic Act which provided far better incentives to improve hotel facilities. The Irish government had specified its aspirations for tourist development and the means to achieve them. What was the result?

As it turned out the year 1949 was the high water mark for revenues in the ten years following. Revenues fell from £27 million pounds in 1949 to a low of £22.6 million in 1954, finally recovering to £27.7 in 1959. In 1953, the year the *Programme* had hoped to generate $13 million on a total tourist revenue of approximately $217 million, the actual figure was $6 million on a total revenue of approximately $100 million. The number of American tourists projected for 1953 by the 1951 tourist report was 70,000, the actual figure was 33,000. The Tourist Traffic Act of 1952 was no more successful with its incentives as the reports were in their estimates. In the period 1952 to 1957 the number of hotel and guest house bedrooms in Ireland actually *decreased* from 17,000 to 16,000 (Kennedy and Dowling 1975: 143). It was not until after 1959 that tourism in Ireland was to increase under a program of improved incentives.

Along with agriculture and tourism a most important area of the economy was industrial development. The aspiration of the Irish governments in the immediate postwar years were limited to capital investment, requesting Marshall Plan aid, protectionism, and hewing to the conservative line that economic growth would be generated by the private sector. Leaders were not yet persuaded by the Keynesian approach.

In fact the policy toward industrial growth was operating at two levels. On the one hand the government, sparked by balance of payments crises, adopted constrictive economic policies throughout the fifties. On the other hand government institutions were created to generate growth, acts were passed to provide government incentives, reports were produced that called for a more active role on the part of the government, all of which finally culminated in the famous *Economic Development* report of 1958.

We can review the latter record as it bears on the changes in government policy in 1958 and contrast it with the actions of successive governments in the early 1950s. A comprehensive articulation of Ireland's goals for the immediate postwar period is in the *European Recovery Programme* of 1948 in the section on Industry excerpted above.

This part of the *European Recovery Programme* report is more in order of a lament about lack of industrial development in the past coupled with a hope for the future: "Proposals" have been approved for "many new factories" which government industrial policy encourages to locate "in provincial towns and country districts" and will be protected from foreign competition in light of "the well known justification for protection of infant industries" (*European Recovery Programme* 1948: 21). Local authorities are prepared to welcome and "arrange for Local capital participation" where required.

The creation of the Industrial Development Authority (IDA) triggered a wave of criticism, partly due to a struggle over bureaucratic turf (Finance opposed it) but also because it was supported by McBride. In fact the suggestion that an authority might actually plan industrial development or use the authority and funds of government to encourage industry flew into the harsh winds of the coalition traditionalists and opposition leaders like Lemass who did not want an agency created that would challenge his old bailiwick of Industry and Commerce.Ireland's participation in the Marshall Plan did lead to two developments which were to blossom later. The first was the creation of the IDA in 1950. The second was the creation of the Dollar Exports Advisory Committee which became the Export Board in 1951. The former was to come to encourage new industries in Ireland, the latter to encourage exports.

An additional progeny of the *European Recovery Programme* was the IBEC Report. In 1951 the IBEC Technical Services corporation of New York was commissioned by the Irish government, in conjunction with the IDA, to chart the industrial potential of Ireland. The resulting report *Industrial Potentials of Ireland* was completed in 1952. The tables mentioned in the text are not included in this excerpt.

*INDUSTRIAL POTENTIALS OF IRELAND*
*AN APPRAISAL*
*1952*

*On the industrial side the progress made in Ireland since 1938 ranks near the top of European achievement as is shown in Table 10 measuring comparative progress and industrial production at constant price levels between 1938 and 1950.*

*Without disparaging the Irish industrial accomplishment in any sense, it is realistic to note the factors which combine to make the Irish record in this field one that should induce further continuing effort rather than self-congratulatory complacence:*

*(1.) It is relatively easy to show impressive percentages of gain at the beginning stages of any development, and increasingly difficult as the development stage matures. Ireland's industrial life is relatively new and small. As Table 10 shows, Ireland accounts for only 1/2 of 1% of the combined industrial output of the nations in the tabulation, and in absolute terms the volume of its industrial output exceeds only that of the Saar, Luxembourg and Portugal.*

*volume of its industrial output exceeds only that of the Saar, Luxembourg and Portugal.*

*(2.) Ireland is one of only a few nations in the list that did not suffer severe damage to its industrial facilities in World War II and its dislocations, while severe enough, were mild compared to many of the others. Accordingly, the Irish problem was essentially one of building up from a small base while many others were faced with a large reconstruction problem before production could be brought back to the pre-war level.*

*(3.) The tempo of Ireland's progress from 1947 to 1950, while still relatively good, is much less spectacular than its comparative standing over the 12-year period as a whole. From 1947 to 1950 industrial progress in Ireland was somewhat below, rather than above, the average for the whole group. From 1947 to 1950 Ireland increased her industrial output about one-third compared to a 50% average for the twenty-three European countries on the list. Its present pace, accordingly, is not sufficient even to hold its present relative position.*

## *PART II*

## *A COMPARATIVE ANALYSIS OF IRISH INDUSTRY*

### *Review of findings in Part I*

*Part I has set forth the general economic background against which an industrial development program for Ireland must be considered. Briefly it has been shown —*

*That the level of Ireland's production output is low, absolutely and comparatively, and the same is true for living standards except with respect to food consumption.*

*That progress is being made in lifting the level of incomes of a stationary population.*

*That all of the upward momentum in physical output terms has come from industry, since agricultural production has remained static.*

*That industry measured by output per worker has produced far more than has agriculture, and that hence the continuation of the employment shift that has been taking place should be further encouraged.*

*That there are, however, serious limitations upon the continuation of such shift imposed by shortages of domestically produced materials, a limited domestic market for manufactures, and competitive problems in producing for export manufactures based on imported materials.*

*That Ireland is faced with a progressively worsening balance-of-payments situation that dictates a greatly increased emphasis upon production for export, with particular attention paid to dollar exports.*

*That the expansion of agricultural output is crucial both to provide direct exports and to increase domestic materials available for manufacture and processing.*

*That the degree of Ireland's economic linkage with the United Kingdom is greater than is consistent with her status of political sovereignty, and that both her stability and her opportunities for economic growth will be forwarded through the taking of progressive measures to broaden her area of trade.*

*That capital formation in Ireland is too low and too concentrated upon immediately non-productive ends to provide the lift that its production requires to fulfill National aspirations.*

*That its concentration under Government auspices is so marked that Government must assume a major responsibility for its rechanneling, although the need for establishing an active domestic capital market that could direct domestic savings into productive uses without Government intervention is strongly indicated.*

*That the problems of adequate capital formation and trade policy are complicated by the fact that investment funds and imports generally are currently being financed to an important degree from accumulated foreign investment that will soon be exhausted, and that swift and sweeping actions must be taken to avert what are certain to be drastic and damaging dislocations if they are postponed.*

*That there are related and complicating problems of inflation that must be handled without sacrificing the flow of investment funds to productive uses upon which economic progress in Ireland depends.*

## *PART III*

## *CONCLUSIONS AND RECOMMENDATIONS*

### *A. General conclusions of this study*

#### *The need for clearly defined economic goals*

*There is clearly definable national aspiration to increase the return realized from Ireland's economic activities, expressed as the official policy of Government and opposition parties, in the editorial comment of the Nation's press, in the pronouncements of organized labor and business groups, and in the conversation of the "man in the street." There is widespread acceptance of the aim to increase the level of economic return not only of the present population, but of the expanding population that would result if Ireland could offer sufficient opportunities to check (1.) the considerable net emigration that has drained off a significant fraction of the most vigorous and ambitious youth for more than a hundred years, and (2.) the postponement of marriages to a degree that makes the average age of contraction in Ireland almost uniquely high.*

*Paradoxically, along with this actively voiced ambition for economic betterment there runs an undercurrent of pessimism or lack of confidence in the prospects for achieving the pronounced aims. The talk is of economic expansion, but the action of Government, business, and labor alike is too often along the lines of consolidating present positions rather than of accepting the hazards inherent in changed practices upon which expansion depends. There are few evidences of boldness or assurance in economic behavior to give substance to expressed economic aims. In fact, the declarations of expansive purpose are frequently qualified by expressions of a conflicting, anti-materialist philosophy, of an asceticism that opposes material aspirations to spiritual goals, and hence writes down the former as unworthy.*

*The first need in Ireland's economic programming is for a clarification of aims, and for a confident and wholehearted commitment to their fulfillment.*

*The need to decide whether or not private enterprise is to be a major instrument*

*a. Present procedures cramp private initiative*

*Similarly, whatever economic goals are accepted there is need for a sharpening of decision upon the system of economic institutions, through which they are to be attained. In the contemporary world there is certainly no hard and fast line that can be drawn between the areas of economic activity of Government and private initiative. But our study has shown that in Ireland, despite a general assumption of opposition to the socialist credo, the state has assumed a far larger role in the channeling of investment funds than in England under a Labour Government. The heavy hand of Government controls has extended widely over all business operations in a manner that has tended to stifle private initiative. Price controls, exercised not as an emergency measure but as a continuing instrument, have tended to become profit controls, justified not as a means of controlling inflation, but on the ground that profits beyond a certain minimum are an evil that should be penalized regardless of whether they result from monopoly or from superior efficiency of operation in a fully competitive situation.*

*Again, Ireland must make up its mind as to the direction it wants to take. If it elects to place major dependence upon socialist procedures, that is certainly within its proper prerogative. But if it means to depend importantly upon individual initiative in the accomplishment of its development aims, it cannot hope to be successful unless it is willing to allow sufficient differential returns to elicit extra effort, imagination and operating effectiveness. Without such incentives, the system of private competition won't work.*

*B. OVERCOMING HANDICAPS TO MANUFACTURING*

*The factor of low investment*

*Low investment, in turn, is the result of a variety of influences.*

*a. Profits from manufacturing enterprises in Ireland in general have not been sufficiently high to attract domestic private investment upon a scale consistent with a vigorous industrial development in its initial stages, or to encourage the thorough modernization of existing equipment needed to make Irish manufacturing genuinely competitive. This has been an important influence in retarding the growth of a healthfully active domestic securities market, and accounts in important measure for the considerable volume of Irish investment funds that have been invested abroad over a period of years.*

*b. An elaborate system of Government regulations and controls has exercised divergent and sometimes conflicting influences upon private business initiative. Thus, (1.) The laudable and imaginatively conceived efforts and generally businesslike operation of the Industrial Credit Corporation to promote industrial activity through direct investment and loans have not been conspicuously successful in the important aim of marketing its securities to the investing public. Thus the operations of the ICC have been restricted to a relatively modest scale. At best, such a quasi-governmental program should only be expected to complement, rather than substitute for, an active private investment market. (2.) The protective tariff policy of Government has automatically carried with it the presumption of price controls, and there has been a tendency to maintain unnecessarily higher protection rates with the elaborate control machinery kept in operation to protect consumers instead of lowering customs rates, or other import barriers, to a point where consumer exploitation could be prevented by simple import competition. (3.) The entire price control machinery has seemingly been operated from a highly moralistic approach that has tended to turn into a profits control system — attacking high profits as an inherent evil, to be directly prevented by complicated and diverse measures of unit markup controls, total profit controls and other devices with little regard for their impact upon incentives for industrial efficiency and in some cases (as in shoes) resulting in multiple prices for goods of the same quality. (4.) The business tax structure, while lower than that of the United Kingdom or the United States, and about the same as that in Holland and Sweden, has probably been too high for Ireland's stage of industrial development, amounting to about 40% on the profits of moderate sized manufacturing corporations. (5.) The ostensible weight of this tax burden has been increased by what appears to be an inadequate allowance for depreciation and depletion, when consideration is given to the great need for strong modernization. (6.) Customs duties on import materials in several fields add to the existing handicaps under which the industries dependent upon such materials labor. (7.) Finally, there has been a very heavy hand of Government regulations placed upon foreign trade through numerous import controls and export licensing provisions of the type that has been discussed in connection with meat exports.*

*Not sufficient Government initiative for socialism — nor sufficient incentive for private enterprise*

*In sum, under Irish procedures, there has been built up a system of practices that have limited and importantly displaced private initiative without the corresponding assumption of a vigorous Government initiative and responsibility for promoting a direct expansion of domestic production and foreign trading activities that are characteristic of socialist economies. The result has been to saddle Ireland with many of the disadvantages of both the private initiative and the socialist approaches, without realizing the full advantages of either.*

*There is need for a re-examination of Government economic policies across the board with the view of rationalizing them in order that they may promote a consistent incentive toward a consistent set of economic aims. The same might be said of almost any other country — certainly of the United States. If the need is greater in Ireland than elsewhere, it is only because Ireland has fewer natural economic advantages than many others and, hence, less margin for muddling. This sorting out and definition of major purposes is not something that can be done by outsiders. Ireland must decide what it wants to do, and once having done so, her own people are quite as capable of appraising the impact of specific measures upon central aims as are any outsiders. There is in the Irish Government however, an exceptional degree of compartmentalization. We found in a number of fields critically important to industrial development, that there was little central policy guidance from the agencies charged with formulating industrial development policy, and often a lack even of specific information as to what was being done in the ancillar lines. Thus the Ministry of Agriculture has seemingly exercised an almost autonomous voice in negotiating the cattle provisions of the Trade Treaty, although the issues are of crucial importance to industrial development prospects. Some workable mechanism, at least for assuring the reasonable coordination of economic policy, would seem to be badly needed.*

*E. THE NEED FOR INDEPENDENCE OF THE IRISH ECONOMY (Sections C an D are not included in this excerpt.)*

*We return, at the end, to a theme that has run like a chain of linked traffic signals throughout our analysis of the Irish economy — the degree of Ireland's economic linkage to the United Kingdom which is inconsistent with its passionate commitment to political independence. The effectiveness of political sovereignty will continue to be vitiated while the Irish economy remains so decisively dependent upon the United Kingdom as a market for its exports, as the purveyor of its shipping services, as its major source of import supply, and in its financial and fiscal services.*

*The influence of this status of economic dependency dominates the design and color of Ireland's economic life in myriad ways that rob it of independent initiative. Her currency is tied to sterling, and sterling crises affect Ireland by the inevitable process of infusion. Ireland's investment funds both public and private have flowed to the United Kingdom in the absence of a developed and active market for home investment. She is almost entirely dependent upon Britain for dollar exchange. She is forced to buy an important part of her processing materials upon terms that are competitively disadvantageous, and to sell an important part of her output in a form that serves the convenience and interest of England's economy rather than her own. Almost every decision and bargain with respect to Ireland's foreign trade is conditioned by the stern necessity of accepting the best terms that Britain will offer, since no tenable alternatives have been fashioned.*

*The status of economic dependence permeates the psychology and outlook of all but a few of the boldest spirits who are concerned with the management of Ireland's economic affairs. Procedures in most economic fields continue to be modeled upon British procedures even at a time when, demonstrably, they are working far from well in the country of their origin.*

*Irish business is generally hesitant to meet British competition head-on. Premium aged Irish whiskey is exported at prices competitive with ordinary Scotch, which leaves neither much by way of incentive for exporting or margin for promoting its sale. Irish pottery and most Irish textiles are styled to imitate British designs instead of developing a distinctive character of their own. There is an enormous good-will toward Ireland in many parts of the world, partly generated by its forced emigration of population, that could be capitalized if Ireland could develop export products that were both excellent in quality and recognizably Irish in their characteristics.*

*For the Irish economy to come of age, it must be placed in a position of independence comparable at least to that which to date has been achieved in the political field. That, too, will require time and effort. Independence can only be achieved through building alternative markets and finding alternative sources of supply. It emphaticially cannot be forwarded by merely giving up long established relationships with the British economy, a process that would leave Ireland weaker rather than stronger. The best economic policy for Ireland is to hold fast to profitable trade exchanges with the United Kingdom, but to assiduously cultivate trade and trade relationships with other nations as well. Thus, upon an expanded trade base, independence in the form of multiple alternate opportunities may gradually be built, without sacrificing the volume of trade that flows in the traditional channel. The first prerequisite is a recognition of need strong enough to stimulate a consistent drive for its achievement on the part of government and private interests alike.*

*The exploration of specific development potentials recommended in this report represents one line of procedure. It is an important line, and one that deserves full and vigorous implementation. It involves the meticulous study of market opportunities and comparative cost structures in Ireland and all potential manufacturing competitors. In this connection, the operating comparisons between manufacturing in Ireland and the United States are far from irrelevant, since successful development in the notoriously unsentimental arena of world trade will depend upon Ireland's ability to meet the toughest competition in sight.*

*But it should be recognized that there are no magic formulae for selecting either new lines of manufacture, or existing lines that can be expanded, with certain success. There are few, if any, specific fields of processing or manufacture, (except perhaps the field of meat and cattle by-product production and fabrication) in which Ireland may truthfully be said to have great natural advantages. On the other hand, there are few enterprises based on the fabrication of domestically produced materials, or even on imported materials provided that their bulk, weight and cost are low in relation to the value of the processing applied to them, in which Ireland could not compete successfully if production were organized with the requisite efficiency.*

*If Ireland were to establish a general economic climate favorable to private initiative, with institutions that provided strong incentives for investment in the modern capital equipment upon which high productivity depends, and equally attractive rewards for managerial and worker performance, development of the more promising lines of manufacture would follow almost automatically. Foreign capital likewise could be attracted in considerable volume to what would amount to a haven from the state-imposed restrictions that are so widely prevalent in Europe. In the absence of such an encouraging atmosphere to enterprise, it will be difficult to nurture successfully even those ventures which are most wisely selected in terms of Ireland's development needs.*

*The greatest need in Ireland's economic life is confidence — the will to establish a framework of economic institutions geared to dynamic growth, the independence to cut loose from usages modeled upon European practice that is defensively restrictive. In short, Ireland, in the economic sphere, needs to adopt the independence of spirit that it has applied to the political and cultural fronts. Its economic development calls for the boldness of individual initiative and the healthy gusto for the good things of life that characterize the Heroic Tradition. That tradition is sufficiently a part of the fabric of Irish culture to warrant confidence that Ireland will build an economic future, upon its already considerable progress in the industrial field, commensurate with the potential of its fine human and by no means negligible natural resources.*

When released the Report was ignored by the then Fianna Fail government and the proposed aid from IBEC in prompting investment in the "potentials" identified never took place. The report was prescient in several ways that should be highlighted in the face of what occurred later.

harbored a "conflicting anti-materialist philosophy" and a propensity for deadening government controls. The suggestions to invest the government's capital in growth producing manufacturing rather than public works, encouragement of foreign investment through tax incentives, and liberalization of price controls to promote exports, addressing the problem of employment and emigration, all prefigured the approaches adopted in later government programs.

The IBEC is not the only report to seek government action to stimulate industrial growth and employment. The 1953 *Committee of Inquiry into Taxation on Industry Report* was convened to consider a increase in the depreciation allowance so as to allow a closer relation of "wear and tear" to replacement costs. The larger argument embedded in this particular tax issue was whether the government was going to use tax policy to stimulate industrial growth.

*COMMITTEE OF INQUIRY INTO TAXATION ON INDUSTRY REPORT 1953*

*INTRODUCTORY*

*At our first meeting on the 26th October, 1953, Mr. MacEntee addressed the Committee. In the course of his address he said:*

*"For many years past representations have been made to successive Ministers for Finance concerning the incidence of taxation on industry. The substance of these complaints was that, in its present form, taxation was proving an obstacle to the modernisation and extension of productive capacity or, to put it more succinctly, to the investment of capital in industry.*

*The part which industry plays in our economic life is now undoubtedly substantial: but if we are to provide reasonable opportunities for our people it must become very much greater. Therefore, the suggestion emanating from responsible — though admittedly not wholly disinterested — quarters that existing taxation, particularly in the shape of income tax, gravely impedes its proper development, has had the close attention of the Government for some time past. Income Tax, however, has become such an indispensable and important source of revenue that any change in its incidence, even for the benefit of industry, cannot be considered in isolation and without regard to its consequences. The needs of the Exchequer cannot be ignored; for if they are the public services may suffer. Regard must be had also to the extent to which the burden on other classes of taxpayer will be increased, as, in general, concessions in favour of one class of taxpayer operate, in their early stages at least, to shift the cost to other shoulders. These considerations must be borne in mind even though the ultimate result of the change may be to benefit the in mind even though the ultimate result of the change may be to benefit the community as a whole. In tax matters the benefit must be proportionate to the cost to the ordinary individual taxpayer."*

*9. On the other hand, the inadequacy of wear and tear rates based on historical costs has been argued at length.*

*The general case presented on behalf of industry has been to the effect that present methods of computation, and rates of income taxation, constitute serious deterrents to the natural growth of industry by depriving it of the liquid funds required for the maintenance, modernisation and extension of industrial capacity, at current inflated price levels.*

*A review of the evidence shows the exceptional emphasis placed by industrialists on the inadequacy of present wear and tear rates in relation to the problem of replacement costs. It is scarcely an exaggeration to say, that their main case for a change in the method of computation is concentrated on that issue.*

*10. Essentially, what industry appears to be seeking, is an easement of the total tax burden currently imposed on it. In so far as the main emphasis has been placed on a change in method of computation of industrial profits, it is, in effect, seeking differential treatment.*

*Any relief given to industry will admittedly result in an immediate loss of tax revenue. This loss, it is contended by industrialists, can be justified on the grounds of an expected expansion in industrial productivity and in the national economy generally, which will compensate the Exchequer by a greater ultimate yield of tax.*

*Unless and until such increased compensatory revenue materialises, however, the immediate loss will create budgetary problems which may affect the interests of the general body of taxpayers over the intervening years.*

*18. In a community which accepts private enterprise, industrial profits should require no general justification. Protected industries have, however, to submit to a certain measure of Governmental supervision and control in return for the fiscal privileges they enjoy.*

*In the interests of consumers the State has deemed it necessary to keep under review the profits earned and prices charged in a wide range of industries. Many manufacturers are restricted to maximum profit "targets," and maximum price orders are enforced in the case of certain commodities under the Supplies and Services (Temporary Provisions) Act, 1946, which has been renewed annually.*

*These controls are regarded by industry as restrictive and irksome. In particular, it has been represented to us that, where actual manufacturing costs are conceded as a datum in determining a profit "target," a positive disincentive to reduce costs and improve efficiency is created. It is in our opinion desireable, that the emphasis should be on efficiency rather than on the actual limitation of profits.*

The very carefully hedged statement by Sean MacEntee indicates the caution with which tax policy was approached at the time. Section 9 outlines the case for tax relief and its effects, while section 18 reargues the classical protectionist position but with the goal of improved "efficiency rather than on the actual limitations of profits" (*Committee of Inquiry* 1953: 7). The final section relents and, though foreseeing a potential loss of £1 million to £1.5 million in tax revenue, suggests the depreciation rate be changed, thus recognizing it as a deterrent to industrial expansion.

In a similar vein, the IDA in 1952 was given the authority to attract foreign industry and develop indigenous industry. But the most express use of government incentives for industrial development was the setting up of the Underdeveloped Areas Board. The Board had the power to give grants to new industries of up to 50 percent of machinery and up to 100% of the cost of the land, structures, and employee training.

In 1953 the Fine Gael party in *Blueprint for Prosperity* called for a laissez faire approach to industrial growth, and the Fianna Fail government in power was engaged in deflationary policies leading to contraction in growth. Still a clear call for more direct government stimulation of the economy was sounded in *The Commission on Emigration and Population Problems 1948 - 54 Reports*. The Commission was asked to examine population trends and policy. Noting that emigration had deprived Ireland of half its population in the past century, and that the principal cause was the lack of jobs, the commission viewed agricultural development as necessary but not as a source of new jobs.

*COMMISSION ON EMIGRATION*
*and other*
*POPULATION PROBLEMS*
*1948-1954*
*REPORTS*

*1954*

*384. Earlier in this chapter we concluded that agricultural development was unlikely to cause any significant increase in the size of the population on the land, but was nevertheless essential to raise the low level of productivity and the low agricultural income, to relieve unemployment and under-employment on the land and to improve the unsatisfactory marriage pattern in rural areas. An increase in agricultural productivity and income would also increase the demand for goods and services, thereby providing a larger market for industrial and commercial expansion. Furthermore, greater agricultural output would mean a greater supply of materials for processing and consequently a greater possibility of industrial expansion on the basis of home-produced raw materials. It is principally in these ways that a prosperous and efficient agriculture is of vital consequence to our demographic problems. Our examination of the employment possibilities in afforestation, turf development and fishing suggests that while the maximum development of these activities could provide a basis for some increase in population, it would have only a limited significance in relation to our general population problems. These considerations point to the need for expanding industrial and commercial activities so as to provide the additional employment opportunities which are required and without which our population cannot be expected to increase to any great extent, the volume of emigration cannot be substantially reduced and the other demographic weaknesses cannot be eliminated.*

*385. That there is appreciable scope for industrial expansion and development is, in our opinion, unquestionable. We do not consider it necessary to instance and examine the particular cases where such development is possible to show that this is so, nor do we consider it within our competence as a Population Commission to decide which industry or branch of industry could advantageously be established or expanded. There are abundant considerations of economic and demographic significance which indicate that the limit of industrial expansion has not yet been reached and we confine our attention to some general considerations which not only demonstrate the possibility of further development but also, in broad terms, indicate its extent.*

*The Need for Assisting Industry*

*396. With such handicaps and against such competitive power as we have described, few, if any, new industrial enterprises would have been established in the Twenty-Six Counties since 1922 or would be possible in the future without adequate protection. Protective measures for industry are and have been a feature of Government policy. The principal measure applied up to the present time have been tariffs and restrictions on imports. This kind of protection has been used to assist industry to develop the home market. Efforts to develop export trade in the future may make it desirable to rely to a greater extent on other forms of assistance such as cheap power, cheap transport, special export facilities, or, in some cases, direct State assistance. Without measures to protect or assist industry, it would be difficult to conceive of industry on any wide scale maintaining itself or developing further. In the international sphere countries are being urged to abolish or relax protective measures in the interests of world trade and there have been international conferences and agreements designed to achieve this aim. We consider it of prime importance that in entering into international agreements of all kinds regard should be had to the importance of maintaining our freedom to develop our industries as we think fit. While the effect of abolishing or relaxing protective measures of various kinds by international multilateral agreement may well be of benefit to a few great and firmly established industrial counties*

*— the system of bilateral agreements may work out to the distinct advantage of the Twenty-Six Counties — we consider that the risks accepted by other countries in the interest of international trade cannot reasonably be expected from this country because of its special position. For historical reasons we have had a late start in industry and hence have not had enough time for development. Our economic structure is unbalanced through having insufficient industrial production. We are at the doorstep of a powerful industrial and exporting economy, and our general position is reflected in our grave demographic problems. In short, we cannot afford to risk either impairing our existing structure or losing the opportunity to develop our natural resources to the full.*

*397. The effect of protective measures requires constant review in the public interest. A primary consideration is that protective measures at an adequate level should assist the home manufacturer to secure as much as possible of the domestic market. Some tariffs may be too widely drawn and, in consequence, may require to be re-defined so as to protect only what can be manufactured here. Again, the ineffectiveness of a tariff, which is reflected in continued imports, may be due to the failure of manufacturers to take advantage of their opportunities to meet the full market requirements for the protected articles. It is equally important that protected industries should provide a reasonable range and variety of goods of satisfactory quality and that prices should never become excessive merely because of protection. On the question of price, some protected Irish industries are selling their products at prices equal to, and in some cases lower than, British prices for comparable goods, and hence protection is in such cases a provision against dumping or preference for imported products. Others are not in this position and numbers of industries may find that because of extra costs of raw materials and other factors the prices of efficiently produced goods will not be competitive with the landed prices of imported goods, so that reliance on a tariff is necessary. In such cases the granting of protection should depend on the balance to be struck between the extra cost to the community and the value of the industry from a national standpoint, and particular care should be taken not to place avoidable burdens on agriculture and other industries by increasing the cost of materials needed by them for further production. It would be obviously undesirable to protect an industry in which the probable balance in the long run did not lie clearly to the advantage of the country as a whole. Furthermore, it is possible that protection may engender complacency and help to stifle initiative and efficiency. The object of protection is to help industry to develop to the point where it can satisfy home demand and if possible provide an export trade as well. Protected industries should not be allowed to take advantage of their privileged position to do less than is required of them. It is only by periodic review of the protective measures adopted that such dangers can be averted.*

*423. With maximum development of agriculture, with industry providing as much as possible of the requirements of the home market and with energetic development of export trade in industrial products, additional employment should result, without which the amelioration of our main demographic weaknesses and economic problems will not be possible. Such development is essentially a long-term policy. Immediate results cannot be expected, as is evident in the case of afforestation and fisheries. A quicker response may be obtained from agriculture but social tradition and habit may delay the full results. Since the policy is long-term it follows that it should be framed so that emphasis is placed on those objectives which can be most easily attained. The case for giving a high place in the order of priorities to agriculture rests on the fact that, by encouraging agriculture, use is made of physical attributes which give the country a natural advantage in competition with other countries; exports to pay for additional imports required for industrial and other development are increased; under-employment and unemployment on the land are reduced and the income of the agricultural community is raised, thereby providing a larger home market for industrial products, greater possibility of extending commercial and ancillary services and additional savings for investment. It should be pointed out, however, that there is a tendency in developed countries for the agriculturally-occupied population to decline in numbers. Agricultural development, therefore, is unlikely to bring about a substantial increase in the size of the agricultural community. Hence it is mainly expansion in industry and services which will provide the additional employment without a reduction in living standards. The volume of this employment will depend on the extent to which greater agricultural prosperity can provide a wider market for industrial products at home, on the ability of industry to meet home-market demand and on the possibility of developing exports. Development, agricultural and industrial, and the rising standard of living which the population seeks, call for a programme of large-scale and long-term investment which far exceeds the present volume of domestic savings. The Commission believes that, within the capacity of the country and its population, there is scope for such an expansion in production as would make a major contribution to solving our demographic and economic problems. In the final analysis, however, the solution of these problems depends on the tenacity of the community's resolution to solve them and on the amount of effort it is willing to put forth in this endeavour.*

The commission emphasized the fact that despite the handicaps to the growth of Irish industry, it is the only area in which an increase in employment can stem the flow of emigration. The commission accepted a protectionist position but held that protection is not to retard development but promote it and that exports are vital to job creation.

In the period of the mid 1950s, despite constrictive policies, specific acts and reports supplied the foundation for more direct government stimulation of industrial development.

Despite the growing accumulation of evidence that the policies adopted were not generating industrial growth or agricultural growth both political parties appeared to be competing in adapting regressive policies. When the Inter-Party coalition lost power in 1951, Fianna Fáil returned to govern from 1951 to 1954. Except for Sean Lemass this is generally judged to be one of the worst Fianna Fáil governments. Sean McEntee, Minister of Finance, prevailed over Lemass to pursue deflationary policies. The economic stagnation, depression, and emigration provided no comfort to the Irish voters who in 1954 returned a coalition to power. It was composed of Fine Gael, Labour, and Clann na Talman, a farmers' party. This coalition ruled until 1957 and as noted below passed some significant legislation for the foundations of the period of growth in the 1960s.

In 1956 the Industrial Grants Act was passed, an elaboration of the 1952 act, in which the IDA was empowered to give up to 66 percent of the cost of land and buildings for industrial development in rural areas. But more dramatic in the long term was the 1956 Finance Act which granted a 50 percent tax relief from profits earned on increases over the export sales of the previous year. That largesse was increased in the Finance Acts of 1957 and 1958 to the point that new or increased manufacturing exports were tax free for ten years. These incentives were increased by the improvement of depreciation rates on plant and equipment in 1958 and on increase in the availability of credit from the Industrial Credit Corporation in 1958. Finally in 1958 the protectionist measures embodied in the 1932 and 1934 Control of Manufactures Act, designed to keep Irish ownership of industry, were relaxed. The strategy of seeking foreign investment to develop foreign owned industries in Ireland was facilitated.

The last report to be noted in constructing the foundations of an active interventionist Keynesian government policy of development is the *Capital Investment Advisory Committee Third Report* of 1958. The Committee had been set up in 1956 to evaluate the capital budget of the government in light of balance of payments difficulties and employment and emigration. The third report was preceded not surprisingly, by the first in 1957 concerned with reducing the deficit, and the second in 1957 concerned with housing.

The third however addresses government stimulated economic growth.

*CAPITAL INVESTMENT ADVISORY COMMITTEE*
*THIRD REPORT*

*1958*

*III. RECOMMENDATIONS*

*42. This report has been concerned with the general economic principles which should guide capital investment in Ireland. In making recommendations, we have to bear in mind the limitations of our terms of reference (which mean that our recommendations must be concerned with the public capital programme) and also the fact that we were not appointed as experts in particular fields of industry, trade or agriculture and have not taken evidence about particular productive schemes. As individuals we could, no doubt, produce numerous detailed suggestions for action of varying degrees of authority; but as a Committee our corporate judgment can only at this stage be expressed in general proposals related to the public capital programme, coupled, where possible, with suggestions about the way in which they should be made specific.*

*43. We believe that, with the resolute and continuous application of a vigorous and intelligent policy, Ireland can overcome her economic difficulties. This might best be done by bringing together the various proposals for State action in a broad programme which would be both effective and internally consistent. The resolute application of a known programme for development, step by step over a considerable period, would do much to create confidence. We therefore recommend:*

*(A) that the machinery of Government for preparing and coordinating economic policy should be reviewed and where necessary strengthened. A broad programme of economic development should be prepared, designed to discover and implement productive investments and provision should be made for its continuous and systematic review in the light of changing circumstances. The essentials of this programme should be made widely known: so far as is consistent with effective action, industrial, farming and trade union bodies should be consulted about it; and the public should be kept fully informed about its progress.*

*44. The very multiplicity of past attempts to foster economic development may have stood in the way of their success. There is a critical minimum effort, without which development is not self-sustaining, but tends to peter out. This effort is more likely to be attained and is more likely to lie within the compass of our material resources and our available enterprise if it is concentrated on a narrow front. It is better that the efforts of the State should be few but highly effective rather than numerous and only partially effective and that assistance for private industry and agriculture should encourage self-help rather than passive reliance on subsidy. We therefore recommend:*

*(B) that the Departments concerned with grants, loans, subsidies and services for industry, agriculture and transport should be asked to consider means of concentrating them on purposes likely to increase production capable of being sold abroad, or otherwise 'productive' in the sense defined in paragraph 8, and to suggest a narrow front on which a concentrated effort should be made.*

*As a suggestion for an enterprise of high priority which might benefit from this policy of concentration, we put forward the following recommendation:*

*(C) that the State should help agricultural credit societies to finance agricultural development either directly by loans or by guaranteeing the repayment of loans made to them by the Agricultural Credit Corporation or by the commercial banks. The State should direct attention towards productive kinds of agricultural development by providing for differential rates of interest on the loans which it makes or guarantees.*

*45. Next we recommend:*

*(D) that the carrying out of productive capital projects should not be frustrated by prejudice either in favour of or against public enterprise. In other words, we should welcome the setting up of new State enterprises in fields which private or cooperative enterprise is unable or unwilling to develop; but we do not consider that development in any field should be reserved to State enterprise without special reason.*

*(E) that projects undertaken for economic reasons should not be distorted or frustrated by attempts to make them achieve non-economic ends. For instance, while recognising the strong grounds of social policy for diverting industry from Dublin to the western counties, we would not wish to see such a diversion enforced if it endangered the success of a new productive enterprise. This is not to say that economically sound projects should not be encouraged.*

*46. These recommendations express our general attitude to the problem of achieving rapid economic development; that there should be a programme of State action; that strong effort should be concentrated on a limited range of productive projects; and that care should be taken to avoid the obstruction of these projects.*

*47. Investment depends first of all on enterprise and secondly on means of finance. Enterprise must be encouraged and freed from restrictions. The finance of more investment demands higher savings or the return to Ireland of capital held overseas or the attraction of foreign capital. The increase in the funds available for future investment would probably follow successful development; the question is whether such an increase can be obtained now as a means of encouraging the difficult first stages of development. As one practical means of dealing with these matters we recommend:*

*(F) that the taxation Commission should be asked to report as a matter of urgency on the possibility of encouraging enterprise by changes in taxation and of increasing tax incentives for the investment of savings at home, for the investment at home of past savings now held overseas and for the attraction of foreign capital.*

*48. A reduction in Government current expenditure is another way of releasing funds for investment. We think, however, that it is an illusion to suppose that a substantial reduction can be achieved by a collection of minor economies; large reductions involve policy decisions to give up whole sections of Government activity.*

*49. Current savings and inflow or repatriation of capital from abroad together set a limit to the total amount of investment which can be made by the State and private and cooperative enterprise. We do not think that any question of excessive productive investment by private enterprise is likely to arise in the next few years, but we recognise that it may be necessary to vary the State capital programme so that no waste or excessive demand is caused by fluctuations in private investment. We recommend:*

*(G) that the State capital programme should be fixed each year at the highest level which is consistent with most productive use of the available resources and with the productive investment intentions of private and cooperative enterprise.*

*For this facts are needed, and we recommend:*

*(H) that improved statistics and fuller information about actual and intended private investment in agriculture and industry and about actual and intended investment by State enterprises should be obtained.*

*50. Within the State capital programme thus determined, there should be a marked increase in the proportion devoted to productive purposes. This change of emphasis from redistributive to productive investment is most important and we consider that Ireland must be willing to defer certain desirable forms of social investment, mainly redistributive in their effect, in order to give a fair chance to productive investment in the first and most difficult stages of new development. It is difficult to express this in a precise recommendation and we content ourselves with saying that for a period the urgency of new social projects, without a productive element, should be very high before they find a place in the capital programme. We do not, of course, contemplate the ending of all redistributive investment; a Government social policy must continue. Nor would we wish to see men thrown into unemployment by the deliberate termination of existing redistributive investment until compensating productive investment is in prospect (this would not necessarily be in the same area or trade). We are simply concerned to point out that once productive investments have been devised they must (for the sake of future employment prospects) have a very high priority.*

*51. It is also important that the productive investments of the State should contain no waste or unnecessary redistributive element. Such waste may arise, for instance, in the attempt to maintain an over-extended transport system; or in failure to devise a rates structure which causes the best use to be made of the capital equipment of public transport or of power industries; or in failure to ensure that land is made available to vigorous and efficient farmers; or in failure to ensure that improvements made to land at State expense are fully maintained; or in overlapping of investment and effort in educational institutions which are helped by public funds. We recommend:*

*(I) that the continuous and systematic review of the State programme mentioned in recommendation A should include a review of the productivity of State investment. As a means of encouraging better use of that most important capital resource, the land, we recommend:*

*(J) that lands held by the State should be rented where suitable on short leases to young men who show evidence of competence and zeal. Those to whom these lands are rented should be required to use them in accordance with the priorities set out in the programme for economic development described in A above.*

*52. Finally we come to the question, mentioned in our terms of reference, of 'the general order of priority appropriate for the various investment projects'. This we cannot at this stage give in relation to particular investment projects but it may be of some help if we list the sectors of economic activity within which productive investments are, in our view, likely to be found.*

*Agricultural marketing, grading and processing; market intelligence and market research agencies overseas for both agriculture and industry.*

*Research into production methods in agriculture (e.g., by means of demonstration and experimental farms) and industry.*

*Education - technical, technological and scientific.*

*Land improvement, e.g., fertilising and the provision of shelter belts.*

*Provision and improvement of farm buildings.*

*Development of pedigree cattle and pig farms and encouragement of new lines of agricultural production, e.g., fruit and vegetables.*

*Encouragement of private enterprise, e.g., capital for enterprising young farmers to whom land is rented under recommendation J.*

*Development of new manufacturing activities, especially in fields ancillary to agriculture.*

*Fishery development, forestry and tourism.*

*Encouragement of agricultural cooperatives; limited success has, however, attended such schemes in the past.*

The report places the onus of responsibility for generating growth on the government and identifies the tools: planning, coordination, capital investment, taxation, and education. Whether the government would take the responsibility for direct stimulation of economic development was another question. The importance of the report by T. K. Whitaker, *Economic Development* put forth in November of 1958 is that it was accompanied by a white paper *The Programme for Economic Expansion* which the government of the day supported and was willing to implement.

In retrospect there appears to be many foreshadowings of the government committment to direct economic development, to abandon protectionism and seek foreign investment that were proposed in the *(First) Programme.* Sean Lemass' son claimed it sprang from a speech made by his father in 1955 in which he advocated planning to create "100,000 jobs" (McCarthy 1990: 27). Basil Chubb and Patrick Lynch emphasize the paper given by Whitaker in May of 1956 before the Statistics and Social Inquiry Society in Dublin in which the outlines of *Economic Development* were presented (Chubb, Lynch 1969: 48-76).

In the event the goals and the tools which had been slowly cumulating in the acts and reports cited above came to be crystalized in the report *Economic Development* and the accompanying *(First) Programme*. At this point the shift to government incentive planning proceeds, and fortuitously, it is accompanied by significant growth after 1959.

*ECONOMIC DEVELOPMENT*
*CHAPTER 1*

*1958*

*INTRODUCTION*

*1. How this study originated is shown in the documents reproduced as Appendix 1. It is well to reiterate here that the aim is not to draw up a detailed five or ten-year plan of national development. For a small country so exposed to the perpetual flux of world economic forces there would be little sense in trying to establish a rigid pattern of development. The aim is rather (a) to highlight the main deficiencies and potentialities of the economy and (b) to suggest the principles to be followed to correct the deficiencies and realise the opportunities, indicating a number of specific forms of productive development which appear to offer good long-term prospects. One must be prepared at all times for fluctuations and upsets. A readiness to adapt to changing conditions is a sine qua non of material progress. Nevertheless, one may reasonably hope to find some guiding principles which it would be advantageous to follow through thick and thin.*

*2. While planning in a rigid sense is not useful in our circumstances, there can be no doubt about the wisdom of looking ahead and trying to direct national policy along the most productive lines. A year is too restricted a frame of reference for policy decisions. Their effects overflow such arbitrary boundaries. It is, of course necessary to seek Parliamentary approval year by year for financial policy as indicated in the annual budget. But this yearly process, if it is to be fully effective in contributing to national development, must be set in a much broader framework. An attempt should be made to secure a more general coordination of financial and economic policy with a view to the maximum progress being made in the years immediately ahead. Otherwise, unintended but damaging inconsistencies and conflicts can only too easily arise.*

*3. To think ahead the mind needs the support of facts and figures. The present position and the immediate prospects are the safest starting-point but as one ventures further into the future the estimates on which one must rely become more and more doubtful. This cannot be helped. One can only try to ensure that, here and now, the most competent estimates are made. In this study, care is taken to explain how any forecasts have been arrived at. No more can be done — their ultimate validity cannot be assured.*

*4. Apart from its obvious value in making policy more long-term and logical, forward thinking is particularly urgent and necessary for other reasons. It is apparent that we have come to a critical and decisive point in our economic affairs. The policies hitherto followed, though given a fair trial, have not resulted in a viable economy. We have power, transport facilities, public services, houses, hospitals and a general "infrastructure" on a scale which is reasonable by western European standards, yet large-emigration and unemployment still persist. The population is falling, the national income rising more slowly than in the rest of Europe. A great and sustained effort to increase production, employment and living standards is necessary to avert economic decadence.*

*5. The possibility of free trade in Europe carries disquieting implications for some Irish industries and raises special problems of adaptation and adjustment. It necessitates also a re-appraisal of future industrial and agricultural prospects. It seems clear that, sooner or later, protection will have to go and the challenge of free trade be accepted. There is really no other choice for a country wishing to keep pace materially with the rest of Europe. It would be a policy of despair to accept that our costs of production must permanently be higher than those of other European countries, either in industry or in agriculture. Our level of real incomes depends on our competitive efficiency. If that must be lower than in the rest of Europe we should have to be content with relatively low living standards. With the alternative of emigration available we are unlikely, either as a community or as individuals, to accept such a situation for long unless it is seen as an essential part of a programme of national regeneration. The effect of any policy entailing relatively low living standards here for all time would be to sustain and stimulate the outflow of emigrants and in the end jeopardise our economic independence. Any little benefit obtained in terms of employment in protected non-competitive industries would be outweighed by losses through emigration and general economic impoverishment. If we do not expand production on a competitive basis, we shall fail to provide the basis necessary for the economic independence and material progress of the community. Even a spectacular increase in efficiency and output will still leave us for a long time at a relative disadvantage to Britain and many other countries in respect of real income per head of the population. Indeed, if we are to catch up at all, our annual rate of improvement must exceed theirs.*

*6. Our economic progress requires that more resources be devoted to productive purposes. But there is as yet no agreement on a systematic programme of development. There is need for urgent determination of the productive purposes to which resources should be applied and of the unproductive, or relatively unproductive, activities which can, with the minimum social disadvantage, be curtailed to set free resources for productive development.*

*7. It is well to state that by "productive investment" in this study is meant investment yielding an adequate return to the national economy as a whole. Private investment is not normally undertaken unless there appears to be a fair prospect of financial success, that is, of the investment producing commodities saleable at competitive price. In the case of public investment, the term "productive" cannot be limited to investments yielding an adequate direct return to the Exchequer. It extends also to investment which enlarges the national income by creating a flow of goods and services which are saleable without the aid of subsidies; for this will result indirectly in revenue to pay debt charges. Whether the first test is satisfied is easy to establish, but the second is often a matter of doubt. It is clear that, where neither test is satisfied and part, if not all, of the cost of servicing the capital must be met by a levy on the taxpayer, the investment results in a redistribution rather than an increase in national income. Progress in the building up of real national income depends on capital and labour being devoted to industrial and agricultural development, particularly for export, rather than to the provision of welfare services for home consumption. In an expanding economy, where real incomes are rising and the demand for goods and services is growing, opportunities for useful and continuing employment will arise automatically and, as has been shown in Germany since the war, a progressive improvement in social amenities will be possible without undue strain on the economy.*

*8. It should be added that there is no conflict between what are termed "socially desirable and "economic" objectives. "Socially desirable" objectives will not be permanently realised merely by increasing "social" investment. The erection of houses, schools and hospitals — socially desirable in themselves — will, of course, provide employment but the employment ceases once the period of construction is over and the unemployed man is then left with an amenity which, if he remains unemployed, will contribute but little to his standard of living. Investment which is not productive may provide employment but it does so only for a time and at the cost of weakening the capacity of the economy as a whole to provide lasting and self-sustaining employment. For these reasons the emphasis must be on productive investment, though not, of course, to the exclusion of all social investment. The permanent increase in employment associated with an expansion of real national output is to be preferred to the purely temporary increase which is all that non-productive investment, entailing a mere redistribution of existing incomes, can bring about.*

*9. Without positive action by the Government, a slowing down in housing and certain other forms of social investment will occur from now on because needs are virtually satisfied over wide areas of the State. This decline in building will cause a reduction in employment. The continuance of large-scale investment in housing or other forms of social building would not, however, be justified merely to create artificial employment opportunities. If the objective of an expanding economy is not to be jeopardised, the right course is to replace social investment by productive investment which will provide self-sustaining and permanent employment. This means that no time can be lost in devising a realistic long-term programme of productive investment.*

*10. In the context of a programme of economic development extending over five years or longer, it would be easier not only to avoid inconsistencies between individual decisions but also to secure acceptance of decisions which, presented in isolation, might arouse strong opposition. It would be more apparent to all sections of the community that certain adjustments of present policy were necessary and it would be less difficult to have efforts made and sacrifices borne if they were seen to be a necessary contribution to national welfare and were not in danger of being nullified by neglect or extravagance elsewhere.*

*11. A further reason for careful mapping of future economic policy is that we have no longer the surplus resources with which to meet deficits in external payments. Our wartime accumulation of sterling reserves has been run down. Our post-war dollar borrowings have been spent. But our balance of payments remains unstable. The present state of balance is exceptional — the year 1957 being the first year since 1946 in which a deficit was not recorded — and it is insecure. The equilibrium attained is at a depressed level of domestic economic activity and is due in part to the using up of stocks. A reduction in supplies of cattle, a fall in their export price, and rising money incomes and expenditure, due to wage and salary increases, are only some of the factors capable of disturbing this precarious balance and causing renewed loss of national capital. In fact, the import excess has been tending to increase since August, 1957. It is, therefore, of the greatest importance that policy be concentrated henceforth on the development of productive capacity, so as to sustain and strengthen our economic position and external purchasing power. To allow social services or non-productive forms of expenditure priority over productive projects would cause a misdirection of resources and increase the difficulties of development by raising our production costs, artificially stimulating our imports and putting us in deficit again with the rest of the world.*

*12. There is also a sound psychological reason for having an integrated development programme. The absence of such a programme tends to deepen the all-too-prevalent mood of despondency about the country's future. A sense of anxiety is, indeed, justified. But it can too easily degenerate into feelings of frustration and despair. After 35 years of native government people are asking whether we can achieve an acceptable degree of economic progress. The common talk amongst parents in the towns, as in rural Ireland, is of their children having to emigrate as soon as their education is completed in order to be sure of a reasonable livelihood. To the children themselves and to many already in employment the jobs available at home look unattractive by comparison with those obtainable in such variety and so readily elsewhere. All this seems to be setting up a vicious circle of increasing emigration, resulting in a smaller domestic market depleted of initiative and skill, and a reduced incentive, whether for Irishmen or foreigners, to undertake and organise the productive enterprises which alone can provide increased employment opportunities and higher living standards. There is, therefore, a real need at present to buttress confidence in the country's future and to stimulate the interest and enthusiasm of the young in particular. A general resurgence of will may be helped by setting up targets of national endeavor which appear to be reasonably attainable and mutually consistent. This is an aspect of good leadership. But there is nothing to be gained by setting up fanciful targets. Failure to reach such targets would merely produce disillusionment and renew the mood of national despondency. Realism also demands an awareness that, at present, and for a long time ahead, the material reward for work here may be less than that obtainable elsewhere but that there are many countervailing advantages in living in Ireland. No programme of development can be effective unless it generates increased effort, enterprise and saving on the part of a multitude of individuals. Its eventual success or failure will depend primarily on the individual reactions of the Irish people. If they have not the will to develop, even the best possible programme is useless.*

*13. A concerted and comprehensive programme aimed at a steady progress in material welfare, even though supported by the Churches and other leaders of opinion, could only be successful if the individual members of the community were realistic and patriotic enough to accept the standard of living produced by their own exertions here, even if it should continue for some time to be lower than the standard available abroad. Otherwise the possibility of economic progress scarcely exists.*

*14. For all these reasons the importance of the next five to ten years for the economic and political future of Ireland cannot be overstressed. Policies should be re-examined without regard to past views or commitments. It is desirable to remind ourselves that at all times in a nation's history decisions have to be taken; that there is no guarantee when they are taken that they will prove right; and that the greatest fault lies in pursuing a policy after it has proved to be unsuitable or ineffective. What matters above all is to understand the present position and find the best and quickest ways of improving it.*

*15. This study is intended to help in the preparation of a programme of economic development. Information which may be useful in this connection is assembled for ease of reference. The general scheme of the work is, first, to outline the present economic position, concentrating on the main deficiencies and opportunities. Then, before making a closer analysis of the four main heads under which progress can obviously be achieved — agriculture, fisheries, industry and tourism — it is necessary to examine the extent to which resources may be expected to be available for development needs and the financial policy needed to assure the maximum rate of economic progress. No programme of development can be regarded as realistic which is not founded on a reasonable assessment of the resources likely to be available to finance it. The closer analysis of agriculture, fisheries, industry and tourism is intended to indicate the general lines of development which can most effectively be followed over the next five years or so. Some specific possibilities are also discussed but as illustrations only. The conclusions of the study are summarised in the final chapter.*

*16. It may, perhaps, be said here that problems of economic development are exercising the minds of statesmen, economists, scientists and administrators all over the world. It is clear that development can be accelerated by Government policy but how this can best be done is by no means obvious. It is reasonable to suppose that the solution must vary according to the circumstances of individual countries. Economists have not so far developed any general theory of economic development. The present state of thought in the matter is summarised as follows by Professor A. K. Cairncross in a recent article*:*

> *Economists would agree on the central importance in economic development of capital accumulation and technological progress, but they would not necessarily agree on the precise role played by either, for both are simultaneously causes and symptoms of development. Some are impressed by the barrier that illiteracy and ignorance interpose and would lay most stress on education as a means of securing the rapid spread of modern ideas. Some represent industrialisation as the key to development, and regard agricultural improvement as consequential; others would reverse the order of priority and emphasise the difficulty of expanding the market for industrial products so long as agricultural incomes are low and food relatively expensive. Sometimes it is the heavy industries alone that are picked on as the spearhead, or the machine tool industry is assigned a special role; sometimes the theory runs in terms of balanced growth and the simultaneous building up of a variety of industries, each generating income and providing, directly or indirectly, a market for the others. There are differences also about the possibility of absorbing, without loss to agricultural output, large numbers of workers from the countryside. To some economists the existence of a vast rural surplus of man-power implies the need for a corresponding expansion in industrial capacity, financed, if need be, through drastic taxation; while, for others, the gains to be expected from taking up any slack in the economy are not very significant so long as the existing technological frontiers are not advanced.*

**Economic Development and the West — The Three Banks Review, December, 1957.*

*17. Professor Cairncross later in the same article states, and most economists would agree, that "the nerve centre of the whole forward movement may lie, not in finance, but in entrepreneurial capacity." He points out that "it is doubtful whether investment in public utilities and facilities in countries that lack other essentials of development will automatically gear itself to the expanded transport, power and other services that have been brought into existence." He points out that "historically, the initial advance has rarely been the result of capital expenditure: it has far more commonly followed the expansion of markets, especially foreign markets, the discovery of new mineral resources, the introduction of new techniques involving only a moderate capital outlay, the arrival of foreign immigrants eager to make a place for themselves by a display of enterprise." The usual sequence of events is that a step forward is made in one sector of the economy and that this makes it easier for the rest of the economy to advance.*

*18. These observations are not without relevance to the problem of economic development in Ireland. A dynamic has to be found and released and it is not necessarily increased capital investment, though this may be called for to support a higher rate of development once it is set in motion. It would, indeed, be a mistake to think that a faster rate of increase in output is a matter simply of stepping up the volume of home investment. It is true that there is a close relationship between output per head and the amount of capital per head but there are other conditions of economic progress no less important than increased capitalisation. The first of these is the development of a better appreciation of the dependence of material progress on individual output. Others are a raising of the general level of education, health and skill, the loosening of restrictive practices, whether of employers or employees, the practical encouragement of initiative and enterprise, the adoption of improved methods, techniques and principles of organisation and management both in agriculture and industry, and a greater readiness to apply scientific advances. Attention to matters such as these may yield even greater increases in production than direct capitalisation in the form of new plant and machinery though this does not, of course, imply that increased capitalisation is not also required. It is essential for sustained and balanced progress that an increase in productive capital should be supported not only by advances in education and technical training but also — though these are not short in Ireland — by the provision of basic utilities and amenities, including power supplies, good housing and transport services. Harmonious development calls also for suitable fiscal and monetary policies designed to increase the supply of savings and the incentive to invest in productive enterprises. As between countries, differences in climate, political institutions, educational and technical facilities individual attitudes to work, trade union outlook and policy can be as important as differences in natural resources or in the volume of investment in causing divergent rates of development. Economic growth is, in fact, a complex process depending on social, psychological and political as well as economic and technical factors. In Ireland, the trend of population is an important factor inasmuch as dynamism and flexibility are rarely associated with a declining home population, whereas even a stable population would have good prospects of economic advance if its exports were competitive.*

*19. This study suggests that, given favourable public policies and private dispositions, a dynamic of progress awaits release in agriculture, fisheries, industry and tourism. It is hoped that it will be possible to set this force to work simultaneously in these major branches of the Irish economy. The opportunities of development may not be great enough to give all who are born in Ireland a standard of living they would accept — though there are advantages of living here not to be reckoned in money terms — but such as they are they should be exploited. It is not unreasonable to hope that sufficient advance can be made in the next decade not merely to consolidate our economic independence but to enable us to provide higher material standards for a rising population.*

*20. At the end of this introductory chapter it may be permissible for the Secretary of the Department of Finance to introduce a personal note. I wish to express my grateful recognition of the advice and comments received, on particular aspects of the study, from the Governor of the Central Bank, the Chairman of the Industrial Development Authority, and from colleagues in other Departments, including the Secretaries and other senior officers of the Departments of Industry and Commerce, Agriculture, Lands and Education. For more general criticism I am grateful to the Secretary of the Department of the Taoiseach, the Director of the Central Statistics Office and the professional economists on the Capital Investment Advisory Committee (Professor C. F. Carter, Mr. P. Lynch and Dr. W. J. L. Ryan). To Mr. C. H. Murray of the Department of the Taoiseach and to officers of my own Department (especially Messrs. M. F. Doyle, S. O. Ciosain, M. Horgan, D. O. Loinsigh, J. Dolan, T. O. Cobhthaigh and Dr. B. Menton) I am indebted for preparing much of the groundwork. All this generous assistance made the task of co-ordination and synthesis much less difficult. I must personally accept the responsibility where I have not followed the advice received and it is necessary to say that no Department as such, nor any individual other than myself, is committed to the whole range of views and suggestions put forward.*

*21. In pressing on with this study, despite the claims of ordinary office work, it has been an inspiration to turn to the following words of the Bishop of Clonfert, Most Rev. Dr. Philbin:*

> *Our version of history has tended to make us think of freedom as an end in itself and of independent government — like marriage in a fairy story — as the solution of all ills. Freedom is useful in proportion to the use we make of it. We seem to have relaxed our patriotic energies just at the time when there was most need to mobilise them. Although our enterprise in purely spiritual fields has never been greater, we have shown little initiative or organisational ability in agriculture and industry and*

*commerce. There is here the widest and most varied field for the play of the vital force that our religion contains.*

*(Studies, Autumn, 1957)*

*This study is contribution, in the spirit advocated by the Bishop of Clonfert, towards the working out of the national good in the economic sphere. It is hoped that, supplemented by productive ideas from other sources, it will help to dispel despondency about the country's future. We can afford our present standard of living, which is so much higher than most of the inhabitants of this world enjoy. Possibilities of improvement are there, if we wish to realise them. It would be well to shut the door on the past and to move forward, energetically, intelligently and with the will to succeed, but without expecting miracles of progress in a short time.*

## *CHAPTER 24*

## *CONCLUSIONS*

### *Employment Considerations*

*1. Throughout this study, while there have been some general references to employment, attention has been directed primarily towards productive development. This has been deliberate and has not been due to any lack of concern about unemployment. It is from productive development that the employment worth having from a national viewpoint, i.e., lasting employment, will arise, and the study advocates the maximum productive development which our financial and material resources will allow. It is possible that even this maximum development may not provide a permanent job at the wages he is prepared to accept for everyone wanting to stay in Ireland.*

*2. It would have been quite unreal to approach the question of development from the aspect of employment, that is by setting out the number of jobs required and then attempting to plan how these might be created. There is no sure way in which development works can be planned to produce self-sustaining jobs for a specified large number of individuals of varying capacity and skill. The number itself would be a formidable one if it were to cover not only those now idle who are able and willing to work in Ireland but also those who add to the potential labour force every year but are at present involuntary emigrants. Self-sustaining jobs, i.e., jobs producing goods or services saleable at competitive prices, cannot be created to order. The jobs that can be created, to a limited extent, by public works have no lasting basis; they add nothing to the national output of saleable goods and services and they can survive only as long as the works themselves last or other works, involving a similar redistribution of the community's income, are substituted for them.*

*In any case, the capital available for public works of any kind is not unlimited and can be used for one purpose only at the expense of others. In a very real sense the direct provision of work on unproductive schemes prevents the provision of lasting and useful work in as much as scarce capital is used up for wasteful ends, the burden of taxation is made heavier, costs are raised and productive enterprises hindered and discouraged.*

*3. The fact is that neither full employment nor unlimited supplies of capital can be procured to order. Stress has been laid in this study (Chapters 2 and 4) both on the question of the acceptability of the standard of living afforded by home employment — no plan could in any circumstances guarantee full employment at whatever standard of living the employees chose to name — and on the question of the capital resources likely to be available for development, of which an optimistic assessment has been made. It is reasonable to expect that additional employment of a lasting and acceptable character will be provided by following the general lines of productive development indicated in the study. There would be nothing to be gained by setting up fanciful employment targets; failure to reach such targets would only produce disillusionment. On the other hand, the comprehensive exploitation of the opportunities of development which do exist would inspire confidence in the country's future and would lead both directly and indirectly to an expansion of employment on a permanent basis.*

*SUMMARY OF PRINCIPLES AND SUGGESTIONS*

*General*

*4. The principles emerging from this study and the specific suggestions put forward for future development may now be summarised. A rigid five- or ten-year plan would not be suitable to our circumstances. Nevertheless, it is necessary to look outside the framework of year-to-year budgeting and effectively to coordinate financial and economic policy over longer periods. We now lag so far behind most other European countries in material progress that even a spectacular increase in efficiency and output will leave us at a relative disadvantage. If we are to catch up at all, our rate of improvement must exceed theirs. There are also important psychological reasons for having an integrated development programme. Realistic and mutually consistent aims can stimulate the interest, enthusiasm and resurgence of will which the nation's progress now demands. (Chapter 1)*

*5. The outstanding features of the country's general economic position are the low income per head of the population and the related phenomena of high emigration and high unemployment, and low production and productivity. External reserves have had to be depleted in order to finance investment at a higher level than that warranted by current savings. Private investment has been small and public investment though on a relatively large scale, has been primarily social in character and for that reason has failed to give that significant expansion in basic industries which is necessary for real and continuing development of the economy. The high rate of social investment has involved heavy charges for the service of public debt and these charges, together with the increased cost of social services and other forms of redistributive public expenditure, have entailed relatively high taxation which is a disincentive to saving and private enterprise. (Chapter 2)*

*6. From this background emerges the main general principle that, if we are to avoid economic stagnation and continual loss of population, public and private development of a productive character must be stimulated and organised so as to overshadow the non-productive development which now bulks so largely in public investment and in national capital formation as a whole. The raising of output in agriculture and industry on a competitive basis should, therefore, have a much higher priority than at present in the allocation of savings. The volume of current savings must not only be maintained but increased and the utmost use made of means of raising output which are sparing of capital, so as to make the savings go as afar as possible. The opportunity to switch from non-productive to productive investment will occur in part automatically with the satisfaction to a major degree of social needs (e.g., housing) but it should be reinforced by a positive curtailment of non-productive outlay. (Chapter 2-Section II)*

In 1957 Fianna Fáil had returned to power and picked up the impetus of the *Capital Investment Advisory Report* and *Economic Development*. It is important to note, however, that since the War, or "The Emergency," until 1959, Ireland had been governed by both Fianna Fáil and coalition governments in 1948-1951 and 1954-1957. While based upon different interests their policies had a grim similarity.

The surfacing of this subterranean pressure in late 1958 reminds us that *Economic Development* is an important departure because these goals and tools were not chosen by the governments from the late 1940s forward. What was the performance in the decade from 1949 to 1959 before the adoption of explicit planning?

The first impulse of the post war governments was sound in that they sought to restore demand and provide the facilities for improving output. In 1947 the amount of public capital expenditure was small, but two thirds of it was directed to machinery and transportation. By 1951 the amount had risen to about £100 million but two thirds of the expenditure was on building. While assisting in creating demand this did little for stimulating the growth of manufacturing output or encouraging exports. In fact the opposite happened. With exports low the increased demand created a flow of imports which helped exacerbate the balance of payments problem.

The overall effect, however, was positive as in the period the GNP grew to match prewar level by 1947 and thereafter grew at a rate of three percent per year. Agricultural output rose as did tourism. But the strongest growth rate was in manufacturing which grew from 1946 to 1951 at a rate of nearly eleven percent (Kennedy, Giblin, and McHugh 1988: 58).

The balance of payments deficits were in part compensated for by the infusion of Marshall Plan funds. Ireland received £40 million in loans from the United States at the rate of 2 1/2 percent and £6 million in direct grants.

The progress made in the first six years after the war was impressive (Kennedy and Dowling 1975: 212). The numbers which triggered the government's curtailment of growth occurred in the balance of payments. Blessed by substantial reserves after the "Emergency," Ireland had the capacity to pay for imports though revenue from exports did not match the cost of imports. Ireland's Marshall Plan funds and tourism continued to keep reserves high. But in 1951 the Marshall Plan funds ended and the cost of imports soared, creating a balance of payments crisis. Ireland had little or no control over the rising costs. The U. K. devalued the pound, and Ireland followed suit, while the cost of imports had risen by one-third due to the Korean War and the creation of stockpiles by the U. S. government. "Thus the major cause of the massive deterioration in the balance of trade was the rise in merchandise trade prices" (Kennedy and Dowling 1975: 207). The overall borrowing requirement of the government went from £20.2 million in 1949 to £35.5 million in 1951.

Responding, and perhaps overreacting, the government in the 1952 budget cut current expenditures and revenues were deflated. Taxes were increased and subsidies were cut on tea, butter, and sugar. As Ireland already was in depression the effect was to curtail economic growth and to exacerbate unemployment and emigration. Other than in agriculture, recovering from a slump, there was no increase in economic output. These policies were pursued in every budget thereafter until 1959. Capital expenditures by the government declined in absolute figures over the period from £42.9 in 1952 to £31.3 in 1958 contributing to the lack of investment in manufacturing. That figure had risen rapidly until 1951 and then declined and stayed depressed until 1960.

An excessive preoccupation with the balance of payments both in 1952 and in 1955 helped to preserve these restrictive policies. In the 1952 balance of payments crisis the government had acted to constrain demand at home when in fact the trade deficit was already beginning to improve. In 1955 when another deficit emerged in the balance of payments the government acted to constrain imports by imposing, in March of 1956, a 37.5 percent import levy (with a 25 percent preferential rate for U. K. goods) and credit was curbed on consumer purchases. Whatever the positive effects on the balance of payments the effect on employment was sharply negative as imports, which contributed to the manufacturing sector in Ireland, were hit with these levies. In July the levies were increased to 60 percent (and 40 percent) and applied to a wider range of goods. Manufactured exports, which had been growing during the years after the 1948 Trade Act with Britain provided access to tariff free market in Britain, declined.

Fiscal orthodoxy prevailed in the 1957 budget as again the government cut capital expenditures and retained the import levies. The 1958 GNP was 2.5 percent lower than that of 1955. Employment in industry and agriculture dropped from 1951 to 1958 by over 12 percent leading to massive unemployment. The effects of the slow and stunted growth in the economy were felt in two areas in particular. The first was emigration which rose steadily during the 1950s to the point that the largest decrease in the Irish population since the 1920s (-4.9), some 400,000 people, occurred in the period 1951 to 1961. It produced the lowest population figure the Republic ever had, 2.8 million (Sexton 1986: 31). As Kennedy notes, it is estimated that two of every five children under fifteen in 1946 had emigrated by 1971 (Kennedy and Dowling 1975: 41).

The psychological effects on the people of Ireland in the 1950s have frequently been noted. A declining rural population, young people jobless and emigrating, a stagnant economy, and a conservative government, society, and church led to the sense that Ireland was a dying culture. It is not surprising that many observers see that the changes wrought by *Economic Development* and the *(First) Programme* having as much a psychological impact as economic.

What was the aggregate performance over the period from 1945 to 1959? What was the outcome of the policies adopted during the period? The record is mixed and much of the positive development elements are independent of government policy, whereas the negative elements often stem from government policy. To be fair to the government, Brendan Walsh notes "there were a number of obstacles to better decision making such as delays in data availability." He also states: "Moreover the degree of sophistication in Irish policy making could not with impunity outpace the international banking community which still viewed an independent Irish economy as a dubious proposition" (Walsh 1979: 3).

In the period from 1947 to 1949 the growth in GNP was five percent. The pent up demand of the postwar period contributed to this growth, as did an agricultural recovery from low yields in 1946 and 1947. By 1949 total GNP had recovered to the prewar level (Kennedy and Dowling 1975: 6). This favorable growth rate dropped to 1.8 percent for the period 1949 to 1955. As noted above, the policies adopted for agriculture, tourism, and industry for this period were not expansionary. The constrictive policies of increased taxes and import levies imposed in the 1955 to 1958 period led to a severe depression. The drop in GNP was -1.3 percent in 1955-1956, followed by a growth rate the following year of .6 of one percent, and followed again by a drop of -1.8 percent in 1957-1958.

Sectoral patterns within the overall pattern of change in GNP indicate a changing role of agriculture. From 1949 to 1961 agricultural growth contributed only .3 percent to GNP growth and employment dropped 1.1 percent in that sector. As F.S.L. Lyons notes: "The volume of agricultural output had remained stagnant since 1909 and there are grounds for believing that it was not significantly greater than it had been in 1861" (F.S.L. Lyons 1972: 626). The greater sectoral contribution came from industy which contributed one-half of GNP growth for these years.

On the surface the record for the period is less than startling. The initial postwar growth is followed by a long depression. That depression was coupled with and exacerbated a high rate of emigration. The cumulative effect on the Irish was a loss of confidence and the sense that independence had not fulfilled the promise of economic prosperity. Beneath the surface, however, the building blocks of industrial growth, increased foreign investment, and the rejection of protectionism were being put in place in legislation, in reports, and in the minds of policy makers (Chubb and Lynch 1969; McCarthy 1990).

## *Four*

# From the Advent of Planning to Entry into the European Community, 1959–1972

It has become commonplace to assign a special significance to the year 1958 in the annals of Irish economic development. Events of that year are often seen as representing a break with the past and the beginning of a new, energetic, outward-looking orientation. In this view, T. K. Whitaker's *Economic Development* was the central document in a series of proposals for economic expansion spanning the next decade. To show how widespread that opinion was, Ronan Fanning begins his essay on "The Genesis of *Economic Development*" with two pages of quotations attesting to the importance of Whitaker's work (Fanning 1990: 74-76)! F. S. L. Lyon's statement is perhaps the best known: "It is hardly too much to say, indeed, that even today it can be seen as a watershed in the modern economic history of the country" (F. S. L. Lyons 1972: 628).

Current scholarship is reassessing both the abruptness of the change and the significance of the plans themselves as a driving force behind the rapid growth of the Irish economy in the 1960s. As we have seen in the previous chapter, a number of key development institutions were already in place by 1958. And on a conceptual level, a 1949 paper by Patrick Lynch contained the essential elements of the "new" approach (Fanning 1984: 154). In addition, several observers have argued that it was a set of fortuitous circumstances, rather than the development programs themselves, which propelled the economy forward.

Despite these reservations most agree that *Economic Development* and the *(First) Programme for Economic Expansion* are historic documents. At the very least, they had a beneficial psychological effect by helping to establish a consensus on what to do. There are several additional reasons for their importance: the return to free trade after twenty-five years of protection, the encouragement of foreign investment, the revival of a policy centered on export-oriented agriculture, and the acceptance of the view that the government must take a greater role in directing the economy (Lee 1989: 344). That is, the Irish government now appeared more willing to use demand management techniques to stimulate economic growth.

There can be some confusion about the sequence of documents associated with Whitaker's efforts in 1958. There was the initial statement of proposals contained in a "Memorandum for the Information of the Government" which Whitaker, as Secretary of the Department of Finance, sent to the Minister for Finance on 12 December, 1957. The contents of this memorandum formed the basis for two further documents: *Economic Development* (the "Grey Book") published for general distribution in November 1958, and the "White Paper" which contained the proposals "Laid by the Government before each House of the Oireachtas, November 1958." This was the (First) *Programme for Economic Expansion* sections of which are reproduced below.

T. K. Whitaker set the tone of these documents in his "Memorandum":

> Various commissions have surveyed the Irish economy most thoroughly and it would be a waste of time and effort to cover the ground again. What is urgently necessary is not to know that more resources should be devoted to productive rather than non-productive purposes but rather to know what are the productive purposes to which resources should be applied.

## *PROGRAMME FOR ECONOMIC EXPANSION*
## *PART I. INTRODUCTION*

*1. The programme of economic development contained in this White Paper has been prepared in the conviction that the years immediately ahead will be decisive for Ireland's economic future. Several factors, some outside our immediate power to influence, have helped to bring about this situation.*

*2. The establishment of a Free Trade Area in Europe will, whether we join or not, and irrespective of the conditions on which we become a member, call for a special effort on our part if output and living standards are not to lag behind those of neighbouring countries. Apart from this, the difficulties associated with a restricted home market will become more serious if the population fails to rise. Production has not been increasing fast enough to provide employment and acceptable living standards for growing numbers of our people; large-scale emigration has been accompanied by a high level of unemployment. Emigration will not be checked nor will unemployment be permanently reduced until the rate of increase in national output is greatly accelerated.*

*3. On the basis of existing policies, the capital programme of public authorities will fall in the coming years, mainly because social needs, such as houses and hospitals, will soon be overtaken in most of the country. It is an urgent necessity to make sure not merely that there will be no consequential drop in employment but also that our available resources of labour, land and capital, including those released from social investment, will be employed as fully as possible in promoting sound national development.*

*4. The first essential is to redefine the objectives of economic policy in the light of present-day and probably future conditions. This can best be done in the form of a realistic and systematic programme of economic development covering a period of, say, five years. The publication of such a programme will, it is hoped, help towards the achievement of maximum progress by stimulating public interest and support, ensuring coordination of effort and limiting the scope for misunderstanding and inconsistency.*

*5. In a country in which private enterprise predominates and which is so exposed to fluctuations in external trade, there would be little point in drawing up a detailed plan based on predetermined production "targets". The programme should be read as an outline of the more important contributions, direct and indirect, which the Government propose to make to economic development in the years immediately ahead. The programme is a flexible one, capable of modification to meet changing circumstances or unforseen needs.*

*6. Except to the extent to which it may be State-financed, the vital contribution which the private sector can make to economic progress is not expressly dealt with. The programme is, however, based on the principle that, in the future as in the past, the private sector will be the principal source of new productive projects. It is hoped that the publication of the programme will act as a stimulus to industrialists in the formulation of new projects and will be of assistance to them in the preparation of their production plans.*

*7. There is general agreement that productive capital expenditure—productive in the sense of yielding an adequate return to the community in competitive goods and services—must receive a greater priority than at present in the public capital programme. It is on this fundamental principle that the present programme of economic development is based. The social capital investment of past years has given us an "infrastructure" of housing, hospitals, communications, etc., which is equal (in some respects, perhaps, superior) to that of comparable countries. What is now required is a greater emphasis on productive expenditure which, by increasing national output particularly of goods capable of meeting competition in export markets will enable full advantage to be taken of that infrastructure and in due course make possible and, indeed, necessitate its further extension. The expected decline in social capital expenditure in the coming years will afford an opportunity—and underlines the necessity—of switiching resources to productive purposes.*

*8. As capital is scarce, it is desirable both to conserve existing capital assets and to obtain the utmost value for new outlay. With full regard to the need to avoid hardship to existing tenants, rent controls will gradually be relaxed so as to encourage the greater and more economical use of the existing stock of houses; as a first step, it is proposed to remove control from owner-occupied houses and houses newly-converted into self-contained flats.*

*Attention will be given to the coordination of building programmes of State and semi-State organisations. Policy generally will be directed towards economy in the use of capital.*

*9. Our problems will not be solved merely by additional productive capital outlay, whether public or private. While capital is a condition precedent to, it is not a condition sufficient for, economic progress. More is required—the adoption of improved methods and techniques, the loosening of restrictive practices, the raising of the general level of technical education, the stimulation of new ideas, etc. No programme of economic development will be successful unless the people have the will to work and are prepared to accept the living standards to which their efforts entitle them. This means, in particular, that wage standards must be realistic, having regard to the level of productivity in this country and the need for ensuring competitive costs per unit of output.*

*10. The capital we need for productive development must come mainly from our current savings, supplemented by voluntary repatriation of past savings, by foreign investment here and, within due limits, by borrowing from international lending agencies. The facilities provided by the banks, financial institutions and the stock exchanges are of great importance in securing that capital is placed at the disposal of productive enterprise. It is, therefore, the Government's desire that these facilities will continue to be improved so as to promote industrial and agricultural development. Specific reference is made in the programme to the credit requirements of agriculture and industry. It will be the concern of the Government to make sure that capital for productive development is available as cheaply as possible. Saving will be encouraged and any tendency for consumer spending to cause an external payments deficit, and thus reduce the availability of capital for development needs, will be checked. Subject to this, financial policy will favour the application of all available resources to productive home purposes, not to the accumulation of further external reserves or investments. In this connection, the Government welcome the recent steps taken by the commercial banks to make available finance for the long-term capital requirements of industry and to meet the growing needs of agriculture. They also view with approval the trend towards a more active exercise of its functions by the Central Bank.*

*11. Fiscal policy also will be guided primarily by the need to encourage production and saving. In particular, the Government's aim is to create conditions permitting as soon as possible of a reduction in direct taxation. This would be a tonic to the economy, a stimulus to personal and corporate saving and an encouragement both to native and foreign enterprise to undertake new projects. High taxation is necessitated by high expenditure and can be reduced only if expenditure is reduced, or if taxable incomes are raised by increased production and the cost of current services is at the same time held rigidly in check. As well as encouraging increased production, the Government will strive to reduce the effective burden of taxation by moderating the growth in net debt service charges, by achieving the maximum efficiency in administration, by relating further improvements in the social services to increases in real national income and by reducing subsidies to the minimum necessary to secure a permanent increase in economic production.*

*12. The programme proposed for each of the major fields of development is outlined in Parts II to V of this Paper. In Part VI the cost is estimated in relation to the financial resources likely to be available and an indication is given of the economic benefits which may reasonably be expected if the programme is realised.*

There was a sense of urgency in the proposals, stemming partly from the fact that the emerging free trade area in Western Europe threatened Irish living standards. To make matters worse, this threat came at a time when Ireland's economic condition and morale were already depressed. As noted above, the Irish voters had not found much difference in the policies of the 1950s despite an alteration in power and the renewal of Fine Gael as an opposition party. More important, by far, was the change within Fianna Fáil as in June of 1959 Eamon deValera stepped down as Prime Minister and head of the party. He was elected President of Ireland, a predominantly ceremonial position. His successor was Sean Lemass, a senior Fianna Fáil politician steeped in the nationalist tradition who, however, recognized the dismal economic status of Ireland in the 1950s. Lemass set his own growth goals in agriculture and industry, to be promoted by both the private and the public sectors. There was large scale unemployment and emigration—the perennial cloud over the country—and improvement could only come with an acceleration in the growth rate of national output.

The *Programme* proceeds cautiously here. It avoided stipulating specific targets or setting "fanciful" goals that would simply aggravate disillusionment if unattained. The *Programme* envisioned a 2 percent annual increase in real national income over the coming several years. Moreover the *Programme* affirmed the central role played by the private sector in the economy and made no suggestion that "rigid" economic planning was in the offing. Government policy was calculated to encourage private enterprise to undertake "productive capital expenditure." This was the basis of the *Programme* and the key to the successful attainment of its aspirations regarding employment and international competitiveness (Sec. 6 and 7). There were assurances that industrial and agricultural entrepreneurs would have their capital requirements met by existing financial institutions, by attracting foreign investment, and by such bodies as the Industrial Credit Company (Sec. 10). While it was not stated directly, a question arose as it did in the nineteenth century and in the 1920s: was there a capital shortage in Ireland or rather was there a shortage of entrepreneurial initiative which failed to take advantage of existing financial facilities?

Although the *Programme*'s opening pages emphasize industry, it is worth noting that agricultural policy remains at the center of the proposals. The aim is to form a policy that "enables output to be increased at costs which make exports profitable without subsidization. On this depends not only the possibility of a higher income for the agricultural community but the future development of the whole economy." All in all, the *Programme* represented a new approach to old problems. But the aspirations remain the same: to increase national output and thereby reduce unemployment and emigration.

Whether due to the *Programme* or not, it is clear that economic growth in Ireland did accelerate at that time. Real Gross National Product increased at an annual rate of 4.5 percent between 1959 and 1962. This rate was dramatically greater than the *First Programme*'s aim of 2 percent per year. It was also greater than the rate registered during previous decades. Growth averaged about 1 percent per year in the period 1926-1960. Between 1951 and 1958, employment in industry fell from 282,000 to about 250,000. It had moved to 259,000 by 1961 and to 274,000 in 1963. The latter figure represented 26 percent of total employment. Agricultural employment continued to decline in absolute terms and relative to industrial employment. In 1961, 380,000 held jobs in agriculture, 36.1 percent of total employment. The 1963 figures for that sector were 360,000 employed, 34.2 pecent of the total. This impressive performance appeared to be making inroads into a chronic Irish problem: stemming the emigration of underemployed farm workers and those entering the labor force. In the early 1960s Irish population began to rise again after decades of almost continual decline.

Still, there was grumbling about some aspects of the economy's performance. The Bank of Ireland worried that the size of government expenditure and the "unproductive" nature of some public spending would create budgetary and balance of payments problems. The Bank also pointed with alarm to wage agreements that exceeded productivity gains, a phenomenon that threatened to make Ireland's exports less competitive in world markets (*The Economist*, vol. 208, p. 169, 7/15/63).

One had to consider, too, the likelihood that extraordinarily favorable external circumstances had contributed significantly to the economy's progress between 1959 and 1962. Buoyant foreign demand, improvement in the terms of trade, and an increase in direct investment by international firms all bolstered the Irish economy in the years of the *First Programme* (Kennedy, Giblin, and McHugh 1988: 65-66). The Irish government acknowledged this point in August 1963. Nonetheless, it argued that "these achievements demonstrate how effective a positive, integrated statement of attainable objectives, backed by State aide and incentives, can be." In their survey, Kennedy, Giblin, and McHugh agree with this view, maintaining that "domestic influences also played a major role in sustaining expansion." This was particularly true of "a consistently expanding fiscal policy" which bolstered domestic demand (Ibid).

With that sense of accomplishment, in August 1963 and July 1964 the government proposed a two-part *Second Programme for Economic Expansion*, to run from 1964 to 1970 inclusive. Taken together, the *First* and *Second Programmes* would span the 1960s, designated the "decade of development" by the United Nations and the Organization for Economic Co-operation and Development.

The overall growth rate between 1959 and 1963 masks important sectoral differences. Industry accounted for most of the gain while agriculture had made little progress in that period. This experience had a significant impact on the orientation of the *Second Programme* which made industry the key to development (Daly 1981: 167). The projected annual growth rate for industry in the *Second Programme* was 7 percent against only 2 percent for agriculture. Overall, the economy was expected to grow at a rate of 4.4 percent year.

*SECOND PROGRAMME*
*PART I*
*IMPORTANCE OF EXPORTS AS CONDITION OF GROWTH*

*7. In Ireland, more than in countries of larger population with a stronger industrial sector, a critical importance attaches to exports. Because of our small home market, it is mainly through exports that economic expansion can be achieved. For us, domestic policies and practices must be such as to keep our output adjusted in price and quality to the need to secure a progressive increase in exports of both goods and services. This is the essential condition of growth and it must govern our whole approach to programming.*

*8. Because of the dependence on exports as a source of growth and because of the rapidly increasing degree of international economic interdependence, it would be unrealistic to prepare any economic programme for Ireland without considering what is likely to happen in the major countries with which we have close economic relations. Through our membership of the OECD we are in constant touch with developments and objectives in North America and Western Europe. Moreover, our desire to enter the EEC, as soon as it is possible for us to do so, envisages an even closer degree of coordination and harmonisation of economic policies with the Community. It is impossible to predict when the way will be open to membership of the Community but for the purposes of this programme it is assumed that Ireland will be in the Community before 1970.*

*9. A 50% increase in real income by 1970 as compared with 1960 (equivalent to an average annual rate of increase of 4.14%) was adopted as a collective growth target for the countries comprising the OECD at the first meeting of the Ministerial Council of the Organisation in November, 1961. The promulgation of this target by the Organisation was intended not merely as a psychological stimulus but as a positive aid to the achievement of high rates of growth in individual countries, on the principle that only in a general climate of expansion can individual countries, particularly those in process of development, hope to make maximum progress. We have in fact maintained more than a 4% average advance over the whole period since 1958, a greater rate of growth than was achieved during any similar period in the history of the State. Allowing for the increase in GNP in 1961 and 1962, the average annual rate of growth required over the period 1963 to 1970 in order to advance 50% in the decade is 4.4%. It is necessary to sustain this rate on average over the coming years in order to provide the increased employment and rising standards which will be expected by our citizens; and the studies undertaken show that it is possible, though by no means easy, to realise this aim, despite the downturn in 1962 and the initial difficulties of adjustment to greater competition and other economic changes, provided there is sufficient unity and strength of purpose.*

*EMPLOYMENT AND EMIGRATION*

*20. The second programme is more specific and ambitious than the first concerning the desired improvement in employment, as well as in living standards. Net emigration, as measured by the net outward passenger movement by sea and air, has already declined substantially in the early years of this decade — from 43,000 in 1960, to 27,000 in 1961 and to 21,000 in 1962. At this figure — the recent level is lower — emigration no longer causes population decline. Its progressive reduction is one of the basic aims of the new programme. There will always be some voluntary emigration from Ireland but in time this should be increasingly offset by immigration. In modern conditions the tendency is for business firms to move into and to expand within communities where labour is abundant and the EEC Commission have expressed themselves as supporting this desideratum. In a Europe in which manpower shortage has become the most serious impediment to growth, Ireland will have a special opportunity in the future to create, by intensive promotion of industries and services, an increasing number of home outlets for those leaving the land and for young persons newly seeking work, and, in time also, for some of the Irish workers now living abroad who may wish to return home.*

*BASIC PRINCIPLES OF THE SECOND PROGRAMME*

*21. Though the second programme is more comprehensive than the first and the economic and social environment will be different, the basic principles of the first programme, as set out in Part I of the 1958 White Paper, will remain fully applicable. It is still expected that the private sector, stimulated and guided by public policy and supplemented where necessary by State initiative, will be the principal source of new productive projects. The main emphasis in public activity will be on productive expenditure which will increase the national output of goods and services capable of meeting competition in export markets. Earning and saving will continue to be encouraged by fiscal policy. Higher productivity and greater competitiveness remain the key to permanent improvements in employment and community welfare.*

*SUMMARY OF OBJECTIVES*

*22. The second programme will, therefore, be distinguished by the following principal characteristics:*

*(i) It will cover the period to the end of this decade.*

*(ii) It will have as its chief objective the raising of the real income of the community by 50% in the 1960's, in line with the collective target of the OECD.*

*(iii) Its complementary aim will be to secure the progressive reduction of involuntary emigration so that by 1970 net yearly emigration will be reduced to 10,000 at most. The net increase in employment envisaged in the decade is 78,000.*

*(iv) Special attention will be given to education, training and other forms of "human investment".*

*(v) The obligation of Ireland to give increased aid to less developed countries will be recognised.*

*(vi) The basic principles underlying the first programme will continue to be respected.*

*50. The development of inland fisheries will continue with a view to increasing exports and improving angling as a sporting amenity and tourist attraction. An annual grant-in-aid of £75,000 has already been assured to the Inland Fisheries Trust for the next few years for the development of game fishing, coarse fishing and sea angling. The promotion of inland fisheries will also be fostered by the Department of Lands, Board of Conservators and the ESB; the growing number of local angling organisations will be encouraged to participate in this work. It is confidently expected that these developments, coupled with the tourist promotion activities of Bord Failte, will attract growing numbers of angling visitors and, in conjunction with the expansion of salmon fishing, fish farming and eel fishing, will contribute to increased exports.*

*INDUSTRY*

*51. The main contribution to the future expansion in GNP, both by way of increased employment and increased production, is expected from industry. If agricultural growth for any reason falls short of 2.7% per annum, industry will have to step up its contribution further. Industrial expansion will have to be achieved in a world which is moving towards freer trade in manufactured products and in which competition is becoming more intense. In these circumstances our industrial economy faces two problems; adaptation and development. There must be adaptation of existing industries so that their products will progressively achieve the highest standards of competitiveness on both the home and export markets. This was an urgent task when membership of the EEC seemed imminent. It is no less urgent now that the prospect of membership has been postponed for some time, for postponement of itself does nothing to improve the prospects of Irish goods in export markets, rather the reverse. Exports are the key to national prosperity; it is only by winning sufficient export orders against growing competition from other countries that the expansion of production and employment envisaged in the programme can be realised.*

*52. In all Irish industries there are firms whose outlook is dynamic, whose equipment and methods are up-to-date and whose output is expanding. The reports of the Committee on Industrial Organisation, however, have shown that these firms, thought they may account for a high proportion of output in their respective industries, may be in a numerical minority. The Committee found that in many industrial concerns buildings were unsuitable, procedures and equipment obsolete, direction and management unenterprising, operative training inadequate and the range of variety in production too wide. In these firms the urgent need of reorganisation is receiving insufficient attention, and, even since publication of the Committee's reports, there has been no convincing indication that sufficient thought is being given to preparing for the more acute competition that lies ahead. In a number of the industries surveyed, only the minority of progressive firms has made sustained efforts to develop exports. In many concerns there is great scope for improving efficiency,and the recommendations of the CIO indicate the direction in which they, and the industries of which they form part, should move. Plant and machinery must be modernised, the organisation of work improved, modern techniques of management introduced; the level of technical skill must be raised, restrictive practices by both management and labour removed, a greater degree of specialisation introduced, market surveys undertaken, and the possibilities of joint action in export marketing and other fields explored. Adaptation Councils can play an important role in carrying out the adaptation measures necessary to prepare industry for freer trade and all industries which have not already done so should urgently and seriously consider the establishment of Councils.*

*53. During the second programme the emphasis will be placed on securing the widest and most effective use of the inducements offered by the State to firms to increase their efficiency. Generous grants and special loan facilities are available towards the cost of re-equipment and adaptation. Under the Technical Assistance Scheme, recently extended in scope and size, grants are available of up to 50% of the cost of engaging industrial consultants and of sending management and labour on training courses. These activities will be supported because experience both here and in other countries has shown that very substantial increases in productivity and efficiency can be obtained by applying expert advice, frequently at very little cost in additional investment. If industries are to become and remain competitive, it is vital that they keep abreast of new knowledge and its implications. There must also be greater emphasis on research and development, and this may require co-operative effort because of the relatively small size of most Irish firms. This co-operative effort will be assisted and supplemented through the Institute for Industrial Research and Standards whose growing research facilities should be availed of by industry to the fullest extent possible.*

*54. The improvement in the efficiency of existing industries, and in particular the development of industrial exports, is of such vital importance to continued economic expansion that, besides aids and inducements, other measures must be applied to ensure adequate progress. A 10% cut in protective tariffs was made on 1st January, 1963. A further cut will be made on 1st January, 1964, and the general aim is to achieve a reduction of the order of one-third by 1st January, 1965, the process of reducing protection to be continued thereafter, with due regard to developments in our trading relations and to the conditions affecting particular industries. Indeed, a progressive reduction of protection, apart from being a stimulus to efficiency, is the price we must expect to pay, in any international context, for improved outlets for our own exports. More selective action may be needed to quicken the pace of change in any industry in which costs are high because effective steps towards modernisation and improvement have not been taken.*

*55. Tariff reductions and the efforts by industrial concerns to increase their efficiency will reshape our industrial economy. These economic changes will not be achieved without difficulty for the individual businessman and the individual worker, but they must be carried out in the interest of the community. Continued expansion depends on the necessary changes being made quickly and smoothly. In these circumstances, it is reasonable that the community should encourage and facilitate economic change by contributing to the costs which it imposes on individuals. As this process of change develops, some firms and industries may meet insuperable difficulties and serious problems will be posed for the towns and localities which are now largely dependent on them. These problems are being tackled in three ways. Firms are being encouraged to switch to new lines of production by grants, special loans and accelerated depreciation allowances. Industrial grants will be applied to attract suitable new enterprises to the areas which are adversely affected. Arrangements will be made to provide that workers who lose their employment are retrained for employment in industries which are expanding and that they are assisted in resettling in the places in which these expanding activities are located.*

*56. The improvement in the competitiveness of existing industries must proceed side by side with the broadening and deepening of the industrial base. There are differences between the industrial structures of countries which are now at a higher stage of economic development than Ireland. The differences are slight, however, when compared with the similarities. All these countries have diversified industrial structures in which almost all of the main branches of industrial activity are represented. The second programme will attempt to strengthen our industrial structure by an active promotional campaign to secure the establishment here, where economically feasible, of major industries which we now lack.*

*57. In attracting new industries to broaden the industrial base, the main inducement will be industrial grants, which have proved their effectiveness during the first programme, supplemented by fiscal incentives to greater efficiency and higher exports. The scale of capital grants will be maintained at current levels but additional flexibility will be exercised by An Foras Tionscal in the assessment of grants for industries which are needed to lay the base for further activities. The Committee on Industrial Organisation has recommended that industrial grants policy should be amended so as to promote the growth of major industrial centres; a special examination is being made of this recommendation and the related question of establishing industrial estates at these centres. Additional resources will be given to the Industrial Development Authority so as to enable the pace of industrial promotion to be accelerated. The Government will, in due course, submit proposals to the Oireachtas for the repeal of the Control of Manufactures legislation; no obstacle must be placed in the way of the external investment which will complement our own efforts to achieve the growth targets.*

*58. The objective of the second programme is to increase industrial output at an average annual rate of 7%. This expansion is of the same order as that realised during the years 1958-62. It is expected that this rate of growth will be achieved by an average annual increase in productivity of nearly 4% and in employment of 3%. If these expectations are fulfilled, industrial output in real terms will be 97% greater and output per industrial worker will be 47% greater in 1970 than they were in 1960, and over the decade industrial employment will rise by 86,000. A net increase of 86,000 in the numbers employed in industry will require the creation of a much larger number of new jobs: new jobs will be needed for the workers now engaged in industry who will have to transfer to different employment as conditions become more competitive, as well as for the new entrants to the industrial labour force who will come either from agriculture or from increases in the population of working age. The expansion of the industrial sector is a key objective, because the reduction in emigration, the improvement in productivity and the expansion in services all depend primarily on its achievement.*

*RELATIONSHIP OF INCOMES TO OUTPUT*

*104. It is essential to establish a coherence both between the objectives of the programme and our attitudes to work and productivity, and between the national output of goods and services and the reward we seek for our work. Each member of the labour force — employer and employee alike — must put into the economy at least as much as he seeks to take out. It is well to recall the words of the first programme —*

*"No programme of economic development will be successful unless the people have the will to work and are prepared to accept the living standards to which their efforts entitle them."*

*A programme for economic expansion requires of the community that it adopt an incomes policy which is consistent with the programme's objectives; "the ability of the authorities to pursue an ambitious expansionary policy untrammelled by the need to resort to stop-and-go policies can be seriously limited if money incomes are pushed up excessively." The 50% growth target will not be achieved unless our costs are fully competitive with those of our competitors. Costs have little chance of becoming, or remaining, competitive if money incomes outstrip production. Money incomes will outstrip production, and economic growth, social welfare, and improvements in living standards will be threatened, if we fail to recognise that an increase in output is the only safe and lasting basis for an increase in incomes. Although hourly labour costs (including social security payments and other wage supplements) in Irish manufacturing industry are generally lower than in most other European countries, the factors mentioned in paragraph 52 depress output per head so that labour costs per unit of output compare unfavourably with those of our competitors. Because of the leeway we have to make up, the argument that a rise in money incomes must at least be matched by increases in productivity would still hold good even if inflationary wage increases were taking place in Europe.*

*105. It is essential that there should be widespread public acceptance of the need for a sound incomes policy, and full co-operation between the Government and sectional interests in carrying it out. Such a policy requires that the increase in all types of income — wages, salaries, profits and rents — should not exceed the realised increase in national production. If the objectives of the programme are realised and national output is raised by about 4% a year, incomes and social benefits can increase correspondingly in real terms. It is important that at least part of the benefit of increased productivity should emerge in the form of lower prices or better quality, first, to ensure that more Irish products become competitive and exportable and, second, to ensure that the benefit will be shared by all sections of the community.*

## *CHAPTER 4*
## *CONCLUSION*

*110. In Chapter 1 the aims of the second programme have been outlined and the general approach to the achievement of these aims defined. Chapter 2 has shown to what extent the various sectors of the economy are counted upon to contribute to the overall growth rate. Chapter 3 has indicated how the real income gained may be divided as between investment for future growth, on the one hand, and consumption, on the other. At various points attention has been drawn to the need for consistency between the various elements of the programme but it is necessary, in conclusion, to say something more on this vital condition of success.*

*111. The framework of the second programme is determined by the growth rate. The rate chosen, as being both what we should aim for and what our best endeavours should realise, is a 50% increase in real national income in this decade — representing over a 4% average annual advance. If a higher rate proves to be attainable without excessive deficits in the balance of payments, it would, of course, be foolish to neglect to work for it. But if it is thought that a sufficiently bold target has not been chosen at the outset, the grounds for this view must be established by showing under what particular heading — agricultural or industrial production, tourism or other services — there are opportunities realisable within the next seven years, in the conditions, internal and external, likely to obtain, which have been overlooked or underestimated.*

*112. Similarly, when it comes to the broad division of the fruits of the progress achieved, it is impossible to claim more for consumption without curtailing investment or for community services, such as education, unless there is a corresponding abstention from private consumption. Increased investment, bringing about the greater productivity of a larger workforce and thus enabling exports to be expanded in competitive conditions, is the principal condition of progress. If investment is reduced below the level envisaged because too much is being consumed and too little saved, production in the future will be affected and there will be less goods and services coming forward either for consumption or investment. A particular importance attaches to the presence or absence of a rational incomes policy, because it is primarily through wages, salaries and profits that the fruits of progress are distributed and the allocation of additional purchasing power in any of these forms without regard to the trend in national production can pull the framework of the programme apart. It is important also that there should be general acceptance of the tax or other changes needed to effect any agreed redistribution of incomes or increases in community benefits. In fact, if steady progress is to be made towards the target set, the relationships indicated in Chapter 3 between consumption (public and private), savings and investment need to be maintained. If the growth rate aimed at were not realised, the dependent aims would also have to be modified. Less would, for instance, be available for improvement of public services, or for increased private consumption, than has been postulated. It would, moreover, be indefensible to incur the projected deficits in external payments except in association with the projected upward trend in real national product and in expectation of a continued advance, in incomes and employment, beyond 1970 which would be less dependent on external resources.*

*113. If the framework set out in this publication is accepted, the detailed programming for agriculture, industry, tourism and the other services must conform to it. It is obvious that a programme would not be worthy of the name if it were not intelligently fitted together in this way.*

*114. An economic programme is necessarily expressed in terms of employment and production, savings and investment, exports and imports. It must endeavour to relate changes under these heads to the main divisions of economic activity, namely, agriculture, industry and services. These are convenient terms for describing complicated economic processes and analysing their inter-relationship but the importance of these processes lies in their implications for the individual members of the community, not as statistical units but as human persons. In the last analysis, the success of the new programme will be measured by the contribution it makes to human welfare in the widest sense by affording increased opportunities to Irish men and women to develop their full potential as individuals and as members of the community. The Government in drawing up this programme are fully conscious of their responsibilities in this respect, but they can only assist, guide and persuade; they cannot guarantee that the desired degree of progress will be achieved. The targets set out are aims, not promises, and the realisation of these aims will depend on the degree to which all members of the community co-operate in their individual, as well as their representative, capacity. It is, however, a heartening characteristic of national economic planning that, the more people who plan on the assumption that the target will be realised, the more certain it is to be realised. Courage and consistency in planning are the first requirements; general acceptance and co-operation will then promote success.*

*115. This, therefore, is the appropriate point at which to obtain the views of the principal functional organisations, representing the trade unions, industry, agriculture and the other important sectors of economic activity. Having before them a clear exposition of the objectives of the second programme, of the main assumptions on which it is based and of the necessary conditions for its fulfillment, these organisations will thus be in a position, at the formative stage, to consider the reasonableness and practicability of the programme and to advise on the best means of realising it. The Government hope, in this way, to secure the maximum degree of common acceptance of the aims of the programme and of common purpose to achieve them.*

*116. In the light of the views received, progress will be made with the further elaboration of the programme. The results of the first programme are being analysed as a guide to the most effective way of obtaining, in the conditions that may exist in the years 1964-70, the specific contribution required from the major sectors to the achievement of the new target. It is intended that this more detailed exposition of the proposed lines of progress in agriculture and other major sectors should be published early in 1964.*

The *Second Programme*'s design was more comprehensive than its predecessor, as these specific growth targets indicate. It stressed the key role of exports as a source of economic expansion (Part I, sec. 7). The *Programme* also sought the participation of trade unions, employer associations and State institutions through the newly established National Industrial Economic Council. This was a step towards an incomes policy, which sought cooperation between the Government and sectoral interests to ensure that "the increase in *all* types of income— wages, salaries, profits and rents— should not exceed the realized increase in national productions" (Part I, sec. 105).

In line with policy developments elsewhere, Keynesian demand management techniques were more in evidence than in the earlier *Programme*. The same can be said of the *Programme*'s emphasis on "human capital" —government support for training, education, and the like—as a way to preserve and enhance competitiveness in international trade. Still, the private sector remains "the source of new productive projects" to provide a net increase in employment and to reduce emigration.

Part II of the *Second Programme* revised slightly the annual growth targets set down in Part I, from 4.4 to 4.3 percent. It also restated the importance of tying income gains to "rates of increase in incomes and national productivity" in order to keep Irish goods and services competitive in international markets (Part II, sec. 8).

*SECOND PROGRAMME*
*FOR*
*ECONOMIC EXPANSION*
*PART II*

*4. It was stated in Part I that the chief objective was an increase of 50% in real Gross National Product (GNP) between 1960 and 1970, made up of increases of 31% in agriculture, forestry and fishing, 97% in industry and 43% in the "other domestic" sector. In the agriculture, forestry and fishing sector, agriculture accounts for virtually all the output. The target for the sector as a whole has been revised as a result of the determination of separate targets for each of its sub-groups, agriculture (33%), forestry (66%) and fishing (75%). The revised figure for the sector as a whole is 33%. This has the effect of increasing the projected rate of increase in GNP from 50% to 51%, equivalent to an annual average growth rate of 4.2%. Allowing for the increases achieved to date, the target for the period of the second programme, 1964 to 1970 inclusive, is 35% or 4.3% a year. This compares with the growth of about 4 1/2% a year achieved during the first programme.*

*INCOMES POLICY AND INDUSTRIAL RELATIONS*

*8. Realisation of the programme's targets will enable real incomes to be increased correspondingly. Part I drew attention to the danger that rising costs and prices could jeopardise achievement of the targets, and to the need for adopting an incomes policy which would establish an orderly relationship between the development of money incomes and output. Since Part I was published, the ninth round of post-war wage increases has been negotiated and is being implemented. The formula for the increase agreed on by national representatives of trade unions and employers provided a valuable guide for wage negotiations, while at the same time the widespread acceptance and implementation of the formula strengthened the authority of the national representative bodies. In the central negotiations, the Government's assessment of the wage developments compatible with the economic situation was put before the two parties so that their deliberations could have regard to the public interest. The agreement finally reached in January, 1964, provided for a maximum increase in basic wages of 12% during the period of two and a half years covered by the agreement. Expressed as an annual average, this increase — approximately 5% — exceeds the annual average increase in productivity contemplated throughout the period of the programme. If rising costs are not to threaten the growth targets of the programme — in particular the exports targets — it is essential that productivity should rise at a faster rate during the currency of the agreement than is contemplated throughout the programme as a whole. Since the full wage and salary increases are being paid in 1964, money incomes will rise more quickly than national output in that year. It is essential that this imbalance be rectified as quickly as possible. Unless there is a close correspondence between increases in money incomes and national output, production and living costs are raised and goods and services become less competitive in home and export markets. To avoid these consequences, it is desirable that, in general wage and salary settlements for a term of years, there should be an approximation from year to year of the rates of increase in incomes and national productivity.*

*9. In the evolution of incomes policy, the National Industrial Economic Council will have an important role. In advising on measures for the development of the economy, the Council is expected to have regard to the trend in the general level of incomes with a view to including in its reports, where relevant, policy recommendations in this connection. These could be of considerable value in securing conformity between the development of incomes and the requirements of the programme.*

*10. If the programme is not to be retarded by recurrent industrial disputes, satisfactory labour-management relations are essential. In our democratic system of free negotiation this depends, primarily, on the willingness of both labour and management to discuss and settle their mutual problems in an enlightened and progressive spirit of co-operation with full regard to the national interest. This spirit of co-operation is evident in the coming together of both sides in the National Employer/Labour Conference and their participation in the work of public bodies such as the Irish National Productivity Committee and the National Industrial Economic Council. It is the Government's policy to promote such co-operation and to encourage and assist the interests concerned in resolving their mutual problems. Steps are also being taken to review, in the light of experience and in consultation with employer and labour interests, the legislative machinery provided under the Industrial Relations Acts and the Trade Union Acts, to ensure that it is adapted to present-day national needs.*

## *CHAPTER 15*
## *GENERAL FINANCIAL POLICY*

*1. Part I of the programme states that it will be the objective of financial policy to maintain adequate — while avoiding excessive — demand as a basis for maximum economic advance. It is desirable that total community spending — capital and consumer spending in due proportions - should be sufficient to keep productive activity at the highest rate consistent with a competitive level of prices and costs and a reasonable degree of external balance.*

*2. Adequate demand in this sense cannot be expected to be automatically maintained. Indeed, it is constantly in danger of being upset by both external and internal forces. In our case, the former are particularly important, since the external demand for Irish goods and services accounts for more than 40% of GNP. We cannot, of course, determine the economic and trade policies of other countries but we can influence the volume of our external sales by the extent to which we maintain a competitive position and take advantage of the opportunities available. The level of internal demand can be more directly influenced but care must be taken to ensure that action in this field does not adversely affect the level of external demand. It is total demand, external and internal combined, that we need to keep right.*

*3. Deviations from the appropriate level of demand may occur, either by way of a fall in total demand, lowering the rate of growth below its true potential, or by way of an excessive increase in demand, leading to a rate of growth which, being dependent on excessive deficits in external payments, is not sustainable. Both situations are disruptive of economic progress and require remedial action.*

*4. Failure to maintain the desired (and sustainable) growth rate because of a falling off in demand would mean that part of the country's productive resources was lying unused and opportunities of producing more in order to raise living standards and provide employment were being foregone. Moreover, the running of industrial plant below capacity tends to have adverse repercussions on costs. Experience here and in other countries has shown that a high level of domestic demand helps to reduce unit costs and to stimulate exports. Wide fluctuations in the growth rate are also undesirable from the psychological point of view since they tend to undermine confidence and prevent or upset the sensible planning which is the objective of a programme for economic expansion.*

*5. If, therefore, because of a slackening of activity in the private sector, total demand should begin to fall below the desirable level as defined above, the Government will be concerned to ensure that appropriate action is taken to make good the deficiency. Various fiscal measures are available. For instance, taxation on incomes or expenditure might be temporarily reduced, at the expense of greater Government use of credit, thus making more resources available for investment or consumption. Investment can also be stimulated by specific reliefs and incentives.*

*6. Another method by which demand can be stimulated, should the need arise, is by increased capital expenditure on the part of public authorities. The capacity to increase the volume of such expenditure in any short period is limited and depends on a number of projects being always at the "ready to go" stage. The alternative of increasing current expenditure is unsatisfactory since, in practice, it cannot be reversed.*

*7. What particular method or methods of stimulating demand should be employed if the occasion arose would depend on the circumstances of the particular situation. Any action taken would, of course, have to be consistent with the "essential condition of growth" laid down in paragraph 7 of Part I, namely that "domestic policies and practices must be such as to keep our output adjusted in price and quality to the need to secure a progressive increase in exports of both goods and services".*

*8. It is not only inadequate demand but also the opposite situation that must be carefully guarded against. Excessive pressure of demand, whether it be due to excessive credit for the private sector, excessive Government borrowing, or increases in money incomes which outrun increases in productivity, can push up prices, lessen the competitiveness of our exports and cause a rise in imports, with consequent disturbance to the balance of payments. Since reliance must be placed on an expansion of exports for the main impetus to the growth of national production, the trend of internal costs and prices in relation to those in our principal export markets must be watched carefully. So also must the balance of payments, as a large continuing drain on external reserves or accumulation of external indebtedness could not be sustained. If the pressure of internal demand became so great as to cause unmanageable deficits in the external accounts or a damaging increase in domestic costs and prices, corrective measures would be required. Provided, however, that personal consumption does not increase at a faster rate than that projected in the programme, this situation should not arise.*

An important assumption underlying the *Second Programme*'s strategy was that restrictions on international trade would decline throughout the 1960s. As a central consideration, the *Programme* envisioned Ireland's entry into the European Economic Country (Common Market) before the end of the decade. Although membership did not come about until 1973, both the *Programme* itself and related initiatives emphasized the need for Ireland's physical and human capital to be on their mettle in a new trading environment.

One such initiative was the formation of the Committee on Industrial Organization (CIO) in 1961. Its members came from the Federation of Irish Industries, the Irish Congress of Trade Unions, the Federated Union of Employers and the public service. The group's charge was "to make a critical appraisal of the measures that might have to be taken to adapt Irish industry to conditions of more intensive competition in home and export markets." In view of the fact that tariff protection would no longer provide a remedy, the Committee was asked to "formulate positive measures of adjustment and adaptation" for those industries where difficulties might arise.

A *CIO Interim Report on State Aid* (February 1962) said that "In their present state, many Irish firms and industries could not survive competition from imports." The Committee suggested several ways to improve competitiveness and recommended a variety of State aids to encourage industry to "adapt." Echoing points made by the Fiscal Inquiry Committee in the 1920s, the CIO indicated that improvements in design, purchasing, and marketing were effective ways for Irish firms to become more competitive. In its Interim Reports, the Committee on Industrial Organization clearly felt that much of Irish industry lacked a sense of urgency in dealing with the new conditions. The government attempted to overcome this inertia by expanding the existing program of grants and loans. As an added spur, the Control of Manufactures Acts of the 1930s were repealed. This legislation, which limited foreign investment in Ireland, proved an embarrassment to the Industrial Development Authority in its attempts to attract firms from abroad. Finally, the CIO recommended the formation of "adaptation councils" in each industry to keep the issue of competitiveness alive and to help shape policies geared to that industry's specific problems.

Unilateral tariff cuts of 10% each by the government in 1963 and 1964 and the Anglo-Irish Trade Agreement, effective July 1, 1966, strengthened the Committee's position that time was running out for inefficient Irish firms. A *Report on Progress of Industrial Adaptation* (March 1966) assessed the work of the adaptation groups. It concluded that, despite successes, much remained to be done. Many firms "have made very little effort to build up any export trade. In conditions of free-trade the continuance of such inertia will inevitably lead to extinction."

The CIO's activities in the 1960s were aimed at strengthening the competitive position of domestic firms. At the same time, and for the better part of a decade, the Industrial Development Authority was engaged in "the initiation of proposals for the creation of industries and the attraction of foreign industrialists to the country." The IDA was established in 1950 and a variety of measures involving grants and tax relief supported its efforts.

The creation of these bodies and the two plans of the early 1960s were carried out, it should be noted, by a minority government. From 1961 to 1965, Lemass ruled with the necessary votes of independents in the Dail. Lemass not only governed with confidence during these years but also managed to effect the most significant change in economic policy since 1932. And when the programs proved to be inappropriate to the circumstances, they were changed as well. The end of the *Second Programme* coincides with his departure from office in 1967.

Recall that these actions were undertaken during the life of the *Second Programme for Economic Expansion. A Review of Progress 1964-67* covered the first four years of that *Programme*. Part of the *Review* examined the extent to which outcomes had deviated from targets. At the outset, however, the *Review* indicated that, whatever the achievements, the *Second Programme* was no longer an appropriate development plan. This judgement stemmed from the uncertain status of international trading relations, particularly the yet-to-be-realized entry of Ireland into the European Economic Community. The *Programme's* targets were based upon the assumption of membership before 1970, with attendant benefits to Irish agriculture. Now it was deemed better to abandon the *Second Programme* rather than modify it, and to establish a *Third Programme* for the years 1969-1972. Before turning to that document, we will survey *Second Programme* outcomes as they appeared at the end of 1967. (Figures for 1967 were treated as provisional estimates.)

The actual annual average GNP growth rate in 1964-1967 was a full percentage point below the target for that period: 3.3 percent vs. 4.3 percent. Agricultural growth was particularly disappointing: 0.8 percent against a target rate of 3.8 percent per year. Industry fared somewhat better, registering a 5.8 percent rate instead of the targeted 7.0 percent. In the face of the variations, it was inevitable that the *Second Programme* would fall short of its overall employment targets. With 1,052,000 employed in 1963, the *Programme* projected total employment to be 1,133,000 in 1970. By 1966, however, total employment stood at 1,066,000 and a revised target of 1,081,000 was incorporated into the *Third Programme*.

The *Second Programme* also projected a continued shift in the composition of employment in Ireland. Whereas 34.2 pecent of those employed were engaged in agriculture in 1963, the anticipated figure for 1970 was 28.9 percent. Comparable values for industry were 23.5 percent and 29.5 percent. As events unfolded, however, revised targets anticipated an even greater change: the 1972 projection called for agriculture and industry to account for 25.6 percent and 30.9 percent of total employment, respectively.

The *Second Programme Review* provided a sobering reminder of the fragile nature of Irish economic development. That cautious tone carried over (as was the intent) into the *Third Programme for Economic and Social Development 1969-72*, presented by the government in March 1969. This document placed Ireland's recent progress in the context of the unprecedented growth experienced generally throughout postwar Europe. The government warned that such historically high rates may not be sustainable and should not be used as targets.

Moreover the *Third Programme* emerged from a Fianna Fáil government that had undergone some changes since the departure of Lemass. The new Prime Minister, Jack Lynch, was not as skilled in, nor as committed to, economic policy as Lemass. In 1969, the year the *Third Programme* emerged, Lynch had won an impressive election victory which provided him with a strong mandate. The Labour Party had hewed to a more socialist line in this election and had suffered a loss of seats to the middle class, market-oriented parties. The Irish voters were happy enough with the economic growth of the 1960s stimulated by government planning. However, they had no taste for a larger dose of Labour Party socialism.

Despite the disappointments and early demise of its immediate predecessor, the *Third Programme* was not presented as a hastily assembled replacement. Rather, the Government promulgated the *Third Programme* as a logical extension of the other two. In this view, the first programme's "aim was to accelerate progress by strengthening public confidence. The object of the second was to achieve the maximum sustainable rate of growth in order to provide the rising standards which had come to be expected as a result of progress under the first programme." While it does not claim that "an acceptable level of national prosperity has been achieved," the government maintained that the time had come to consider "how the fruits of progress are to be used." On a more mundane level, the document addressed the problems of implementing a development plan, a concern raised in the *Second Programme Review*.

While the very existence of the *Third Programme* stemmed from the fact that Ireland was not yet an EEC member, the Government clearly had not abandoned that expectation. Accordingly, the *Third Programme* continued to emphasize the challenges and opportunities associated with a wider and freer trading environment. "The Government's aim is that the end of the programme period will see Ireland economically much stronger, socially more concerned and psychologically more prepared for membership of the European community of nations."

## *THIRD PROGRAMME ECONOMIC AND SOCIAL DEVELOPMENT 1969-72*

*Laid by the Government before each House of the Oireachtas, March, 1969.*

## *CHAPTER 1 INTRODUCTION*

### *PAST ACHIEVEMENTS*

*1. Ten years have passed since the Government published their first programme for economic expansion. In that period the nation has made substantial advances in material prosperity. The gross national product in real terms (the volume of goods and services produced every year by the nation) has during those ten years grown by nearly 4% a year —three times as fast as during the preceding decade and nearly four times as fast as in the years leading up to the Second World War. These are increases in real terms —that is, after allowance has been made for changes in the purchasing power of money —and represent in the period since 1958 a rate of growth which, if sustained, would double the nation's standard of living in less than twenty years.*

*2. This achievement must be put in its proper perspective. Much the same pattern has been evident in almost all countries in Western Europe. Even in those countries where the rate of growth has been comparatively low, growth since 1945 has compared favourably with performance over the previous fifty years or more. For all the variation from country to country, the record of post-war growth in Western Europe as a whole, when viewed historically, may well be unprecedented. This judgment applies not merely to the total economic growth achieved but also to its pace, which has, since 1945, been both faster and less subject to fluctuation than at any other period in modern history.*

*3. This means that in Ireland, as in Western Europe generally, standards of "normal" economic growth and expectations of the future have been set by reference to achievements which are historically exceptional. This is not to say that plans to achieve similar rates of growth are not well-founded. It does, however, suggest caution in extrapolating past trends into the indefinite future. While the recent pace of development seems capable of being sustained in the years immediately ahead, it is lower than the 5 1/2% a year growth rate which the National Industrial Economic Council thought would, on certain assumptions, be required to reach full employment by 1980.*

*4. The continued existence of large numbers of underemployed on the land means that for some time to come progress towards the goal of full employment will consist of transferring people from low-income, part-time occupations to better-paid, full-time work, rather than of registering substantial increases in the numbers actually recorded as being at work. Before these increases become possible a considerable and sustained effort will be needed over a wide field in order to raise the long-term rate of growth to as high as 5 1/2% a year. To a great extent the rate of growth is, as the Council pointed out, subject to collective decision by the community. Thus, if a slower growth in monetary incomes is accepted, the dangers of inflation and the retarding effects of measures to correct them can be avoided; if more resources can be made available through savings, greater investment is possible, leading to faster growth. These points are discussed further in Chapters 12 and 18 below. The size of the task, however, and the collective disciplines that it would impose are such that clear understanding and agreement are necessary on the purposes for which economic growth is pursued. Growth cannot be achieved without sacrifice; present consumption must be sacrificed so that resources can be devoted to the investment needed to produce future wealth, and present contentment and settled habits must be sacrificed to the change, innovation and technical progress needed if growth is to be achieved.*

*NEED FOR ECONOMIC GROWTH*

*5. In Irish circumstances, growth is needed so that sufficient job opportunities can be created to enable Irish men and women to develop themselves as individuals to the limits of their ability without being compelled to do so in an alien environment. In this sense, growth is required to achieve full employment.*

*6. Growth is also needed to raise the general standard of living. Wealth and standards of living are, to a large extent, comparative matters. Unless standards in Ireland are seen to be not markedly different from those obtaining generally throughout Western Europe, especially in Britain, dissatisfaction with our economic progress —and its outward manifestation, emigration —will remain. Since those who emigrate are often the very people who bring about change and growth in the economy, there is a double loss here, because their departure means diminished capacity to increase national output. In a sense therefore, growth is needed so that growth can be achieved.*

*7. Growth is needed for an even more fundamental reason. Broadly speaking, the market forces at work in a competitive economy ensure that increases in output are accompanied by increases in income — indeed, one of the main objects of policy is to ensure that income gains do not outstrip production increases to the detriment of our competitive position. Examination of the record of economic growth in all countries shows, however, that market forces direct few of the tangible fruits of growth to the economically weaker members of society —the old, the chronically sick, the very young, the poor, the handicapped and other groups who for one reason or another have not the same bargaining strength as others in asserting their claims to a share in prosperity. To these, the State owes a special responsibility and it is to the State, in modern society, that they must look to meet the shortfall between their minimum needs and their own resources.*

*8. Moreover, in order to avoid a situation of contrast between private riches and public penury, the State must provide for collective needs in environmental improvement - education, welfare, cultural amenities, nature conservation and recreation facilities - which cannot or will not otherwise be met but which are amongst the legitimate and necessary purposes for which growth is sought. Growth is, therefore, needed to meet both the special needs of the underprivileged and the collective needs of the community. Indeed, the extent to which these needs are met can be regarded as a critical test of the uses to which we put economic growth. A rise in economic prosperity is of little value for its own sake; it is only valuable if it makes possible, and is used for, an improvement in the quality of life.*

*ECONOMIC AND SOCIAL DEVELOPMENT*

*9. It is for these reasons that the Government have designated this to be a programme for economic and social development. This follows logically from the previous two programmes. The principal aim of the first was to accelerate progress by strengthening public confidence after the stagnation of the 1950s, indicating the opportunities for development and encouraging a progressive, expansionist outlook. The object of the second was to achieve the maximum sustainable rate of growth in order to provide the rising standards which had come to be expected as a result of progress under the first programme. The inclusion of social development as a major objective of the present programme does not mean that an acceptable level of national prosperity has been achieved, but rather that the stage has now been reached where more thought must be given to how the fruits of progress are to be used. We must avoid a situation where the pursuit of material progress becomes the exclusive goal of economic endeavour.*

*10. As a nation, we have particular responsibilities at our present stage of economic development. Not only have we an obligation to ensure that all members of society share in economic progress; by extension, we incur with progress an obligation towards the underdeveloped countries of the world. We also have, by reason of Ireland's late entry on the path of industrial development, an opportunity of learning from the lessons of other nations. The costs of economic growth —in terms of air and water pollution, traffic congestion, noise, dereliction of cities, destruction of visual amenity and natural life, not to mention the unquantifiable human costs of social and technological change —are only too apparent in the developed industrial countries. We must take care that in fostering the industrial development that is the key to our future prosperity we do not unwittingly destroy the advantages —some of them increasingly scarce in Western Europe —with which we start. We must distinguish carefully between increases in gross national product and improvements in the quality of life of the nation. An advance in one does not necessarily mean an advance in the other; it may even mean the contrary.*

*MAIN OBJECTIVES*

*11. The present programme has been drawn up against the background of the NIEC Report on Full Employment, and is a step on the road to that goal. The national growth rate aimed at is 17% over the four-year period 1969-72. The accompanying rise in employment (16,000) is expected to reduce emigration to an average annual level of 12,000-13,000, so that the total population, which had already begun to increase during the second programme, should continue on an upward trend, and should exceed 3,000,000 in 1972. This, however, is only a beginning. Much more will have to be done before full employment is reached.*

*CONDITIONS OF THE PROGRAMME'S SUCCESS*

*18. The conditions of the programme's success remain basically the same as for the second programme, namely, a favorable external environment, a relationship between the growth of incomes and output which will not prejudice our international competitiveness, and the maintenance of an appropriate balance between consumption, savings and investment. If these conditions are met, the programme's output targets can be realised, and the social development aims —especially in the fields of health, education, housing and income maintenance —will be capable of fulfillment.*

*19. Enjoyment of the fruits of progress is conditional on the acceptance of the proposed general pattern of their distribution. It is not possible for one sector to lay greater claim to the resources made available without the acceptance of a smaller share by other sectors. It is not possible, for instance, within the framework of the projections, for consumption to grow more rapidly than total national output without reducing investment; nor is it possible for private consumption to grow more rapidly than total consumption save at the cost of the resources to be devoted to communal development —an encroachment which would be contrary to the principal aims of the programme. Moreover, since most economic decisions are taken outside the Government's immediate sphere of influence, there is no guarantee that the aims set in this programme can be reached, or that its policies and purposes will not be frustrated by private decision or indifference. The programme's targets can be reached only if the conditions and assumptions on which they are based are fulfilled; they are not self-fulfilling, nor, in a free-enterprise economy, can they be imposed from above.*

## *CHAPTER 19*
## *IMPLEMENTATION*

*1. Earlier chapters have described measures which will be taken during the third programme to increase the capacity of the economy by augmenting the stock of national resources and improving its quality. These aims will be further assisted by the maintenance of aggregate monetary demand at an appropriate level. Actual use of enlarged capacity and realisation of the increased production of goods and services which it makes possible will also depend on the level of demand. Thus, it will be the task of financial policy during the programme to ensure the expansion and utilisation of capacity at the highest level consistent with preserving national price competitiveness and an acceptable degree of external balance.*

### *AVOIDANCE OF FLUCTUATIONS*

*2. The short-term corollary of this is the avoidance of excessive fluctuations in the growth rate. These can undermine confidence, and, by creating uncertainty as to future prospects, frustrate longer-term planning and investment intentions in the private and public sectors. As far as possible, therefore, short-term anti-cyclical policy will be related to the framework of medium-term objectives set out in the programme.*

### *CONSUMPTION AND SAVINGS*

*8. The composition of expenditure envisaged in the programme has been adopted on the assumption that the growth of incomes will be consistent with its requirements. Rises in monetary incomes markedly in excess of real output, apart from their other effects, are likely to upset the projected rates of increase in consumption, imports of consumer goods, and savings. If, however, a reasonable relationship is maintained between the growth of output and monetary incomes, specific measures to influence the growth of personal consumption should not be required other than those described earlier for the encouragement of savings. The growth envisaged for personal consumption, 3.3% a year on average, should be sufficient to satisfy the desire for higher living standards while at the same time leaving room for the savings needed to finance investment and keep the balance of payments deficit within acceptable limits.*

*9. If, as has been happening, incomes increase excessively, it may be necessary for the Government to take action to offset the effect of excessive demand on the volume of consumption and imports and on the price level. Experience indicates that this might best be done through the use of fiscal policy and credit policy, changes in which have had considerable influence on consumer spending in the past. While these policies would not prevent the upward pressure on costs and prices resulting from unduly large increases in incomes, they could contribute to a more even growth in the volume of consumption and the avoidance of secondary price increases and excessive imports arising from the demand effects of higher incomes. The extent to which it would be desirable to use these instruments, and the particular measures to be employed if consumption expenditure were to rise more rapidly than envisaged cannot, of course, be decided in advance. These decisions would depend on the development of a number of other economic variables. Action in the field of fiscal and credit policy will, however, be taken to whatever extent may be warranted to preserve the consistency and balance in development on which the success of the programme depends.*

A *Third Programme Review* appeared in 1971. At that time, the central issue of EEC membership had been rejoined. The fact-finding stage of the negotiations was nearing completion and most signs pointed to Ireland's accession, but not before 1973. That date, of course, lay beyond the then current planning period so that the *Third Programme*'s assumption of nonmembership remained intact. In assessing progress for 1969 and 1970, attention once again focused on unfavorable disparities between *Third Programme* projections and actual outcomes.

The disappointing results associated with the *Second* and *Third Programmes* did not encourage the formulation of a fourth. Attention turned, rather, to the increasing likelihood that Ireland would shortly enter the EEC. In April 1970 the Government had presented its assessment of membership's implications for Ireland.

*MEMBERSHIP OF THE EUROPEAN COMMUNITIES*
*IMPLICATIONS FOR IRELAND*

*Laid by the Government before*
*each House of the Oireachtas,*
*April, 1970.*

*7. The principal implications which emerge are*

- *accession to the Communities would involve an amendment of the Constitution;*
- *as regards the political implications of membership, the EEC is still at an early stage in its political evolution and its members are at present bound only by the terms of the Treaty of Rome, which does not impose specific obligations in the political field. As the Communities evolve towards their political objectives, those participating in the new Europe thereby created must be prepared to play their part in achieving those objectives. Ireland would have a*

*voice in the shaping of the political development of the Communities as in other aspects of their activities;*

- *for industry in general the expectation is that, while there would inevitably be problems in the shorter term, the gains from EEC membership would be progressive and, in the longer term, would significantly outweigh any losses that might occur. It is expected that access to the enlarged Common Market would considerably enhance the attractions of Ireland as a base for new foreign industrial investment. While our grants for encouraging industrial development would come under review in the Community it is considered that they are in keeping with the objectives of the Treaty;*
- *membership would provide improved outlets at remunerative prices for most of our agricultural production. The areas of agricultural production which would be most likely to benefit are cattle and beef, milk and dairy products, sheep and lambs. Producers of pigs, poultry and eggs would have to meet higher feed costs but the effects could be offset by more efficient production. Cereals might show a swing from wheat to coarse grains with perhaps no significant overall change in acreage. Production of sugar beet and potatoes might show little change. Horticulture would be likely to encounter difficulty, due to increased competition from Community supplies;*
- *it is tenatively estimated that the volume of our gross agricultural output by the latter years of the decade could be of the order of 30-40 per cent over the present level;*
- *higher prices for agricultural products could result in an increase of 11-16 per cent in food prices which, allowing for some change in the present pattern of consumption, would result in an increase of 3-4 1/2 per cent in the consumer price index; the increase would be spread over the transitional period;*
- *it is not considered likely that the Treaty requirements for free movement of workers would have any significant effect on the Irish labour market;*
- *as regards fiscal policy, the main implication is the requirement to introduce the added-value system of sales taxation, which could entail changes in the general tax structure;*
- *so far as economic and monetary policies are concerned, membership of the Communities would involve the coordination of Irish policies with those of the other member States but in general our economic policies are consistent with those of the member States;*
- *the cost of implementing the principle of equal pay in the private sector cannot be readily estimated. Abolition of sex-differentiation in pay in the public sector would cost £1.25 million per year; if, in consequence, marriage-differentiated scales were to be abolished*

*and related adjustments made in the pay of grades consisting entirely of women, the total cost would exceed 9 million a year;*
- *it is estimated that Ireland's contribution to the cost of running the Communities could be of the order of £19 million a year as from the end of her transitional period but might well be less. Membership would give rise to a saving of at least £36 million a year in Exchequer support to agriculture.*

*4.34 Attitudes in Irish industry have, without doubt, changed considerably over the past seven or eight years; protectionist, inward-looking attitudes, for the most part, have been replaced by a more progressive outward-looking, export-conscious, approach. These psychological changes are not quantifiable but are nevertheless real. However, there are a number of disquieting aspects. It is doubtful, for example, if, even still, there is everywhere in industry a sufficiently deep appreciation of the realities of free trade or a proper realisation of the changes it will entail in the trading and industrial situation to which Irish industry has been accustomed. More disturbing, however, is the fact that inflationary increases in industrial costs are making our products progressively less competitive in home and export markets even before free trade has become a reality.*

*4.35 In brief it can be said that*
- *industry is now much stronger and more widely-based than it was when the surveys by the Committee on Industrial Organisation (CIO) began in 1961;*
- *this increased strength is reflected in the increased volume of ouput and, more so, of exports, and in the increased employment provided by older-established as well as by the newer firms sponsored by the Industrial Development Authority (IDA).*
- *the extent of the investment in new equipment reflects the increased confidence of much of Irish industry in its capacity to meet free trade;*
- *industry in general is now far less protection-minded than formerly; there is a much better appreciation and acceptance of the need for changes in attitudes and practices but there is room for much further improvement;*
- *adaptation to free trade is a continuous process, the pace of which must now be accelerated in view of the likelihood of or early accession to EEC:*
- *by providing funds, incentives, facilities and services, the State has assisted industry to make the necessary transformation but the State cannot itself effect that transformation;*
- *the responsibility rests mainly with industry to gear itself for free trade; despite the undoubted progress an different fronts of the past seven or eight years, industry's all-round preparedness might be described as uneven and capable of considerable improvement.*

*GENERAL ASSESSMENT*

*4.36 Consideration of the implications of EEC membership for Irish industry must, in the first instance, have regard to the operation of the Anglo-Irish Free Trade Area Agreement. The fifth annual reduction of tariffs under this Agreement is due to be made on 1 July 1970 and we shall then be at the half-way stage in the progression to a free trade situation with the U.K. Indeed, taking into account the two unilateral tariff reductions introduced by the Government in 1963 and 1964, Irish tariffs on most British industrial products have already been cut to about half the level at which they were originally fixed. From now on, the reductions in these tariffs will be progressively more critical. For many sectors of industry, therefore, the impact of free trade will have become fairly fully felt some time before our market would be open to European competition in general. For these industries, the main testing time will be the two or three years immediately prior to 1975. Undoubtedly there will be some industries for which the removal of protection against imports from the EEC and the reduction of protection against third countries would likely be of special significance because of the particular competitiveness of the imported goods concerned.*

*4.37 The EEC obligation to align our duties against non-Community imports with the level of the common customs tariff could involve increased cost for some firms using imported dutiable materials from outside the enlarged Community, and thus affect their competitive position in both the home and British markets. It seems unlikely, however, that this aspect will have serious implications for industry in general. To a large extent the materials used by Irish industry, both for home and export purposes, are bought from countries which will make up, or which are likely to be associated with, the enlarged Community and even where this is not so, it is possible that, in some cases, satisfactory alternative sources of supply within the enlarged Community could be found. Where Irish firms found it necessary to continue to draw basic raw materials from outside the Community, it is likely that, in most cases, the materials would be either free of duty or subject to a fairly low level of duty. However, where Irish producers trading on the home market or in the British market had to meet extra materials costs arising from payment of the common customs tariff or the substitution of materials from more costly EEC sources, this aspect would add to the difficulties arising from the increasing competition in these markets as the Irish and British duties are removed.*

*4.38 Industrial activities at the Shannon Customs-Free Industrial Zone are based to a substantial degree on the processing for re-export of materials imported free of duty from countries other than those which will constitute the enlarged Community. The position of the Zone will have to be the subject of discussion with the Community.*

*4.39 Not every Irish firm can expect to survive in free trade. It is to the potential for exports within the enlarged Community —a buoyant market of over 250 million consumers where the variety of demand will be virtually limitless — that we must look for the gains to offset any losses in the home market and also to permit of the necessary expansion of our industrial base. There would be increased opportunities —*

*(a) for existing firms through access to wider markets;*

*(b) for the establishment of new export-oriented industries to serve the enlarged free trade market.*

*This further widening of the industrial base could be expected to lead in turn, through linkage, to added opportunities for existing manufacturers, including those in the small industry category, and for service-type industries. The necessary switch of labour resources would be facilitated by our scheme for the retraining and resettling of workers, which would be eligible for assistance from the European Social Fund (see Chapter 11).*

*4.40 While it is reasonable to expect that membership of the EEC would considerably enhance the attractions of Ireland as a base for new foreign industrial investment, it is essential that the existing industries should exploit to the fullest extent the new export opportunities which would be open to them. In so far as the EEC duties on industrial products will be at a low level, following full implementation of the "Kennedy Round" reductions, it could be suggested that the additional trading margins arising from the elimination of the duties following or accession to membership would not be very great. It is only part of the answer to this to say that, in the keenly competitive field of export marketing, the margin represented by even a moderate level of duty would very often be critical. Removal of the duties is only one aspect. Membership of the Common Market would require our fellow-members to remove restrictions on Irish products; it would provide common terms of access to raw materials for ourselves and other Community producers; and, in general, progress in the harmonisation of customs procedures, taxation and fiscal policies, and in many other fields, is aimed at the elimination of all obstacles which tend to inhibit trade within the Community.*

*4.41 In 1969, our industrial exports, excluding those from the Shannon Customs-Free Industrial Zone, to the six present member countries of the EEC were valued at approximately £29 million. This represents, at current prices, almost a nine-fold increase as compared with 1960 and these exports expressed as a percentage of our total industrial exports have more than doubled in that period. In the same period, industrial exports to the EFTA countries, other than the U.K., increased from approximately £1.2 million to about £3.6 million. At present, Irish exports to the Community, where dutiable, are subject to the common customs tariff on the full value of the finished goods. As a member of the EEC we would have duty-free access to the enlarged Community for all our exports though any materials of third country origin included in the goods would, of course, have been charged with the common customs tariff on importation into Ireland. This would provide scope not only for a substantial increase in exports in absolute terms but also for an acceleration of the process of diversification of export markets, which would make us less vulnerable to fluctuating conditions in an individual market.*

*4.42 Looking, therefore, at industry as a whole it is reasonable to expect that the gains from membership would be progressive and, in the longer term, should significantly outweigh any losses that might occur. The probable position in the earlier years of membership is more difficult to forecast as it is then that the problems caused by elimination of protection and adjustment to the enlarged market would chiefly arise; but given a determined effort to overcome those problems, it should be possible to maintain in those years an industrial growth rate of the order of that projected in the Third Programme for the period 1969/72. The increasing pressures of trading in a situation where tariff and quota protection of the home market against Community imports would not be permitted, and where traditional export markets would become increasingly competitive, would undoubtedly create serious difficulties in some sectors. However, experience would be likely to vary from sector to sector within industry as a whole and even from firm to firm within a particular industry. In some sectors, the result would often depend on the extent to which a particular firm had adapted its production methods or traditionalised its product policy in sufficient time, and with sufficient energy, to cope with the new situation. Changes in the structure and pattern of Irish industry, partly as a result of increasing competitive pressures and partly as a result of the opening up of new trading opportunities, would seem inevitable —this has been the experience of the operation of the Common Market on the economies of the existing member States of the Community.*

*4.43 The prospect of increased competition at home, and the possibilities of increased exports in an enlarged EEC, underline the need to maintain industrial costs at competitive levels. This applies particularly to labour costs which in 1969 increased at a much faster rate than in the EEC or in any of the other applicant countries. If the benefits of membership are to be maximised, and the disadvantages minimised, this trend must be corrected.*

*4.44 It is necessary to face up to the fact that membership of the EEC would pose problems, possibly of a serious nature, for some sectors of industry as well as for individual firms. Nothing must be left undone, either at the appropriate levels in industry or by the State agencies concerned, to solve or at least mitigate these difficulties. But it would be an unbalanced reaction to become obsessed with the difficulties and not attempt to view the situation in wider perspective.*

*4.45 The dominant feature of our accession to the EEC must be seen to be the opening up of much wider markets and greater opportunities and not the increased competition in the limited home market. For many industries the additional competition from EEC countries would be unlikely to add greatly to the competition they are already committed to face in the Irish market under the Anglo-Irish Free Trade Area Agreement. Therefore, viewed from our present position, the balance of advantages in the industrial sector favours membership of the EEC and the benefits may be expected to increase as time goes on.*

*4.46 The Confederation of Irish Industries, indeed, has recognised ("Challenge" —February 1968) that, in certain respects, the full implementation of the Anglo-Irish Free Trade Area Agreement without membership of the EEC would be even more severe on Irish industry than if combined with membership of the EEC. Among the reasons mentioned are*

- *Membership of the EEC would make it possible for industry to diversify into new markets, thereby reducing our dependence on Britain and specifically the danger of disruption of our economy from economic fluctuations in Britain.*
- *If Britain were a member of the EEC, many British firms would be looking towards Europe as well as towards Ireland for new markets instead of concentrating their attention here, as may happen within the next few years.*
- *Membership of the EEC would make Ireland increasingly attractive for new external investment in industry.*
- *The institutions of the EEC involve responsibility by the Community as a whole to safeguard the economic well-being of each member State, both big and small.*

*4.47 The structures, patterns and techniques of industrial production and trade throughout the world are at present in a period of rapid change and development. In this climate even the industrially powerful nations are changing their traditional trading policies in order to achieve their desired economic growth. In our circumstances, it is all the more important that we should adapt ourselves to this situation. The Irish home market, despite an expanding economy, is not big enough to provide adequate outlets for industrial production on the scale necessary to achieve the national objectives of a rising standard of living with full employment and reduction of emigration to an acceptable level. A satisfactory rate of progress in this direction is now almost entirely dependent on our ability to sell more and more of our production on export markets. A European Community comprising the existing member States and the applicant countries would provide a trading environment which would permit of the expansion of our exports in line with our growth objectives.*

## *CHAPTER 16*
## *CONCLUSION*

*16.1 The Government's view of membership of the European Communities has been made clear on any occasions. It is, in the first place, that membership affords an opportunity of participating fully in the movement towards European unity, a movement which evokes a strong and sympathetic response in the Irish people. Secondly, membership of the enlarged Communities would provide conditions more favourable to our economic development than would be obtainable outside.*

*16.2 While the present White Paper gives a quantified assessment of the consequences for Ireland of entry to the Communities in respect of certain areas, it is not possible to demonstrate in national-accounts terms the economic consequences of, on the one hand, membership of the Communities and, on the other hand, not becoming a member. There is, nevertheless, a substantial basis for a qualitative conclusion which indicates that the national interests would be best served by entry to an enlarged EEC which included the United Kingdom. To remain outside would place our agricultural exports at a severe disadvantage and would leave very much in doubt the possibility of maintaining, let alone expanding, our industrial exports.*

*16.3 Because of its small scale, the domestic market does not of itself afford a sufficient basis for the expansion of the economy at a pace and to an extent that will enable the country to achieve its principal economic objectives, namely, full employment, the cessation of involuntary emigration and a standard of living comparable with that of other Western European countries. In Irish circumstances, therefore, economic growth of necessity depends on an expanding export trade.*

*16.4 Approximately half of all agricultural production is sold abroad; it follows that any increase in production must likewise be exported. The difficulties of finding export outlets at remunerative prices for many of our agricultural products are well known. These difficulties would be greatly accentuated if Ireland were not to become a member of the enlarged European Communities. It is only necessary in this connection to advert to the sharp drop in our exports of cattle and beef to the present Community since the coming into operation of the common market organisation for these products. Membership would ensure access for Irish agricultural products to a large market at remunerative prices and enable them to compete on equal terms with those of the other member States. This would result in considerably higher returns for our exports of cattle, beef, dairy products, lamb and pigmeat.*

*16.5 Irish industry has been the main source of growth in the economy over the past decade. The rapid expansion of the industrial sector is a reflection of the rising trend in the value of our industrial exports which has exhibited a striking rate of increase — from £33 million in 1958 to £149 million in 1968. In achieving this increase, Irish industry has shown that it is capable of competing not alone in the British market where it has the advantage of duty-free entry but also in the EEC which now provides an outlet for industrial exports valued at £29 million. The removal of protection in the domestic market could entail difficulties for some sectors of Irish industry. The scale of these difficulties would depend on the response of Irish management and workers, in the firms affected, to the new trading situation as it emerged over the period leading to the assumption of the full obligation of membership. The*

*possible losses in this regard, however, must be viewed in relation to the overall balance of advantage to the economy as a whole.*
*16.6 In the light of the growing strength of the economy and given equitable transitional terms, it is reasonable to conclude that membership of the European Communities would give a strong impetus to production and exports, both agricultural and industrial, and so to the growth of the economy. The enlarged Communities would constitute a market of over 250 million people capable of a high and sustained rate of growth and so would provide an external environment more favourable to economic growth than that in which the Irish economy has heretofore been obliged to operate and substantially more favourable than that which would obtain if Ireland were to remain outside the enlarged Communities.*

This White Paper updated earlier documents bearing upon EEC membership, most notably the White Paper of April 1967. The 1970 Paper restated firmly the Government's position: (1) that membership would permit Ireland's full participation in the movement towards European unity; and (2) that membership would promote the nation's economic development. The document provided some details on the likely impact of EC membership on various sectors of the Irish economy. Overall, it expressed the view that the progress of the previous decade had brought Ireland to a position wherein membership now "would give a strong impetus to production and exports, both agricultural and industrial, and so to the growth of the economy."

The support for entry into Europe was strong, as it had been since the first petition to enter in 1961. But it was not uniform. The left wing groups held that Ireland's economy was already in the grasp of foreign investors, foreign banks, and multinational corporations. This position was augmented by those who saw the traditional culture of Ireland corroded by materialism. These views drew little attention from the Irish public which rather uncritically assumed there would be no negative consequences.

It was true, of course, that not all industries or firms would fare well under the new arrangements. Some had not taken full advantage of opportunities to modernize and restructure. There was also the disturbing fact that "inflationary increases in industrial costs are making our products progressively less competitive in home and export markets even before free trade has become a reality." Still, in appraising the "State of Preparedness of Irish Industry," the 1970 White Paper found considerable basis for confidence. The Paper cites the emergence of a more outward- looking, progressive attitude within Irish industry and the modernization of industrial capital which "reflects the increased confidence of much of Irish industry in its capacity to meet free trade." This survey recognizes the importance of State aid to industry in this transitional period, but emphasizes that the responsibility for successful adaptation rests within industry itself.

As the main source of growth in the economy during the 1960s, Irish industry was the primary object of emphasis and concern in the White Paper of 1970. Nonetheless, agriculture remained important and warranted a detailed, special study: *Irish Agriculture and Fisheries in the EEC* which would assess the implications of membership for Irish agriculture. The White Paper itself expressed no doubt that "to remain outside would place our agricultural exports at a severe disadvantage." In overall terms, the Paper concluded that membership in fact would "give a strong impetus to production and exports, both agricultural and industrial, and so to the growth of the economy." Finally, while membership would entail problems as well as possibilities for the Irish economy, the expectation was that the *Third Programme* industrial growth rate would be maintained.

On the eve of accession to the European Economic Community, the Irish could take some satisfaction in the outcomes of the post-*Economic Development* years. Data in the early 1970s provide a useful sketch of the nation's economy as the new era approached. In price-adjusted terms, per capita output had increased by some 65 percent over the 1960 figure. Emigration had fallen dramatically in comparison to the earlier postwar years. While growth rates of output and employment did not match the most optimistic projections, between 1960 and 1973 they did exceed by a wide margin the figures registered in the 1950s: 6.5 percent vs. 3.1 percent in output and 2.3 percent vs. 0.8 percent in employment. Total employment in 1971 remained at about the 1961 level of 1,050,000, although the unemployment rate had climbed from 5.1 percent to 5.5 percent of the labor force. This occurred, however, in the face of net *in* migration and a population increase of 160,000 between 1961 and 1971.

# *Five*

# From Entry to Europe to the Single European Act, 1973–1990

The beginning and end of the year 1973 marked two significant developments for Ireland: entry into the European Community came in January 1973 and the increase in the price of oil occurred in the latter part of 1973. The first event promised an acceleration of the benefits that had come over the past fifteen years. The advantages of the EC's Common Agricultural Policy seemed to be bountiful for Ireland as well as offering access to the EC market. Irish officials had persuaded the somewhat skeptical six founding member states that Ireland was committed to free trade and developed enough to prosper under those conditions. A tariff reduction over five years was negotiated as well as the retention of special Irish development incentives.

Inflation had been sweeping upward during the prior period from about 4.2 percent to 8.5 percent. The rate of inflation, however, was to receive a whirlwind impetus when the price of oil quadrupled within two years in a country that was over 70 percent dependent on energy imports. The effects on the economy were profound as the government increased borrowing to pay for the oil and the balance of payments was skewed by such a sharp increase on the import side of the ledger. The cost of oil in the production of goods, as well as the heating of homes and powering cars, pushed prices up. At the same time demand was diminished through the cuts in disposable income of Irish consumers as they paid their heating bills.

The increase in the balance of payments deficit as a percentage of GNP went from 3.5 percent to 10 percent from 1973 to 1974, the rate of inflation by late 1974 was 18 percent, and the government's borrowing for noncapital purposes, that is, to meet the current budget deficit, went from .30 of GNP in 1973 to 3.1 in 1974 (nine months) and 6.8 percent in 1975 (NESC #88: 1989:65-66). The government of the day, a Fine Gael-Labour coalition had been elected in February 1973. This "National Coalition" had two distinct features; the degree of electoral cooperation between the two parties and a common fourteen point program with a considerable bundle of promises for everyone. The Prime Minister, Liam Cosgrave, (son of William Cosgrave, Prime Minister from 1922 to 1932) ended up approving borrowing levels that would have brought the wrath of his father. The Minister of Finance, Richie Ryan, inexperienced in this area, sought to soften the blows of the oil crisis by borrowing the Irish government through the oil crisis. The government responded to the drop in growth in the European economies, the rising cost of oil, and the rise in imports, with a White Paper in November 1974 entitled *A National Partnership*. In the paper the government urged a "partnership" during this period of economic retrenchment in which "we must be content with the same volume of goods and services as before to share out among ourselves" (*A National Partnership* 1974: iii). In this atmosphere of low expectations the government recommended energy conservation and development of alternative sources; job conservation and job creation through capital expenditures guided by the Industrial Development Authority; cultivation of European Community resources for agriculture; and controlling inflation through wage agreements.

*A NATIONAL PARTNERSHIP*
*Laid by the Government*
*before each house of the Oireachtas*
*November 1974*

*GOVERNMENT'S PRIORITY*

*74. From the earlier sections of this paper it will be clear that the world economy is likely to face a very difficult time in 1975 and indeed that its problems, unless international co-operation improves, could persist for several years to come. This situation is a reality which cannot be wished away. It is one which Irish economic policy must take into account if it is to be realistic and responsible.*

*75. Because of the dependence of the economy on external trade, we are more open than most to a downturn in world activity. There is little doubt that next year the majority of the industrialised countries, to which we sell the bulk of our exports and from which we receive so much of our industrial investment, will have little, if any, growth. Like ourselves, these countries are at present finding their employment and living standards adversely affected by the deflationary impact of the oil crisis, yet there is a general reluctance to introduce measures to ease the employment situation and protect living standards because of the fear that this might result in higher inflation and greater external deficits. The handful of industrialised countries which are still free of balance of payments difficulties and which could, if they wished, aid those in deficit by increasing their economic activity and their intake of imports, are equally reluctant to do so until international inflation is seen to be brought firmly under control.*

*76. This depressed external situation places an irremovable constraint on Irish economic growth. There is no way in which we can enjoy a high rate of growth when economic activity in the rest of the world is, at best, sluggish. The foreign customers who in normal times help us to improve our standard of living and give increased employment by buying our goods and services are now finding their purchasing power reduced through high domestic prices or because they are themselves out of work. This must inevitably affect our prospects of economic growth.*

*77. So far as Ireland is concerned, a balance of payments deficit of the order of £300 million, representing 10% of our national production, and a rate of inflation of 17-18%, would, in normal world conditions, call for urgent action to reduce internal demand to a level that would lower substantially the rate of domestic inflation and the balance of payments deficit. The reality of any significant reduction in internal demand, however, would be to reduce the home market for Irish-made goods and to cut back on employment, personal incomes, profits of industry and funds for investment. These effects would be bad enough in themselves but in addition it would be the impossible to ensure that they would be evenly distributed throughout the community. Instead, these corrective measures would mean that many now employed would find themselves out of work.*

*78. The Government are not prepared to contemplate policy measures of this nature. They are determined instead to give priority to the maintenance of employment and the preservation of living standards. This will be the core of the Government's response to the present economic situation.*

*79. It will be necessary also to reduce the rate of inflation. Pursuit of the two-fold objective of maintaining employment and preserving living standards is not incompatible with tackling the problem of inflation. On the contrary, failure to pursue this two-fold objective would be likely to lead to further inflationary pressures, as groups in society whose living standards would be hit felt impelled to seek higher money incomes, and as the necessity to support an ever-growing number of unemployed and their dependents raised sharply the cost of Government and the amount required to be levied in taxation.*

*BALANCE OF PAYMENTS*

*80. Efforts to combat inflation must be supplemented by vigilance to guard against a continuing deterioration in the balance of payments which could in time undo much of the economic progress achieved in recent years.*

*81. The external over-spending brought about by the enormous rise in the prices of oil and of many basic materials represents an additional claim on Irish resources which will eventually have to be met by a transfer abroad of a great part of what we produce at home. However, as indicated in paragraph 78, the government do not believe that this additional claim should be met by a sudden transfer of resources at the expense of employment and domestic living standards. Instead they propose that our external situation should be steadily improved by reductions in the deficit phased over a period of several years in this way, instead of precipitating a sudden drop in living standards and a worsening of unemployment, the adjustment will be accomplished by using for this purpose whatever growth in our economy can be secured in the difficult conditions likely to prevail over the next year or so.*

*82. A phased reduction in the deficit is particularly justified in view of the fact that our very large external over-spending in 1974 is in part due to factors which are unlikely to be repeated in 1975. There has been an abnormal increase, of about 40%, in our average import prices for our cattle and beef exports. The measures taken by the EEC including, at the instance of the Government, the adjustment of the Green £, will, however, secure a recovery, both in price and volume, of agricultural exports in 1975. This improvement, together with the expected slowing down of import prices, will ensure that the movement in our external deficit will be downwards. This will help to maintain confidence abroad and thus facilitate the borrowing of the considerable amounts of foreign capital that will be required to implement the Government's policy of maintaining living standards and employment.*

*83. While it is clear that present circumstances dictate a policy of spreading the burden of adjustment of the balance of payments deficit over a period, the government recognise that, at a time when other countries are making strong efforts to lower their deficits, it would be most imprudent to delay making a start with reducing ours. It would be even more imprudent to take any action domestically which would cause the deficit to rise. An increase could be interpreted as any unwillingness to meet our obligations and could endanger our credibility abroad and our ability to borrow the foreign capital so necessary for our further economic growth.*

*ENERGY CONSERVATION AND DEVELOPMENT*

*84. At a time when the high cost of energy is inflating both domestic prices and the external deficit, it is most desirable to economise in the consumption of energy and to accelerate the development of domestic sources of energy.*

*85. Recent measures taken by the Government should help to reduce energy consumption. These include (i)* *expansion of the fuel efficiency scheme administered by the Department of Transport and Power, the fuel efficiency service provided by the Institute for Industrial Research and Standards and the grants schemes available to industrialists from the IDA for conserving energy;*

*(ii)* *improving efficiency in converting fuel to electricity at ESB generating stations;*

*(iii)* *the introduction of heating control systems in public buildings.*

*86. To supplement action in the foregoing areas, the Minister for Local Government commissioned a study by An Foras Forbartha, in conjunction with the Institute for Industrial Research and Standards, of measures to improve thermal insulation in houses and other buildings. An interim report makes recommendations in regard to reduction of heat losses through walls, roofs, doors and windows. This report is being published for comment by interested parties, following which the Minister for Local Government will announce the action to be taken to improve thermal insulation in the construction of grant-aided and local authority housing. The report will be of considerable benefit to householders generally for the information it contains on the steps that can be taken to economise on heating.*

*87. The Minister for Transport and Power has set up an Advisory committee representative of Government Departments and State bodies, to advise on the promotion and co-ordination of conservation measures. In addition, the Government will mount a campaign to impress on all the need and the ways to save precious and costly energy.*

*88. For the longer term, the aim must be to secure the greatest possible use of native sources to energy. A substantial expansion in the production of Bord na Móna is planned. The Bord will develop an additional 40,000 acres of bog to supply 200,000 tons of turf per annum and, in addition, sufficient turf to fuel a new electricity-generating capacity of 160 MW. Expenditure on the new programme is scheduled to begin in 1975.*

*89. The provision of a nuclear power station has been approved by the Government. Steps will be taken to expedite the project but it is unlikely that electricity from nuclear sources will be available before 1982. When completed it will constitute approximately 15% of our electricity-generating capacity and lessen our dependence on oil imports.*

*90. The government are finalising the terms on which exploration licences for offshore gas and oil will be granted. Natural gas has already been found off*

*Kinsale. It has been decided to use about 60% of this find for the generation of electricity, thus achieving an annual reduction of about £20 million in our oil import bill, at current prices. While this reduction is welcome, it is relatively small in comparison with our oil import bill, estimated at £200 million in the current year. There may be further natural gas. It is also possible that oil could be discovered in substantial quantities in Irish off-shore areas, but it would take several years to complete the necessary development works before oil could come ashore. Even if there are further commercial finds in Irish areas, and this cannot be regarded as a certainty, it is unlikely that they would provide a significant proportion of our energy requirements until the early 1980's.*

*91. For these reasons the possibilities of off-shore development do not reduce in any way the need for the most stringent economy in the use of energy in the interim and Government policy will be directed towards achieving the maximum degree of conservation.*

*EMPLOYMENT*

*92. There are two aspects of the maintenance of employment which determine the Government's response under this head to the present economic situation. One is the need to preserve, so far as possible, existing employment; the other is the need to keep up the momentum of new job creation.*

*(i) EXISTING INDUSTRY*

*93. In present circumstances, the preservation of existing employment demands that priority be given to keeping production going. An immediate problem affecting production in the current inflationary situation is the inadequacy of financial resources available to firms.*

*94. In this, as in other countries, the working capital of many farmers and industrialists is in danger of proving insufficient because of inflation. This problem has been compounded in some cases by difficulties in export markets and by increasing competition on the home market as a result of the gradual removal of protective tariffs. The textiles and clothing and footwear industries and industries ancillary to building are, in particular, facing problems; in the agricultural sector, cattle producers are especially affected. Many firms in other sectors could also face problems of inadequate working capital. The Government and the Central Bank are concerned that monetary policy should support the objectives of economic policy by ensuring that enough credit is available to meet the needs of productive activity and help to maintain employment.*

*95. Bank credit for productive purposes increased at an annual rate of about 17% in January-August 1974. This is less than the Government consider desirable and, indeed, is below the Central Bank's guidelines. The Government welcome therefore the request which the Central Bank has made to the commercial banks to respond positively to the short-term liquidity requirements of their business customers. Apart from its general desire to arrange that financial facilities will be available for new and expanding enterprises, the Central Bank is concerned to ensure that credit is available to assist the survival of sound firms and the preservation of the employment they afford, thus protecting the base for further progress in the future.*

*96. Fir Teoranta, which is financed almost entirely by the Exchequer, is an important link in the chain of State assistance for industry. It provides finance for basically sound industrial concerns which may be in danger of having to close down or suspend activities because of inability to raise capital from commercial sources. The Government will ensure that any funds which the Company may require will be made available by the Exchequer.*

*97. Industry will benefit also from moneys made available under the Industrial Development Authority's scheme of grants for re-equipment, modernisation, improvement or expansion of industrial undertakings. Exchequer provision for these grants, which is included in the capital allocation for the Authority referred to in paragraph 99, will amount to over £10 million in 1975 as compared with £5 million for the nine-months' period from April 1974.*

*98. The provision of all these facilities represents a valuable assurance to industry that its efforts to maintain employment will be supported by the banking system and the Exchequer. If it should happen that the resources provided through the channels described above prove inadequate, the Government will discuss with the interests concerned the further remedial action which might be taken.*

*(ii) NEW INDUSTRY*

*99. The principal agency through which the Government will stimulate the creation of new jobs is the Industrial Development Authority. Fortunately, the inflow of new industries is currently running at a high level. To enable the efforts of the Authority to be intensified, the Exchequer provision for it in the Capital budget for 1975 will be £42.5 million as compared with £19.5 million for the nine months from April 1974 (equivalent to about £26 million on an annual basis). The total investment in fixed assets involved will be about £150 million in 1975 as compared with about £90 million for a twelve months' period from April 1974.*

*100. Exchequer finance alone, however substantial, will not guarantee the scale of job creation at which the Government are aiming. At a time when industrial investment throughout the world is declining, we must provide in Ireland an economic environment so attractive that we will, so far as possible, avoid this trend.*

*101. Fundamental to the success of the industrial expansion for which the Industrial Development Authority is striving is a corresponding growth in the provision of basic infrastructural services — housing, water and sewerage, road works, electricity and telephones — which will at once attract and facilitate industrial development. It is accepted that these basic services must be provided in advance of industrial development and not merely move concurrently with the development or follow it. The provision of adequate infrastructure is a fundamental necessity requiring close co-operation between the Industrial Development Authority, local authorities and other bodies. The Government will provide adequate capital to make the necessary infrastructural services available.*

*(iii) TRAINING*

*102. The provision of trained workers is also vitally important for the attraction of new industry. As part of their active manpower policy the Government will make additional resources available to AnCO (The Industrial Training Authority) to enable it to expand its programmes of industrial training. Industrial training is also a valuable instrument of manpower policy in times of rising unemployment. In particular, more places will be made available in training centres for workers temporarily disemployed and for young workers experiencing difficulties in getting jobs. Application is being made to the European Social Fund for grants to expand our training facilities.*

*(iv) THE HOME MARKET*

*103. Action to assist industry must be supplemented by the efforts of industry itself to maintain and, where possible, increase the volume of sales. In addition, the consumer can help support industrial production by the purchase of Irish goods, knowing that thereby he is assisting in keeping other members of our training community in employment.*

*(v) EXPORTS*

*104. The Government's basic economic objective is to ensure that domestic demand is supported at its present level — in contrast to the decline that is evident in other countries — but for an expansion of sales we must look to export markets.*

*105. Our export earnings will be increased by the higher value of agricultural exports which will accrue in 1975 from a larger volume of, and better prices for, our farm products resulting from recent EEC decisions. Direct employment in agriculture accounts for approximately one-quarter of the total number at work. Employment in processing and servicing industries related to food and agriculture accounts for about the same percentage of the total in manufacturing industry. This sector of the national economy makes a very significant contribution to the country's balance of payments because it exports a very large proportion of its total output but requires only a relatively small volume of imported inputs.*

*106. The task facing industry in general will be more difficult. As pointed out in paragraph 75 above, little economic growth is expected in our principal export markets in 1975. Nevertheless, it is heartening that industry is confident that, given a favourable domestic climate, it will be able to improve on its record of rising export sales.*

*107. Our share in any one of our export markets is small in comparison with other countries. Because of this we should, provided we remain competitive, be able to increase our exports to these markets if we make a concerted drive to do so, even in areas which are growing slowly or not growing at all.*

*108. The difficulties likely to be experienced in the coming year in expanding exports to our traditional markets because of reduced demand make it all the more necessary to seek out additional markets where this constraint does not apply. Examples are the countries of Eastern Europe and the Middle East which by reason of the resources at their disposal offer substantial outlets for Irish goods. Trading with these areas presents special problems but these can be overcome by intelligent and energetic marketing. The Government, through the development of diplomatic relations and the work of Coras Trachtala, are taking steps to open up markets in these areas in conjunction with manufacturers and traders.*

*109. Export credit on concessionary terms has been available since 1971 to exporters of capital goods. The credit is provided by the Associated Banks for terms of not less than one or more than five years against the security of an export credit insurance policy. The scheme is now more attractive than when introduced since the difference between the concessionary terms on which export credit is granted and the general cost of bank credit has increased.*

*110. About three-quarters of the resources allotted for the scheme have been paid or committed but it is already clear that continued industrial expansion is likely to require more export credit than was envisaged when the scheme was introduced. The Government consider it essential that additional facilities should be provided and proposals to this end will be discussed with the banks.*

*EUROPEAN ECONOMIC COMMUNITY*

*111. In the agricultural sector the Government, working within the context of the Common Agricultural Policy, will aim at strengthening significantly the income position of farmers. In particular, they will continue to press for better management of the EEC beef market in order to safeguard the interests of beef producers in this country. A short-term scheme of loans at low interest rates has recently been announced to give assistance, mainly through the Agricultural Credit Corporation, towards the provision of fodder for the higher numbers of livestock on farms this winter. In the longer-run, the Government will encourage the Community to establish a more efficient mechanism for identifying potential problems in the market for beef — and indeed other important farm products as well — in order to ensure that effective action can be taken before these problems become acute.*

*112. As regards the other major farm commodities, recent decisions made in Brussels indicate a favourable outlook for 1975. The farm-gate price of milk has been increased substantially during 1974, and present prices should give a considerable incentive for an expansion of output in the coming year. The price of Irish bacon on the UK market — and consequently the price paid to pig producers here is an all-time record, and this should lead to an increase in production of pigmeat for which there is a lucrative market. The Government will continue to press for an EEC regulation for mutton and lamb, and the European Commission have indicated their intention to present firm proposals as soon as possible.*

*113. The recently negotiated 5-year quotas for sugar have laid the basis for an assured price for all the sugar beet that we can produce in 1975. In the case of cereals, the very strong world market is expected to continue and will ensure the maintenance of demand for all the grain that farmers can produce next year. A substantial increase in barley production is urgently necessary and can be achieved without a reduction in livestock-carrying capacity.*

*114. Other recent decisions will also considerably improve the farmer's position in 1975. The adjustment of the Green £ will increase farmers' incomes and will, through the reduction of the monetary export charges, give further substantial help to our export trade in farm products. The farm development scheme, now gathering momentum, will help farmers to make their enterprises more efficient. The Council of Ministers is committed to the introduction of a system of cash payments to livestock farmers in hilly and other disadvantaged areas. The Government have decided to provide the necessary funds (a percentage of which will be recouped from Community funds) and the scheme is planned to come into operation early in 1975. It will help many Irish farmers who have encountered exceptional difficulties this year.*

*115. Failure by the European Economic Community to implement an acceptable regional policy has been seriously disadvantageous to us. In the course of preparations for a proposed Conference of Heads of State and Government before the end of the year, the Government, together with the Italian Government, have pressed for an early decision in favour of the establishment of an adequate and fairly distributed Regional Fund.*

*116. In addition to Community action which has as its purpose general developmental progress, there are Community facilities designed to assist member countries in balance of payments difficulties, notably the system of mutual assistance operated through the European Monetary Co-operation Fund. A welcome further development has been the agreement to raise loans outside the Community to assist in redressing external deficits of member countries caused by the rise in price of petroleum products.*

*INCOMES*

*117. From all that has been said so far it is clear that what is decisive for employment and living standards is the course that we as a people follow in regard to increases in incomes. Unless there is a general world collapse, we can maintain living standards. And we can to a very large degree maintain employment, by securing new jobs to replace those lost in weaker sectors. But these two objectives can be achieved only if all sections accepted the necessary self-discipline which will prevent large-scale unemployment and falling living standards for many — perhaps eventually all — sections of the community.*

*118. The resources which our people have to share are going to remain at or about present levels for some time to come. This means that there should be enough to enable them to maintain their present living standards. However, it also follows that during this period we as a community will not be able to improve our present living standards. If some sections of the community, through, for example, monopoly profits or wage demands in key sectors, were to secure disproportionate increases in incomes, these could be achieved only at the expense of weaker groups.*

*119. The Government believe that those who are dependent on social welfare payments should be cushioned against price rises and should also be assured of at least an adequate maintenance of their position vis-á-vis other sections of the community. To this end, the Government have decided that social welfare payments will be increased in the Budget and revised during the course of the year. Arrangements will be announced shortly for the application of appropriate guidelines for the revision of rates of payment, and for necessary review machinery. The working, and future application of this scheme, which is geared to meet a very real need in a period of rapid inflation, will be reviewed in the context of the continuing improvement of the social services which has the objective of creating a comprehensive social security system covering all citizens.*

*120. The Government recognise also that there may now, at a time of such rapidly rising inflation, be anxiety among workers that living standards may fall. They will examine, with the interests concerned, how best to arrange that earnings under future agreements may be protected, through adjustments in line with the cost of living, against erosion from price increases.*

*121. It will be necessary to ensure that those whose income does not come from wages or salaries observe the self-discipline required by this situation. The Government will consult with both sides of industry and other relevant interests to see how this can best be secured and, if necessary for this purpose, will introduce legislation. The farming community is a special case so far as incomes are concerned; for instance, family farm incomes in the cattle sector have fallen sharply this year and this situation will have to be taken into account in the application of the principles outlined above.*

*122. It is vital that there should be general acceptance of the overall approach to income adjustment envisaged above, subject possibly to limited modifications in its application to particular sectors; for example, in present critical circumstances it may be difficult to justify percentage increases at the very top of the scale as great as those applying to workers lower down. It is also essential that any re-distribution of income through the tax system in order to help the deprived sections of the community, particularly social welfare recipients, is not nullified by the better-off seeking compensation for any additional tax imposed for this purpose.*

*123. The adjustment of incomes in line with cost of living increases could have risks for us. Where other countries who are our competitors on world markets have lower rates of inflation than we have, e.g. Germany (7%), their income increases, if related to rising prices, will necessarily be lower than ours, and the cost of the goods they produce will accordingly be less. These risks are acceptable only as a means of preventing an even higher rate of inflation in the future which would imperil employment and living standards. Indeed for some firms and industries the additional costs involved in giving compensation for increases in the cost of living might so reduce competitiveness as to lead to a laying-off of workers. This problem will clearly have to receive serious consideration in forthcoming income negotiations.*

*124. The scale of income increases has also important implications for State finances through the application of the terms of the National Pay Agreement to public service* pay falling on the Exchequer. At budget time the cost of public service pay for 1974-75 was estimated at £314 million. For the year 1975, the figure will be somewhat above £380 million exclusive of the cost of unprocessed grade claims and of the cost of any general pay settlement that may follow the expirey of the 1974 National Agreement. While some of this increase is attributable to such factors as increased numbers, equal pay and the transfer to the Exchequer of a further part of the cost of health board staff, by far the largest single element in the increase in the carryover effect of the 15th round, including the escalator clause. Rising liabilities of this magnitude limit severely the capacity of the Exchequer to allocate additional resources for the purpose of social development and the promotion of economic growth and employment without recourse to additional taxation. It is essential to the achievement of the Government's objectives of maintaining employment and preserving living standards that full account be taken of these wider implications in the next round of wage negotiations.*

*125. It would be short-sighted to think that action along the lines proposed by the Government lies wholly in the future. The seriousness of the situation demands that the current National Pay Agreement be honoured in the spirit as well as the letter. The fact that the escalator clause of the Agreement, which will shortly come into effect, substantially compensates workers against rising prices should make it easier to show the moderation that is so urgently needed if we are to surmount our difficulties. In present critical circumstances all concerned with wage and salary negotiations and settlements should recognise the need for restraint during the remainder of the 1974 Agreement in claiming any special additions to pay beyond the standard increases it lays down. When the Agreement was concluded in March of this year it was understood (and recorded in clause 18) that the parties considered that anomaly claims under it should arise only in a limited number of cases. It is important that for the remaining months of the Agreement this provision should be adhered to.*

*126. The protection of living standards and the preservation of employment are directly dependent upon public support. A government can provide the leadership and the framework necessary to achieve these objectives; it cannot secure these objectives in the face of a wave of demands and counter-demands by groups seeking to improve their own individual positions irrespective of harm done to the overall interest of the community. There must be strict fairness between all sections of the community if we are to achieve the two immediate national aims of maintaining employment and living standards.*

*Given whole-hearted public co-operation with the Government's leadership we can win through.*

**Civil service, teachers, Garda Siochina, Defence Forces and Exchequer element of health boards' expenditure on staff.*

The aspirations of the Paper were based upon realistic expectations, the policies were based upon the priority of increasing employment and the standard of living rather than attacking the balance of payments and inflation issues. What were the effects?

Unfortunately in each area the performance fell short of even the limited expectations put forth in *A National Partnership*. While the search for alternative energy sources and conservation measures had the effect of dampening the sharpest effects of the cost of oil, it did take time. In 1973 the ratio of the value of energy to GNP was 2.6 percent, it shot up to 7.2 percent in 1974 and was still 6.0 percent in 1977.

The task of protecting jobs and creating new jobs fell to the Industrial Development Authority. The government projected increased capital expenditures and passed legislation which created new IDA programs. In 1973 the Service Industry Program was created to stimulate nonmanufacturing jobs. In the same year the Joint Ventures program was developed to partner Irish companies and foreign firms. The Project Identification Unit was created in 1975 to encourage the provision of manufacturing inputs from Ireland rather than from imported sources. Finally, Dublin was included as a site for industrial development. Moreover the entry into the EC allowed the IDA to promote foreign investment in Ireland as a means for foreign firms to enter the EC market inside the 17 percent external tariff barrier. The IDA opted for an emphasis on electronics and pharmaceuticals, two industries whose growth potential appeared great (Lee 1989: 473,531). The government proposed an increase in capital expenditure in 1975 of £42.5 million (up from £26 million in 1974) to finance job creation.

Nevertheless the number of jobs created did not outpace the growth in population, or the loss of jobs in indigenous Irish firms which closed down in the face of foreign competition. At the same time, there was a drop in agricultural employment as the economy shifted to industry. A closer look indicates that from 1973 to 1978 agriculture lost 34,000 jobs and the labor force grew at a rate of 2 1/3 percent in the 15-24-year-old bracket and at times by 3 percent in the 25-44-year-old bracket. Thus despite the creation of over 53,000 net new jobs, the overall effect was an increase in unemployed from 7.9 percent of the labor force to 12.5 percent over the years from 1973 to 1977.

Within the manufacturing sector there was a shift in employment. The lowering of tariffs hurt inefficient indigenous industry such as textiles and footwear. But other sectors, such as chemicals, plastics, metals, and engineering, grew at a steady pace. Thus the job creation effort was very effective in light of the job losses in traditional sectors and in agriculture.

It was in the agricultural sector that the goals of the government as expressed in the white paper were met or exceeded. While a collapse in cattle prices in 1974 caused a relatively brief crisis, the EC system of price supports under the Common Agricultural Policy helped keep Irish breeders' incomes supported. Thereafter the CAP generated a sharp increase in farmer's incomes while at the same time the number of people employed in agriculture dropped. S. J. Sheehy compared the projected estimates of the impact of EC membership and the actual results and found over the years 1970-1978 that gross output grew 35 percent and real incomes increased 70 percent. While some agricultural outcomes did not reach projected figures, they grew to an extent that would have been unthinkable without EC subsidies (NESC #88:1989: 102).

The government's goal of controlling inflation was no more successful than the call for a national partnership and common sacrifice. The inflationary effect of oil prices, direct and indirect, cannot be denied but wage agreements hardly represented the "moderation that is so urgently needed if we are to surmount our difficulties" (*A National Partnership* 1974: 42). The National Pay Agreements (a succession of negotiated agreements concluded every eighteen months between government, employers, and trade unions begun in 1970) gave a pay increase of 29.4 percent in 1974 and of 16.6 percent in 1975. Both agreements contributed to rates of inflation of 11 percent in 1973, 18 percent in 1974, 21 percent in 1975, 17 percent in 1976, and 13.6 percent in 1977. These figures were substantially in excess of the European average and obviously corroded growth in real income.

In the area of government borrowing, however, the record is even more dramatic and equally disquieting. Whitaker and others had long urged that the government borrow for capital expenditures which in the long term would contribute to economic growth. Borrowing to meet the shortfall between government income and expenditures began in the 1970s to grow at a pace that caused a great degree of concern about the cost of debt service. Not only did the amount of borrowing increase in absolute terms, but the foreign borrowing component increased sharply as well. Ireland, a creditor nation as late as 1973, had accumulated £313 million in foreign debt by the end of 1976 (Lee 1989: 472).

Overall, the period displayed a record of mixed performance in terms of the goals of *A National Partnership* with overall economic growth in the period a strong 4.1 percent per year, significant industrial job creation, and a near doubling of agricultural per capita income. The bleaker side of the ledger reveals increased total unemployment, persistent inflation, increasing government debt, and higher than average balance of payments deficits.

In July 1977 the Fianna Fáil government came to power running on an election manifesto of, among other things, abolishing local property taxes and income taxes, removal of taxes on small cars and motorcycles, and a grant of £1000 to those purchasing their first home. The manifesto not only promised to cut taxes but increase spending on job creation and social programs. The cumulative effects of the Coalition's policies from 1973 to 1977, plus the professionalization of the Fianna Fáil electoral effort, added to the Fianna Fáil victory. Lynch returned to power and was prepared to implement the election manifesto. He relied on the advice of Martin O'Donoghue whom he appointed Minister of Economic Development and Planning. O'Donoghue's plans included an optimistic overestimate of the role of the private sector in generating growth and an underestimate of the amount of debt that would be generated by government borrowing.

In January 1978, the government put its plan *National Development 1977-1980* before the Irish people.

*NATIONAL DEVELOPMENT*
*1977 - 1980*
*1978*

*SECTION 1*

*INTRODUCTION*

*1.1 During the last few years, the Irish economy has tended to lose momentum. Employment has fallen substantially; living standards for many have stood still or declined; the private sector has cut back on investment; inflation rates have been higher than in any previous post-war period; wage levels have increased in a continuing spiral as workers have tried to maintain their real incomes; and the costs of Government programmes have escalated, necessitating rising taxation and heavy overseas borrowing to finance them.*

*1.2 The longer such trends continue, the fewer become the options available to correct them. It is vital, therefore, that planned action be taken and that it be taken quickly. While it is for the Government to provide leadership it is only through effective partnership of all sectors of the community that real progress in economic and social reconstruction will be ensured. There must be agreement on where our national interests lie, and on the steps to be taken and the commitments to be made in pursuit of these interests.*

*1.3 The Government's pre-election manifesto was the first step in meeting this requirement. The manifesto set out the strategy for economic and social progress which they would follow in office. This strategy has two essential features. The first is immediate action to raise employment and output and to curb inflation. This action is designed to revive business confidence and lay the foundation for further growth. The second comprises a wide range of specific policy measures directed in the main towards sustaining and reinforcing this faster growth, making better provision for infrastructural development, and ensuring that economic advance is accompanied by social progress in areas such as education, health, housing and social security.*

*1.4 In the initial stages of implementing the manifesto strategy, a significant increase in Government expenditure and substantial tax cuts are required. However, in the subsequent stages stability will be restored to the Government's finances through revenue buoyancy, control of expenditure and an enhanced private sector contribution to the process of development.*

*1.5 Subject to the need for review and adaptation, referred to later in paragraph 1.9, the manifesto strategy and the action stemming from it will continue to form the basis of the Government's management of the economy over the remainder of the decade.*

*1.6 Action has already been taken since July 1977 to meet the manifesto commitments on job-creation. Increased public expenditure on building and construction and increased employment in the public services is expected to create an additional 15,000 jobs in 1977-1978. The Government's youth employment programme will be directed towards providing the balance of the 20,000 jobs within that period as envisaged in the manifesto. Furthermore, the formulation of the 1978 Budget is being guided by the requirements of implementing the manifesto both in regard to job creation and the wide range of measures to be undertaken in specific policy areas. To make room for the cost of doing so, expenditure under other heads and on existing services will be kept with strict limits. Otherwise the consistency of the Government's strategy would be endangered.*

*1.7 Outside the budgetary area, successful pursuit of the Government's strategy will depend very much on the response of the social partners. This response must include a willingness on the part of the social partners to agree on moderate increases in nominal incomes over the next two to three years. Provided that this reasonable response is forthcoming, enhanced business prospects arising from the successful implementation of the strategy should result in the creation of more job opportunities, a higher level of investment, and the expansion of output both for export and to meet greater consumer demand at home. These more buoyant levels of business activity will be made possible and supported by moderation in pay levels coupled with the tax concessions as envisaged in the manifesto. If the widespread acceptance of the key elements of the Government's strategy were to diminish or if the response from the social partners were inadequate, it would be necessary to review not alone the extent to which implementation of the strategy could proceed but also the continued appropriateness of its economic and social aims.*

*1.8 The measures already carried through and the further action to be provided for in the 1978 Budget will complete the first phase of implementing the Government's development programme. The second phase will build on the recovery set in train by these measures. During this phase the emphasis will gradually shift from existing policies to maintain progress at a high level towards a third phase. This third phase will involve new policies for structural changes in the Irish economy — thus setting the scene for sustained and long-term economic and social development.*

*OBJECTS OF THE WHITE PAPER*

*1.9 The main object of this White Paper is to set out the Government's intentions for the second phase of development. It isolates crucial issues, indicates as clearly as can be done at this stage the measures proposed to deal with them and the broad results expected. While the emphasis of the White Paper is on the Government's contribution to overcoming the problems facing the economy, it is clear that Government measures cannot on their own secure the results that are required. All sectors of the community must make their contribution to achieving success. Because such support may not always be forthcoming at the pace or in the form envisaged, and because other assumptions underlying Government action, e.g., world trading conditions and movements in external prices, might not be confirmed by events, the proposed forms of Government action have to be conditional. The programme of action will, therefore, be reviewed annually in the light of the results achieved.*

*SECTION 2*
*ECONOMIC AND SOCIAL AIMS OF GOVERNMENT ACTION*

*2.1 In implementing their development strategy, Government action will be directed towards achieving, as priority, the national aims discussed in the following paragraphs.*

*INCREASING EMPLOYMENT*

*2.2 A major national aim must be to increase employment. Unemployment is at an unacceptably high level. Numbers on the Live Register rose from 70,000 in February, 1971 to over 118,000 in February, 1977. Since then there has been a moderate decline to the present level of about 107,000. The main factors contributing to the rising trend have been the high rate of job loss since the post-1973 recession, the growth of the labour force, and the ending of net emigration in the period 1971-1976. Job losses have been spread across the manufacturing, building and construction and services sectors.*

*2.3 The absence of a Census of Population in 1976 makes a precise age breakdown of the numbers out of work impossible. Indications are that the bulk of unemployment is concentrated in the younger and older age groups. The available figures suggest that the level of short-term unemployed (measured by those on the Live Register for 27 weeks or more) is at present about 50,000, or less than half the total.*

*2.4 With the cessation of net emigration in the early seventies, the continuation of the population increase and changes in participation rates, especially among married women, a significant rise in the labour force has taken place. At mid-April, 1976, the labour force totalled 1,143,000, having risen by 23,000 since mid-April, 1971. The trends in population movement were of particular significance in the same period with net immigration of the order of 11,000, in contrast to previous experience of net emigration.*

*2.5 It is difficult to estimate future job requirements with accuracy. The estimate has to take account of the reduction sought in the level of existing registered unemployment, the number of persons seeking work but not on the Live Register, the expected increase in the labour force, future redundancies, and the outflow of workers from agriculture. To meet the expected increase in the labour force, redundancies and the outflow from agriculture, about 20,000 new jobs per year would be necessary over the remainder of the decade. If, in addition, a worthwhile reduction were to be made in present levels of unemployment, this figure would have to be increased by half as much again if not more.*

*2.6 Apart from other factors, these estimates could be increased or offset to some extent by variations in the expected pattern of migration in the period. In this connection, it is envisaged that the rate of inward migration will fall off and that the estimated downward trend in the outward movements will continue. The figures could also be affected by differences in the labour force participation rates used in making the calculation. At present these rates cannot be established accurately although refinement of those now used will be possible in 1978 when the preliminary results of the 1977 EEC Labour Force Survey become available.*

*CURBING THE RATE OF INFLATION*

*2.7 Since 1970, inflation rates in Ireland have been consistently above the EEC average. Effective national development requires that they be curbed. The consumer price index rose on average by 14 per cent a year from 1971 to 1976. While the openness of the Irish economy and our dependence on international developments were mainly responsible for the acceleration in the rate of inflation from 1973 onwards, they can hardly be regarded as a sufficient explanation for all price rises. Domestic cost pressures have also accounted for a sizeable portion of Irish inflation. For instance, it is estimated that taxation accounted for about one-seventh of the total increase. This reflects the degree to which increased public expenditure had to be met by raising the burden of taxation in conditions of slow growth.*

*2.8 In a number of EEC member states the level of inflation has been within, and for some, well within, single figures, e.g., 9.5 per cent for France, 4 per cent for the Federal Republic of Germany, and over 5 per cent for the Netherlands. It is agreed Community policy to bring about a convergent reduction in the inflation rate of the member states. The present aim is to achieve an average annual rate of no more than 5 per cent for the EEC as a whole by 1980 and progress is already being achieved in that direction. Against this background it is essential that the Irish rate of inflation be brought down as envisaged in the Government's manifesto. Otherwise, apart from the adverse and potentially dangerous domestic effects of rapidly rising prices, it will become increasingly difficult for Irish goods to compete either in the domestic or foreign markets, the attractiveness of this country as a manufacturing base will be diminished and the strategy of the Government programme will be undermined. The reduction in inflation, therefore, remains a key goal both in its own right and as an important requirement for achieving the primary aim of rapid job-creation.*

*RESUMING THE GROWTH IN LIVING STANDARDS WHILE MAINTAINING COMPETITIVENESS*

*2.9 It is undesirable that the arrest in the rise, and in many instances the actual fall, in living standards experienced by major groups in the community in the recent past should continue. These standards, as measured by changes in real disposable personal income, rose by only 1 per cent a year on average in the period 1974-1976. Moreover, general living standards here are lower than in the UK and lower still than in the continental countries of the EEC. In promoting development it is the Government's intention that real incomes will rise, and that ultimately the gap between such incomes here and those in the other member states will be significantly narrowed. Doing so depends essentially on raising the level of output per head of the population here and more particularly the output per head of the employed population. Achievement of the Government's intention is fully compatible with the income restraint required to maintain the price competitiveness of Irish production. In fact, such moderation is vital to ensure the creation of the conditions for the generation of jobs accompanied by a real rise in living standards for an increasing proportion of the whole population. Provision will be made, therefore, for raising living standards over the remainder of the decade as an integral part of the Government's programme.*

*EXTENDING THE PRODUCTIVE BASE OF THE ECONOMY*

*2.10 The Government regard the extension of the productive base of the economy as a major national goal. It complements that of achieving a sustained rise in employment levels and real incomes. Expansion of demand through general increases in private and/or public spending would have only marginal and temporary effects. Those effects would be nullified quickly as a result of bottlenecks in the productive system, and by the inflationary impact on costs and the burden of debt service. For lasting effects additional productive employment has to be created. Desirable action here needs to be considered against the background of recent industrial trends.*

*2.11 The loss of industrial employment in the recent past has been higher than might have been expected from output performance. The divergence can be attributed to an acceleration in the rate of productivity increase which itself reflected the pressures of international competition and the shedding of labour due to inflation and recession. The divergence also reflected the high incidence of job loss in the vulnerable labour-intensive industries which were adversely affected by the greater access of external competitors to the domestic market.*

*2.12 Development measures in the period to 1980 must be aimed at securing more industrial investment, at exploiting the output and employment potential of important natural resources, such as mining, and at ensuring that the capacity of agriculture to contribute to national income and sustain employment is fully utilised. Progress in those directions will make for increased activity in the services sector, and will provide the resources to meet demands for better public services in education, health and other areas.*

*PROMOTING EFFICIENCY IN THE ECONOMIC SYSTEM*

*2.13 Attracting foreign industry to Ireland, increasing the international competitiveness of Irish goods and expanding exports all depend on the efficiency with which the economy operates. The Government do not envisage that economic growth here and the advantages of the country as a base for production should derive solely from a system of incentives. Their aim is rather that economic advance should be based more and more on a increasingly well-trained labour force, efficiently employed, and a smoothly operating economic system. At a time of greater world-wide competition to attract industrial investment, incentive such as tax concessions and grants are likely to be less effective unless the country offering them also possesses those more basic attractions. For that reason the promotion of efficiency in our economic system must be a central concern of policy.*

*2.14 Comparison of sectoral productivity levels with those in competitor countries points to gaps between productivity in the manufacturing sector in this country and in other EEC countries, including the UK. Latest available estimates show that the level of productivity in Ireland (for 1974) compares unfavourably with other small Community countries. For instance, it is less than half that in Belgium, Luxembourg, Denmark and the Netherlands. This situation has shown little change as compared with 1971. There was a slight improvement in comparison with the UK in terms of overall productivity; in relation to continental Community countries, however, the gap has widened both for overall and sectoral productivity.*

*2.15 The need and scope for greater efficiency and productivity in our agricultural sector has been well demonstrated in studies by the National Economic and Social council (NESC). Figures for the period 1971-1976 show that while there has been an improvement, there is still great scope for further gains particularly through increases in output. There is urgent need not only to narrow the productivity gap between agriculture and the industrial and services sectors but also to improve the performance of the three sectors in the years ahead, especially in view of the achievements of other competitor countries in raising productivity to a high level.*

*2.16 The need for greater efficiency arises not only at the level of individual firms and sectors but also at national level. The Government accept that in areas such as energy, communications, the road-system and transport, the efficiency, quality and cost of the services provided are primary considerations for the users. It is, therefore, basic to the Government's strategy that their responsibilities under such heads are properly met. Likewise, in the area of the public service generally, there has to be full regard for efficiency and cost effectiveness, and it is the Government's intention that any necessary reforms to that end will be carried out. Institutional arrangements outside the public sector will also need to operate so that they assist in the process of development. This is particularly true in the field of industrial relations and pay settlement. Finally, increased efficiency is necessary to ensure a better return from the limited resources available to a small State for national aims.*

*PRIORITY IN AREAS OF SOCIAL CONCERN*

*2.17 The successful achievement of the Government's aims of increasing employment, curbing inflation and creating an environment conducive to work will result in major social advance. However, there are also specific areas of social concern, such as education, health, housing and social welfare, where the Government are committed to furthering social justice through policies designed to meet particular needs. The Government's intentions in these areas are set our in Section 7, but there are some general considerations applying to public social expenditure which should be mentioned here.*

*2.18 One of the most significant influences on such expenditure over the next few years will be the expected increase in population. The increase will call not only for the provision of more employment, but will also have implications for the provision of services such as housing and, through increasing numbers in the dependent age groups, will make significant claims on public funds in areas such as education and social and medical services for the young and the aged. In some areas the mere maintenance of the existing levels of service will involve increased public expenditure in real terms.*

*2.19 Even given rates of economic growth which are high by historic standards, public resources will nevertheless be under tight constraint. Increasing attention will therefore have to be given to costs effectiveness in public social expenditure so that the Government can fulfill their overall obligations.*

*SECTION 3*
*IMPLICATIONS AND CONSTRAINTS*

*THE CURRENT ECONOMIC BACKGROUND*

*3.1 The year 1977 is the starting point for the Government programme to achieve the aims set out in the previous section. The expected economic outturn for that year provides the economic background against which Government action has been prepared. Overall growth during the year is estimated at about 5 per cent. The major contribution has come from the industrial sector with an increase in total production of about 8 per cent, and substantial progress has also been made in agriculture with an expansion of about 5 per cent. In the services sector an increase in activity of about 3.5 per cent is expected. The higher level of economic activity has been supported by substantially higher exports, buoyant investment, and steady growth in consumer demand. In line with this activity there has also been a widening of the external deficit which for the year as a whole is expected to be about £50 million more than in 1976.*

*3.2 The year-on-year increase in consumer prices at mid-November was under 11 per cent or almost half of the corresponding increase for 1976. The price rise for the year as a whole was just over 13 1/2 per cent compared with 18 per cent in 1976.*

*3.3 Developments in employment and unemployment are less satisfactory. For the economy as a whole, the level of employment is likely to be some 7,000 above that of 1976. Manufacturing employment should increase by about 8,000 or 4 per cent and present indications are that employment in building and construction has stabilised. Despite the better employment trends, however, unemployment, as measured by the Live Register, which stood at about 107,000 or 9.3 per cent of the workforce early in December, 1977 is unacceptably high.*

*3.4 The level of domestic economic performance in 1977 has been achieved despite a loss of momentum in the economic activity of this country's main trading partners since the first quarter of the year. In the EEC as a whole, growth has been sluggish with a slowdown from the 4 1/2 per cent increase reached in 1976 to a likely 2 1/2 per cent in 1977. Capacity utilisation is low and, because of the steady rise in the labour force combined with hesitant growth, unemployment has increased to about 6 million or 5 1/2 per cent of the working population. In the larger grouping of OECD countries the general economic recovery which commenced in mid-1975 has proved equally fragile; growth in 1977 is likely to be of the order of 3 1/2 per cent and unemployment about 16 million. Some improvement in inflation has been achieved however.*

*3.5 In the absence of suitable policy action by the member states, the prospects for better growth and for a reduction in overall unemployment in the EEC are not encouraging. Policy action is needed to improve the economic performance of OECD countries also. Governments of the EEC member states are aware of the need for such action and of the growing divergence in most of these states between the rates of growth of output and investment set out in the Community's Fourth Economic Programme as being necessary to meet employment needs and the actual performance of their economies. There has already been broad agreement on the approach required to boost the growth rate to a somewhat higher level in 1978, but action that would restore Community performance to the levels envisaged in the Fourth Programme has yet to be implemented. The probability, therefore, is that the external economic environment in which the solutions to the problems of employment and growth in Ireland must be sought will continue to be difficult.*

*THE PACE AND PATTERN OF DEVELOPMENT NOW REQUIRED*

*3.6 It would be unrealistic to attempt to establish at this stage a fixed line of progress towards the achievement of the Government's goals. As already mentioned, the approach adopted must be flexible in order to allow for new developments or the correction of deficiencies in the underlying strategy. It is possible, however, to define broadly the implications and the degree of progress that will be needed and to identify the pattern of economic relationships that are necessary to maintain the economic and social aims of Government action.*

*3.7 The main economic targets of the Government can be summarised as follows:*

| | *1977* | *1978* | *1979* | *1980* |
|---|---|---|---|---|
| *Reduction in numbers out of work* | *5,000* | *20,000* | *25,000* | *30,000* |
| *Rate of inflation (end year)* | *10 3/4%* | *7%* | *5%* | *5%* |
| *Increase in national output* | *5%* | *7%* | *7%* | *7%* |
| *Borrowing as % of GNP* | *11* | *13* | *10 1/2* | *8* |

*Action already taken has been sufficient to attain the 1977 targets of a 5,000 reduction in unemployment and a lowering of the inflation rate. The Government are confident that the programme now being undertaken will set the basis for the sustained improvement of employment, inflation and public finance in the period up to 1980. They will provide the climate for the implementation of fundamental policy changes to bring down unemployment to acceptable levels.*

## *SECTION 4*
## *INDUSTRY, AGRICULTURE, AND SERVICES*

### *INDUSTRIAL DEVELOPMENT*

*4.1 National growth and employment prospects depend to a high degree on the performance of the manufacturing sector. Recent performance in that sector has been encouraging. Output in 1977 is expected to rise by about 8 per cent following a rise of 10 1/2 per cent in 1976 largely deriving from a continuing improvement in exports. Employment has been increasing since the second quarter of 1976 and it is estimated that at the end of 1977 it will be over 8,000 greater than at the same time in 1976.*

*4.2 On the basis of present policies the manufacturing sector is capable of expansion at a rate of about 10 per cent a year and of generating increases in employment of over 10,000 a year on average. Expansion at this rate will entail export growth on the order of 16 per cent a year, and in view of present prospects for the growth of markets for manufactured goods. The Government's programme will continue to provide support for rapid export growth through the policy to generate a substantial increase in home demand, firmly based on more people at work. The proposed income tax changes and other concessions will also increase spending power, while the campaign to channel an extra 3 per cent of Irish consumer expenditure towards domestic products should, when finalised, further increase sales of Irish products in the home market.*

*4.3 Promotional activities will be intensified in order to increase the level of job creation in 1978-80 in existing industries as well as in new industries of domestic and overseas origin. The rate of job loss in existing industries accelerated during the recent recession as the orderly adjustment of industry to a new free trade environment was disrupted by the severity and prolonged nature of the fall in economic activity. Aids being provided in other countries to firms in the older labour-intensive sectors of industry to prevent job losses are adding to the trading difficulties and redundancies of Irish firms. The damage caused is a source of concern to the Government and possible off-setting action is under consideration.*

*4.4 Emphasis will be placed on the planned and orderly restructuring of industry. The Industrial Development Authority have now been empowered to provide financial assistance for mergers and acquisitions. Consideration will be given to rationalising and extending the role of existing State institutions to ensure that the developing needs of industry and agri-business are adequately met. The imports of State bodies and of IDA-assisted firms will continue to be carefully examined to see what scope there is for substitution of imports by the production of Irish firms. Marketing capacity will be strengthened and developed. The extension of marketing efforts abroad, such as the purchase of trading companies to extend and underpin the markets for Irish products, will be encouraged.*

*NEW INDUSTRIES*

*4.5 There will be a major emphasis on increasing investment by domestic industry. The Industrial Development Act, 1977, provides for the extension of the IDA's powers in providing assistance for the restructuring of industry and for the introduction of a new incentive scheme. This scheme is designed to encourage entrepreneurs who have worthwhile development ideas, but are unable to secure the necessary funds, to bring their ideas to fruition. In addition the Government are committed to doubling within two years the number of projects to be assisted under the Small Industries Programme.*

*4.6 Competition to secure from abroad high-quality investment such as has been attracted here in recent years is now much more intense than it was previously. With unemployment levels stabilising at much higher rates than in the period before 1973, other countries are making greater efforts that heretofore to attract overseas investment and to ensure that the expansion plans of their own major industries make a contribution to the solution of domestic unemployment. In spite of these difficulties, our intensified promotion efforts are expected to result in the provision of approximately one-half of new industry jobs by means of new overseas industries. The programme of advance factory construction will, therefore, be continued and is expected to form an increasingly important part of the range of incentives available to industrialists.*

*4.7 Priority will be given to improving employment in those areas of the country which suffered relatively worse during the recession. Plans for the physical location of industry in the period 1977-80 reflect both this priority and the Government's concern that industrial development strategy should provide for an even spread of development throughout the country.*

The goals of the White Paper were reiterated with slight modification in *Development for Full Employment*, a green paper put forth by the government in June 1978. The green paper called for full employment by the early 1980s and estimated the number of jobs needed to be created annually to be 29,000. The earlier estimate in the White Paper indicated that the current policies could create 22,000 per year revealing a gap of 7,000 jobs per year to be created through policies for development in services, agriculture, industry, and infrastructure.

The White Paper goals were an increase in industrial and service industry job creation of 20,000 in 1977, 20,000 in 1978, 25,000 in 1979, and 30,000 in 1980; to drop inflation from 11 percent in 1977 to 5 percent in 1980; to increase GNP from 5 percent in 1977 to 7 percent in 1978, 1979, and 1980; and finally, to reduce government borrowing from 11 percent of GNP in 1977 to 8 percent in 1980.

The Report indicates the short run strategy. In order "to support the growth rates sought, the Government propose to expand public expenditure in 1978 and to grant substantial tax concessions" (*National Development* 1978: 24). In the longer run the burden for investment and job creation was to fall on the private sector bouyed upon "better business conditions and improvements in profitability" and by capital expenditures and tax incentives in such areas as farm cooperatives, aquaculture, small industries, internal transport, telecommunications, and housing (*Development for Full Employment* 1978: 19-72).

Legislation during this period included the Industrial Development Act of 1977 which allowed the IDA to support new entrepreneurs with working capital. This resulted in the 1978 Enterprise Development program. The persistent conclusion in studies since 1959 was that there existed a lack of research and development in Irish firms (ranked lowest in the EC in 1977). This prompted an increase in 1978 of IDA grants for R & D to £50,000 per project. Finally the IDA created a program for the development of inner city Dublin in 1978. Observers noted the apparent contradiction of increasing government spending for job creation, cuts in taxes to provide incentives, increased spending on social program, and a reduction in government borrowing.

Before assessing the performance up to 1982 two other developments must be considered: the oil crisis at the end of 1979, the second of the decade, and the Irish accession to the European Monetary System. By early 1980 the price of oil had risen 65 percent as a result of the Iran-Iraq war. In the months to come the cost would rise to tenfold over the price in 1972. The effects in 1979 were not unlike those of the 1973 rise in price, an increase in the cost of imports and of deterioration in the terms of trade. The balance of payments deficit went to 13 percent of GNP in 1979 and 11.5 percent in 1980. The high cost to the consumer of heating oil collapsed domestic demand and the recession abroad collapsed demand for Irish exports. Thus evaluation of the performance of the Irish economy and policies discussed below must take oil prices into account.

Ireland in March 1979 opted to join the European Monetary System though the U.K. did not. In doing so the Irish government benefited from loans of £1250 million and grants and subsidies of £250 million to cushion the shock of exposure to the hard currency area of the EMS. It was the first break with sterling since 1826 and ran the risk of substantially affecting the balance of payments as fluctuations of the British pound had an impact on the 47 percent of Irish exports going to Britain, and the 49 percent of Irish imports purchased from Britain. In fact the effect was relatively small as the devaluation of the Irish pound was matched by devaluation of the British pound. The most damaging effect came in the early 1980s when the Irish government did not control inflation, government spending, and balance of payment deficits, which called for devaluation; while at the same time the Irish government was committed to maintaining the value of the Irish Pound in the EMS.

What was the performance in the year 1977 to 1982? Unfortunately the adoption of the short-term strategy of increased government spending and lowering taxes become a long term strategy. Unfortunately the strategy short and long term did not attain the goals set in *National Development 1977-1980* and the subsequent estimates of *Programme for National Development 1978-1981* and *Investment and National Development 1979-1983*.

Table 1 in the Statistical Appendix examines the years 1979, 1980, and 1981 on the key indicators of employment, inflation, growth in GNP, and government borrowing in comparison with the actual results.

The failure to meet employment goals was caused by a number of factors similar to those of the 1973-1977 period, that is, loss of jobs in noncompetitive Irish industries, in agriculture, and a drop in demand due to the global depression caused by the oil price increase after 1979. Credit should be given to the IDA for creating the number of jobs that kept the unemployment rates under 10 percent, an average of 33,000 per year.

Most dramatic was the rate of inflation which in the years considered, save 1978, exceeded the projections by more than two to four times at the time when the GNP was decreasing and purchasing power was eroding rapidly. Thus the wage demands of the unions and public employees escalated and the average wage increase was 16.6 percent in 1979, 20.5 percent in 1980, and 18.4 percent in 1981. Inflated wages, far out of line with production increases, fueled the inflation. As Dermot McAleese put it, "Value for money is not achieved by paying ourselves more for doing exactly the same work as before" (McAleese 1986: 28).

The growth in GNP declined from the high of 5 percent in 1978 to a negative .5 percent in 1982. The steady decline mirrored the overall pattern in Europe and confounded the attempt to create jobs and generate tax revenue. Finally the government continued the pattern of borrowing began in 1973 moving from 9.7 percent of GNP in 1977 to 15.6 in 1982. The repeated deficits began to drive up the cost of servicing the interest on the government's borrowing. The government then increased taxes to pay for social services and the interest on the debt. The decrease in GNP and increase in taxes caused a drop in disposable income of 12 percent from 1979 to 1982 (Lee 1989: 519).

Irish agriculture, as noted above, experienced a major rise in income from 1973 to 1979. However, after 1978, like a rollercoaster, the trip down was faster and more dramatic than the trip up. Farmers' incomes had shot up from FEOGA grants (The EC farm price support system) which paid £102 million in 1976 and £365 million in 1978. A splurge of borrowing for new equipment, animals, and land followed that left the farmers in a very vulnerable credit position. Land prices escalated unrealistically as farmers, bankers, and creditors thought that farm incomes would continue to rise at 1973-1978 rates.

In fact the favorable conditions of entry into the EC and the upward adjustment in Irish prices to EC levels ended in 1978. The EC was financing a surplus production of food and in 1978 this led to quotas on production and decreasing the prices that the EC would support to eliminate the butter, milk, and beef "mountains." Joining the EMS in 1979 also had the effect on Irish farmers of depriving them of their adjustments in prices made by the EC to account for the Irish rate of inflation. The price increases that Irish farmers could command were no different than the other EMS states.

The slowdown in the global economy and the EC constraints on FEOGA payments brought about an agricultural slump. By 1980 income for farmers was more than one-third less than it had been in 1977. The incomes of farmers stayed at the lower level in the early 1980s and, in fact, dropped to less than pre-EC level in 1986. Farm output did not meet 1978 levels until 1983 and then, after rising, dropped to near 1983 levels in 1986. Poor weather and increasing restraint in the EC payments of FEOGA resulted in farm incomes in 1988 that were less than they were in 1978 although the number employed in farming had dropped by one-third.

The structural problems in Irish agriculture prevented the rural agricultural economy from responding to EC incentives or market pressures in an efficient manner. The growth in agricultural output in the 1973 to 1979 period was provided by only one-quarter to one-third of Irish farms. The remainder, because of the age of the farmers, the size of the farm, poor equipment, etc., could not respond in this period of growth. The size of farms and their ownership did not change despite the rising and falling fortunes of farmers under the EC. The number of farm employees dropped from 285,000 in 1972 to 162,000 in 1988, but the number of farms decreased hardly at all. Thus the rising per capita income did not occur because of structural change in farm ownership.

The land tenure system in Ireland is characterized by owner-occupancy and strong psychological attachment to the family farm, both not surprising in light of the late nineteenth-century pattern of land purchase by landless tenants. In addition leases are short term. These features "combine to create a very inflexible tenure system" which makes agricultures structurely unresponsive (NESC #88, 1989: 98). In addition the lack of a well-developed food processing industry has reinforced the sluggish character of Irish agriculture.

The plan *Investment and National Development 1979-1983* pointed out the rapid growth from 1973 to 1978 but warned that price increases "on the scale experienced in recent years cannot be expected to continue" and the report states "the new situation ... demands a greater emphasis than hitherto on productivity as a means of raising farm incomes" (*Investment 1979-1983* 1979: 39). The report was confident that fertilizers, increased herds, and better management would boost gross output by 3 to 4 percent per year up to 1983. However agriculture suffered declines in output in 1979, 1980, and 1981, a slight increase of 6.3 percent in 1982 and 3.3 percent in 1983.

Of the whole period John Blackwell notes first that there was the difficulty of connecting the plans put forward to the policies pursued; second "the difficulty of choosing between the different and conflicting objectives" of the plans; and, third, the misdirected focus as policies were often directed to areas where there was limited possibility of influence or where they were inappropriate. "At the same time little or no effort was made on matters such as pricing, public investment criteria, taxes and subsidies, the integration of taxation and social security" (Blackwell 1982: 57).

The increase in power and funds granted to the IDA for industrial development to encourage foreign investment has been noted above. Since 1969, under the leadership of Michael Killeen, the agency had been aggressive in using foreign investment as an engine of job creation, production for export, and regional development. In 1980 the effects of three decades of IDA activity appeared to have less effect on the Irish industry than might have been expected. The National Economic and Social Council commissioned a study of industrial policy in Ireland by the American consulting firm Telesis. Completed in July 1981 the Report, *A Review of Industrial Policy,* was not published until February 1982. As it was critical of the IDA, and suggested strengthening other development agencies, the report provoked significant bureaucratic infighting and IDA damage limitation (Lee 1989: 32-33).

The principal conclusions were so controversial because they addressed the very heart of IDA strategy and performance. The strategy of emphasizing foreign investment would not succeed in generating sustained economic growth, Telesis concluded, and recommended support of indigenous firms, especially those with export potential. The foreign firms repatriated profits, had few links to the rest of the economy, had no research and development, or engineering in Ireland, and only engaged in assembly or packaging processes. In addition the IDA did not sufficiently emphasize marketing and distribution which were critical obstacles to the success of Irish firms.

More explosive, however, were the Telesis conclusions that the IDA was not effective even in the strategy it had chosen. The capital grants given to firms by IDA were too generous, had no sanctions for nonperformance, did not produce the number of jobs promised, and paid too much on the average for each job created. In fact the number of jobs approved in contracts with foreign firms from 1970-1978 was 96,026 and the number that were created and still existed in 1981 was 28,937 or 30.1 percent (*A Review of Irish Industrial Policy* 1982: 33). Telesis recommended that grants be halved, that foreign firms have an R & D component and seek inputs from Irish suppliers, that Irish firms be singled out for development efforts, and that other government agencies become more involved in industrial development policy.

In 1984 the Telesis recommendations were incorporated in a report *Industrial Policy* and increasingly came to guide industrial development efforts.

*INDUSTRIAL POLICY*
*1984*

*CHAPTER 1*
*THE OBJECTIVES OF INDUSTRIAL POLICY*

*INTRODUCTION*

*1.1 This White Paper on Industrial Policy is designed to give a new impetus to industrial development. Irish economic development has owed much to industrial expansion over the last 25 years. In that period industry has contributed to economic and social prosperity in this country, and has made possible the introduction and maintenance of services which could not otherwise have been contemplated. This success was facilitated in the early years by a favourable world trading environment and later by our membership of the European Community.*

*1.2 But recently our industrial performance has faltered. In the past three years the number of new jobs created in manufacturing industry has been less than those lost. The policies which had clearly served us well in the 1960s and 1970s are now having less success. Competition for a declining volume of mobile investment is constantly intensifying from both industrialised and developing countries. There has been a major decline in the older labour intensive industries. This has been accelerated by the development of the same industries in 3rd World countries, where wage rates are about one third of those in Ireland. Experience elsewhere suggests a likelihood that manufacturing jobs would, even with an economic recovery, grow at a slower rate than in the past. These developments are taking place at a time when unemployment is at its highest ever level in post war history and the labour force is growing by about 17,000 a year. The state of Government finances does not allow for any real expansion of expenditure on job creation. Therefore, we must ensure that we get the best value in terms of jobs, exports and value-added from this expenditure.*

*COSTS AND BENEFITS OF INDUSTRIAL POLICY*

*1.3 The concept of value for money for the State resources devoted to industrial support measures is of crucial importance. As indicated, in Chapter 13.2 430 million was spent by Departments or agencies directly or indirectly concerned with industrial development in 1983. In the same year a further 315 million in tax revenue was foregone through various tax reliefs designed to foster industrial development.*

*1.4 Until the late 1950s industry did not need these direct supports from the community at large. Support was, until then, provided in the form of protective tariffs and quotas which helped industry but involved higher prices for consumers. As the tariffs were withdrawn more direct grant and tax concessions were needed to enable industry to adapt.*

*1.5 Throughout this process there was, until relatively recently, little detailed analysis of the costs and benefits of these various grant, fiscal and tariff concessions. The available data for such an analysis are still scarce. Such analysis is nonetheless necessary. A trade off clearly exists between the benefits of industrial policy and its costs together with the negative impact of those costs on the economy. To the extent that the costs of industrial policies are reflected in higher taxes they run the risk of defeating their object. High taxes can distort the economy to the detriment of industrial development.*

*1.6 The object of this White Paper is to maximise the benefits from the existing industrial incentives and thus ensure that the benefits from them significantly exceed their costs. To this end arrangements must be made to quantify more effectively both the costs and the benefits. Only thus can one provide a criterion for accurately measuring the success of industrial policy. In Chapter 13.6 arrangements are outlined for a three yearly review of policy by the Department of Industry, Trade, Commerce and Tourism. In preparation for the first such review resources will be devoted to the provision of an adequate data base for a cost/benefit analysis of industrial policy. This will meet the criticism in the Telesis Report that data and information systems in Irish industrial policy need to be improved.*

*ROLE OF INDUSTRIAL POLICY*

*1.7 The term "industry" is often understood to apply narrowly to manufacturing. The distinction between manufacturing and internationally-traded services is becoming increasingly blurred. These services have the capacity to generate employment, wealth and export earnings in the same way as manufacturing.*

*1.8 The Government's Industrial Policy consists of the specific incentives and programmes, infrastructural supports and the wider macro-economic measures which are aimed at maximising the employment and economic benefits of industrial development. The government's role in industrial development is to provide:*

*(i)* *incentives and advisory services for manufacturing and international service industries; this must be done in a way that gives the best value for public money;*

*(ii)* *the necessary physical infrastructural support by way of communications, road and sewage services for industrial development;*

*(iii)* *the encouragement in the commercial State sector of activities that provide productive self-sustaining employment; and*

*(iv)* *an economic environment in which all sectors of the economy, particularly those engaged in the production of internationally-traded goods and services, can expand.*

*OBJECTIVES OF INDUSTRIAL POLICY*

*1.9 In performing these rules the objectives of the Government's Industrial Policy will be:*

*(i) to create and maintain the maximum number of sustainable jobs, as many as possible of them high-skilled, in manufacturing and international service industries;*

*(ii) to maximise value-added by these sectors and to capture the wealth thus created for further investment and employment creation in the Irish economy;*

*(iii) to develop a strong and internationally competitive industrial sector in Ireland, made up of both Irish and foreign-owned industry;*

*(iv) to promote the more rapid development of our natural resource-based industries, particularly food and timber;*

*(v) to promote the integration of foreign industry into the Irish economy through greater linkage with Irish industry and educational institutions; and*

*(vi) to improve the rate of return on the Government's investment in the commercial State companies.*

*1.10 The Government through its economic, social and regulatory policies, significantly influence the performance of the industrial and of the productive sectors of the economy. Taxation raised in order to pay for necessary Government services has an inevitable impact on industrial costs and incentives. Regulations designed to protect the environment or to achieve social justice can also influence industry in ways not directly concerned with the achievement of their objectives.*

*1.11 Grants and tax incentives to industry help to offset the disadvantages associated with our peripheral location in Europe and the absence of a large home market. They are also designed to develop Irish firms which can compete on world markets and to attract investment from overseas. This has been the basis of the Government's Industrial Policy for the past 25 years. As these objectives were not then being fully realised the Government in December, 1979 asked the National Economic and Social Council to undertake a fundamental review of industrial policy. The major part of this review was undertaken by the Telesis Consulting Group.*

*1.12 The Telesis Report and the NESC's comments on the report were published in October, 1982. This White Paper represents the Government's response to the recommendations in these reports and in the IDA's Strategic Plan. It also takes account of submissions by the CII, FUE, ICTU, the State agencies concerned with industrial development and a number of private individuals.*

*1.13 We possess many advantages for industrial development. We offer one of the most generous and comprehensive incentive packages available anywhere in the world. There is an adequate supply of graduate, skilled and semi-skilled labour. Increasingly our education system is being geared towards the needs of modern industry. On completion this year of a major investment programme, we will have one of the most advanced telecommunications systems in Europe. The consistency and stability over many years of our policies for industrial development have been a major source of strength. Changes in Government have not resulted in major reversals of policy as has happened in other countries. There has always been a favourable Government attitude towards investment in Ireland by foreign industry.*

*FUTURE DIRECTIONS OF INDUSTRIAL POLICY*

*1.14 In the light of the studies undertaken, the Government have now decided that the following will be the future directions of Industrial Policy:*

- *(i)* *industrial incentives and State advisory services will be applied selectively; this will entail the concentration of resources on internationally-traded manufacturing and service industries, particularly Irish-owned firms;*
- *(ii)* *there will be a shift in State resources from fixed asset investment to technology acquisition and export marketing development;*
- *(iii)* *priority will be given to the attraction of foreign projects which will perform the key business functions in their Irish factories;*
- *(iv)* *through tax incentives, a risk capital market for investment in internationally-traded manufacturing and service industries will be developed;*
- *(v)* *the Government will take all the measures within their powers to improve the business environment with the aim of increasing the competitiveness and profitability of industry and other productive sectors;*

*(vi) they will promote effective education, training and worker mobility measures; and*

*(vii) will seek to retain within the economy wealth generated by industrial development.*

*1.15 This emphasis on the achievement of explicit industrial development goals will be a lasting feature of Government policy and will ensure a stable planning environment for productive enterprise. It will be monitored by enhanced reporting and a comprehensive industrial information framework.*

*REVIEW OF INDUSTRIAL POLICY*

*2.4 The objective of the Telesis and NESC review of the Government's Industrial Policy was to ensure that this policy would lead to the creation of an internationally-competitive industrial base in Ireland which would support increased employment and higher living standards. Set out below is a summary of the Telesis and NESC recommendations with appropriate references to passages in this document.*

*TELESIS AND NESC RECOMMENDATIONS*

*2.5 Indigenous (i.e. Irish owned) Industry*

*(i) Priority should be given to the development of internationally-trading indigenous industry. This would require a "hands on" approach by the State agencies, but only in the initial stages, in a selective number of projects aimed at developing competences within firms themselves. The measures described at Chapters 5, 6, 10 and 12 give details of the action now proposed by the Government in regard to this.*

*(ii) The testing of the "corporate shell" or "development company" concept i.e. a company which would acquire the technical, marketing and managerial capabilities needed for an internationally-trading company but which would sub-contract these services to independent manufacturers. The Government accept this recommendation which, as described in Chapters 10 and 12, will be tested on a pilot basis initially.*

*(iii) There is a need for a more systematic programme for developing linkages between indigenous and foreign-owned firms. The Government accept this recommendation and the*

*National Linkage Programme in Chapter 10 sets out the action now being taken by the State agencies to achieve this objective.*

*(iv)* *There should be better coordination and integration between the primary producer and the processor in resource-based industry, particularly in agriculture and forestry, in order to develop the significant potential of such industries. The Government accept this recommendation and the action proposed is set out in Chapters 7 and 12.*

*2.6 Foreign Industry*

*(i)* *Telesis recommended that there should be a substantial reduction in the level of grants generally offered to new foreign firms. Both Telesis and NESC advocated that there should be positive discrimination in favour of new or expansion projects with "desirable characteristics" such as key business functions, stand-alone projects, significant potential for sub-supply linkages. As set out in Chapter 8, the Government accept the recommendation for greater discrimination in grant levels for "desirable projects" but do not accept the case for a substantial reduction in grants to foreign firms.*

*(ii)* *Greater emphasis should be placed on promoting the establishment or addition to existing projects of complete business entities, rather than production units, which can integrate better into the economy. The Government accept this recommendation and as described in Chapter 8, this has increasingly been the practice by IDA in recent years.*

*(iii)* *NESC also recommended that the attraction of new foreign firms will, of necessity, continue to be an important element of Industrial Policy and that such firms will remain an important source of new job creation. The Government accept this as is stated in Chapter 8.*

*2.7 Basis for Future State Assistance to Indigenous and Foreign-owned Industry*

*(i)* *Telesis recommended that capital grants should not be given to non-traded businesses (i.e. where the key competitive advantage is transport/logistic costs) except in cases of high skilled sub-supply. The Government broadly accept this recommendation in the criteria for grant assistance set out in Chapters 5 and 6.*

*(ii)* *Both Telesis and NESC recommended that there should be greater concentration on incentives to offset specific competitive cost disadvantages. These arise in logistics, product and process development, export markets, linkages and skill development faced by internationally-trading indigenous businesses; off-setting them would involve a reduction in grants for fixed assets. The Government accept this recommendation (Chapters 5 and 6).*

*(iii)* *It was recommended that there be greater use of loans, loan guarantees and equity for particular projects including foreign industry. The Government are satisfied that adequate scope already exists between ICC loans and IDA loan guarantees to provide loan and loan guarantee assistance where appropriate. The NDC, as outlined in Chapter 12, will now have the major role in equity participation.*

*(iv)* *Telesis recommended that tax-based financing should be terminated or arrangements devised to confine these benefits to "desirable projects". Chapter 5 sets out the criteria now to be used in making these forms of assistance available to industry.*

*2.8 Control and Monitoring of Industrial Policy*

*(i)* *Both Telesis and NESC recommended that Departments (i.e. primarily the Department of Industry, Trade, Commerce and Tourism) should reassume their primary role of formulating/monitoring/evaluating industrial policy. They argued that IDA had filled a policy vacuum created by the absence of a sufficient Ministerial and Departmental input. They advised that the Department of Industry, Trade, Commerce and Tourism should be provided with the necessary resources in terms of expertise and support staff in order to reassume its primary policy role. The Government accept this recommendation. Staff resources necessary for the implementation of the proposals in this Paper will be provided within the present guidelines on public sector staffing (Chapter 13).*

*(ii)* *NESC recommended that there should be a review of the allocation of responsibilities between Departments/State agencies involved in industrial development, the objective of which would be to rationalise and streamline the functions of the various bodies. The Government's proposals to achieve*

*better streamlining of the functions of these bodies are contained in Chapter 13.*

*(iii)* *Telesis and NESC recommended that there should be improved statistical information from IDA and CSO sources in order to provide the data necessary for policy planning and appraisal. Adequate resources should be provided to CSO for this purpose. Both Teleisis and NESC expressed concern about the use of job approvals data in isolation as a measurement of performance. They also recommended that there should be regular reviews of industrial policy by the Department of Industry, Trade, Commerce and Tourism. Such reviews (e.g. every three years) are essential to ensure proper policy direction and that the State is getting good value of its aid to industry. The Government accept these recommendations (Chapter 13).*

Elections in June 1981, February 1982, and November 1982 had brought a period of instability to government policy. In October 1982 the government put forth *The Way Forward: National Economic Plan 1983-1987* and found it serving as an election platform as an election was called for in November. It could have served as the economic program of the Fine Gael opposition also as both parties and leaders were acknowledging the necessity for constraining government borrowing, increased job creation, and controlling inflation. *The Way Forward* boldly sought to eliminate the current budget deficit by 1986.

*THE WAY FORWARD*
*1982*

*CHAPTER I*

*THE CHOICE WE FACE*

*1. The Irish nation faces a grave and historic test. In order to ensure the long-term future of our economy certain measures and decisions must be taken now. Timely and well-considered action is needed to protect our economic welfare and security.*

*2. Many of these measures will have to be corrective. Without them, we would be unable to continue to borrow to the extent needed and would have difficulty in servicing our increasing public debt, maintaining the present value of our currency and continuing to import without restriction. This would result in massive unemployment, undermine our social welfare system and essential public services and lead inevitably to a major decline in living standards of long duration. Such a course of events would threaten the economic and social stability of our society.*

*3. Our economic potential, however is great and our capacity to avert the unwelcome consequences, which now threaten us, is clear. We must be prepared, therefore, to accept that our national income depends on our ability to produce and sell goods and services which are competitive in price and quality with those of other nations. To stimulate growth, we must give priority to productive investment over consumption. We must decide that the numbers employed in the public service, their pay bill and public expenditure generally cannot continue to grow on the basis of ever-greater taxation and borrowing in an economy at our present level of output.*

*4. The facts of economic life in the modern world are simple and inescapable. We cannot achieve better standards of living by merely deciding that we deserve them and must have them. Nor can we achieve them by awarding ourselves more money without the backing of new wealth and production. We must earn our living by our ability to sell enough abroad to pay for all the goods we want to import for production, processing or consumption. Public services cannot be provided on the basis of what is desirable. They must be based on what can be paid for by taxation.*

*5. The Government consider that the measures necessary to overcome our economic difficulties and, at the same time, to realise our economic potential should be combined in a National Economic Plan covering the years 1983-1987. Our problems cannot be overcome and our potential cannot be realised overnight. We need to know, therefore, what sort of effort we must make and how much time we need to overcome our present difficulties. We must have before us a comprehensive statement not only of the costs to be endured but also of the benefits to be gained from a courageous and realistic programme of economic and fiscal policy pursued over a period of years by the entire nation with determination and resolve. The basic strategy of the Plan now being put forward will progressively create a modern economy capable of providing employment for our rapidly-growing labour fource, an expanding and more competitive productive sector, the possibility of reduced personal taxation and more efficient and economic public services.*

*OTHER COUNTRIES ARE FACING THE SAME CHOICE*

*6. Our problems are not unique. After two decades of exceptional economic growth and, in many countries, full employment, countries everywhere are faced with the need for severe adjustment and unpalatable corrective action to offset the effects of the worst and most prolonged recession to hit the world economy since the nineteen-thirties.*

*7. The defensive measures taken by other countries up to this period in the recession have been much the same as our own. Taxation and borrowing were increased so as to finance greater government expenditure, to maintain demand, and to finance balance of payments deficits. Otherwise, demand would have been lower and unemployment would have been greater. But in spite of these measures which could only last temporarily, the countries of the developed world are, almost without exception, still in profound economic difficulties. It has not been possible to maintain demand sufficiently to prevent unemployment growing. There are now 11 million persons unemployed in the European Community as compared with 5 million in 1977. The intimidating outlook is for continued increases in unemployment as countries give the necessary priority to cutting back on their high levels of borrowing and to lowering prices and interest rates.*

*OUR SPECIAL DIFFICULTIES AND OPPORTUNITIES*

*8. We have special difficulties in adjusting our economy without causing excessive cutbacks in demand and output. Our population is growing at about four times and our labour force at about twice the European Community average. This measures our need for greater investment and for more new jobs at a time when we must curtail borrowing and correct our large and unsustainable balance of payments deficit.*

*9. Many of the international economic trends are, however, now for the first time in three years beginning to offer us the prospect of increased exports to replace the internal demand we were forced to create temporarily at the height of the recession by internal and external deficit financing. Compared with a fall of over 1.5% last year, EEC imports are forecast to increase by 2.5% in real terms in 1982 and by about 3% in 1983. In the United Kingdom, our largest export market, the volume of manufactured imports, which was static in 1981, is expected to expand by 7.5% in 1982 and by 5% in 1983.*

*International inflationary pressures are moderating. Our imports, which increased in price by nearly 21% in the first seven months of 1981, increased by just over 8% in the corresponding period in 1982. The international trend in interest rates is downward from the unprecedentedly high levels of recent years.*

*10. Against this slowly improving international background, our economic strategy during the recession, in common with other countries, of deficit financing to sustain demand and employment, can now be modified progressively to remedy deep-seated defects in our economic structure.*

*11. Our economy suffers from a number of serious defects which will worsen unless we avail of the improving international outlook to remedy them:*

- *we are losing jobs faster than we are creating them due to our increasing inability to sell competitively at home and abroad all the goods and services we can produce;*
- *we have lost a substantial and growing share of the home market to imported products;*
- *our higher inflation and interest rates are raising our production and operating costs faster than in other competing countries;*
- *our unit labour costs in manufacturing industry have been rising faster than those of our EMS narrow-band partners in the European Community;*
- *because we are consuming more than we produce, we have been running large deficits in our account with other countries. Such large deficits cannot continue without affecting our trade and the value of our currency. We must return to paying our way in the world;*
- *our level of borrowing for public expenditure, including for current expenditure to finance public services, is unsustainably high and must be progressively curtailed;*
- *we still have serious regional imbalances in economic and social growth and opportunity which diminish total output and reduce the efficiency of our economy.*

*OUR POTENTIAL FOR ECONOMIC AND SOCIAL DEVELOPMENT*

*12. Our capacity to overcome our economic difficulties and create a more productive, more competitive and better-structured economy is clear. To do so, we must unite in national will, resolve and action as we have so often done in the past in the face of adversity and challenge.*

*13. We possess a powerful array of both existing and potential economic and social resources which, properly mobilised and organised, in a framework of sound public finances and prudent economic decisions by all sectors of the community, will enable us to correct the defects in our economy which now threaten our economic and social progress.*

*14. These resources and their capabilities are shown by:*

- *our achievement in creating, outside the public services, over 100,000 new jobs in 1979, 1980 and 1981 in spite of the recession. Though these new jobs were offset by loss of existing jobs due to a decline in demand and competitiveness, the fact that they could be brought into being demonstrates our economic capacity to generate new jobs:*

- *our young population with their high and increasing level of education and technological skill created by a greatly expanded and improved educational, technological and vocational training system throughout the country;*
- *the adaptability and capacity for productivity of our work force;*
- *our proven capacity to attract from overseas, to establish domestically ourselves, and to operate, modern high-technology industry, marketing its products throughout the world;*
- *the training and skills of our farmers and the potential of our farms to achieve much greater output;*
- *our developed and efficient commercial, financial and professional services sector;*
- *our comprehensive and impartial system of public administration;*
- *the steady progress being made in improving our economic infrastructure as a result of the high investment policies pursued by the Government;*
- *our natural resources in minerals, oil, gas and marine resources, as yet not fully assessed or exploited;*
- *our membership of the European Economic Community of 260 million persons.*

*15. We should have confidence in the potential of our resources to raise the level and productivity of our economic performance, not only to the extent needed to solve our immediate needs, but also to attain the higher living standards prevailing in the European Community. We currently produce only half the average output per person of the European Community. We can reduce the gap, like other small economies have done, by producing and selling more goods and services abroad and by supplying a greater share of our own needs from home production.*

*16. We must face realistically and overcome resolutely the challenge to our economic and social future which the defects in our economy create and which reduce our production and our competitive capacity.*

*17. The fundamental strategy and measures contained in this Plan will enable us, over the period to 1987, to make the necessary adjustment to the new challenging conditions facing all the Western democracies as they come slowly out of the long recession. The requirements for success are clear. The burdens to be borne are not excessive. The rewards to be gained are more than sufficient to justify the united national effort which the success of this National Economic Plan demands.*

*18. Our economy now stands decisively at the threshold of a new economic era. Selfish attitudes and the pursuit of sectional interests must give way to a more responsible approach which recognises our vital common interest in averting the economic and social dangers which threaten us. By uniting in action and resolve, we can seize the opportunities which this Economic Plan outlines to ensure a secure future for ourselves and our children.*

*CHAPTER II*

*THE NEED FOR ACTION NOW*

*1. Existing basic trends in the economy cannot be allowed to continue without unwelcome consequences. Predominant among these trends are growth in public expenditure which cannot be matched by tax increases; a high balance of payments deficit financed temporarily by borrowing annually to maintain our foreign currency reserves; and uncompetitive growth in wages and incomes, and rates of inflation and interest which are well above the average European Community rates.*

*2. The current budget deficit, if it were not corrected by increased taxation or by reduced expenditure, could rise to almost £3 billion or 13% of GNP by 1987. With a capital budget requiring Exchequer borrowing of 9% of GNP, the total Exchequer borrowing requirement, by 1987, could become £5 billion or 22% of GNP. It is not open to us to borrow on that scale. Our national debt would have risen by 1987 to one-and-a-half times GNP. The cost of servicing that debt would amount to an annual sum substantially exceeding total income tax revenue. A large proportion of these debt payments would have to be paid abroad, draining the resources of the economy. The need to start a programme of action now to avert this outcome is unmistakable and unavoidable.*

*3. If the existing trend in wage incomes were to continue, it would cause a loss of competitiveness which would reduce our export capacity and increase import penetration of the home market. The unit wage costs of our manufactured goods have steadily lost competitiveness against our major trading partners. Our unit wage costs have been rising faster than in the EMS narrow-band countries; over six times faster in 1979, masked our loss in competitiveness, but in 1982, this will not occur because of the stabilisation of exchange rates in general an sterling in particular. Our unit wage costs in 1982 are expected to increase eight times faster than in the United Kingdom. This loss of wage cost competitiveness will not only lose jobs in existing industry but it could adversely affect the foreign investment in export industry which has been the major source of new jobs.*

*4. The combination of rising debt service and reduced competitiveness in foreign and domestic markets would ultimately widen the balance of payments deficit to over £3 billion or 14% of GNP by 1987. This is a deficit which could not be allowed to develop because of its effect on the value of our currency, on our rate of inflation and on our interest rates.*

*5. Unchecked, the adverse trends outlined would cause heavy loss of employment so that by 1987 unemployment would approach 300,000. Eventually inability to borrow would inevitably lead to further substantial job losses in the public sector.*

*6. Such a combination of events would clearly undermine our society and, therefore, cannot be contemplated even if some minority sectors of opinion will oppose the sensible and moderate measures and decisions necessary to avert these events. We need courage, determination and unity of purpose to reverse and correct the present trends. The Government are giving the firm leadership required. They have already initiated, and will continue to implement, the measures necessary to avert the grim consequences we face if we fail to take the sensible and prudent measures necessary. The Government are confident that the cooperation and consent of all responsible citizens will be forthcoming for the cumulatively beneficial course of action they outline in this Plan.*

*THE WAY FORWARD*

*7. The essential objectives of the Plan can be simply summarised:*

- *to halt and reverse the trend in unemployment so that, by the end of the Plan period, employment could be growing twice as fast as the labour force;*
- *by lowering inflation and interest rates and more moderate trends in incomes and taxation, to create a more cost-competitive economy which is the only basis on which we can expand output, increase employment and maintain existing jobs;*
- *to improve social equity in our society by reducing unemployment, making the taxation system more equitable, and ensuring that public services are provided in accordance with need;*
- *to create the kind of economy and society in which sufficient resources can be made available to protect the living standards of those who must rely on long-term social welfare benefits and in which fraud and abuse of the social welfare system are eliminated;*
- *in promoting the equity of taxation, to reduce over the period of the Plan, the burden of PAYE taxation which is excessively*

*decreasing take-home pay, penalising enterprise and increasing inflation;*

- *to reduce Exchequer borrowing progressively to levels compatible with the long-term ability of the economy to borrow and repay;*
- *to effect this reduction essentially by eliminating the current budget deficit by 1986 through a combination of measures including eliminating wasteful and unjustifiable public expenditures, reducing the numbers employed in the public service and moderating the public pay bill, making working methods in the public services more efficient and charging those who can afford to pay for certain public services;*
- *to the extent that the over-riding requirement to reduce Exchequer borrowing allows, to increase public investment over the period of the Plan, and apply more rigorous investment criteria, so as to ensure the high investment which the development of a more productive and efficient economy requires;*
- *to create an economic environment conducive to private investment and to ensure that public aid to encourage private productive investment and innovation is more selective and linked to performance targets;*
- *to bring the balance of payments deficit under control by increased exports, more import substitution and abating the rate of increase in foreign debt service.*

*8. These are the objectives of the Plan. They are the basic requirements to create a more competitive, lower-priced economy in which employment can progressively increase, the grim upward trend in unemployment be reversed and the realisation of a more equitable and expanding economy ensured. The objectives of the Plan are essentially economic, though certain basic social objectives are included. The full working out and development of social policy as such in the new economic context created by the Plan will be the next major task of national policy to be undertaken.*

*9. The succeeding chapters contain the details of the practical policies and measures proposed by the government to give effect to the objectives of the Plan.*

*CHAPTER X*

*WE MUST NOW DECIDE*

*1. This Plan outlines the measures we must courageously take as a nation to recover our full economic strength and achieve our economic and social potential. Constructive comment or criticism of the Plan will be welcomed. Its objectives are not guarantees but indicate what can be achieved if we make the necessary efforts and international trends remain positive.*

*2. The Plan proposes stringent measures to restore balance in the public finances, including elimination of the current budget deficit by 1986, to halt and reverse the trends of the last decade in public expenditure, to moderate the growth in taxation and make it more equitable, to create the competitive conditions essential for growth in employment, to accelerate the productive and economic infrastructure investment programmes essential for development, and to bring new criteria of efficiency to bear throughout the public sector.*

*3. The Government are fully determined to adhere to the strategy outlined in this Plan, whatever the difficulties involved. The Estimates for 1983 which will be published shortly, will reflect this same determination. The progress of the Plan will be continuously monitored so that when necessary, measures to reinforce its operation and to secure the achievement of its objectives, particularly through industrial and other sectoral developments, may be expeditiously introduced.*

*4. This Plan is but a start. It provides the main economic and financial framework for our development over the next five years. But within that framework we must deepen and extend our knowledge and concern about our society. The very fact that our financial resources are limited must make us ensure that our social policies are progressive and not regressive in their application. We cannot afford in our society, with our limited resources, to operate social policies which are wasteful or are not primarily directed to those genuinely in need. Our health, education, social welfare and housing policies must be carefully and compassionately reviewed to ensure that the constraints on expenditure are administered flexibly and not in a way detrimental to those in genuine need. At the same time, eligibility for services and the appropriate degree of support must be openly and objectively analysed with a view to determining clearly those who are in real need. We have scarce resources, given the exceptionally high degree of dependency in our society, and we must be satisfied that these resources are fully used to increase social equity and equality.*

*5. The Government, therefore, propose to establish shortly, in consultation with the principal interests involved, a permanent structure for economic and social planning. Our exceptional economic and social needs deriving fundamentally from our high population growth and dependency ratio, require a national consensus on economic and social growth and, in particular, on its distribution. The National Economic and Social Council, the Economic and Social Research Institute and other research institutes, the National Board for Science and Technology and the economic and social faculties of our higher education system have already done much to clarify our economic and social choices. In the new permanent economic and social planning structure, the expertise and experience of these bodies will be fully drawn upon in designing and developing new social policies more responsive to our special social circumstances.*

*6. The measures proposed in the Plan require us, in many ways, to look at our economic strengths and weaknesses anew. They require us, above all, to understand that in the immediate years ahead our economic progress must be won in a world adapting painfully but inevitably to the new economic constraints that now bind the Western world.*

*7. Income and welfare expectations are now conditioned by the necessity to build more competitive, less inflationary and more technologically-advanced economies. New factors have caused this: the staggering rise in the cost of energy in the seventies, competition from emerging Third World Countries, technological change. All these must be assimilated if economic progress in the West is to continue.*

*8. This requires vast new investment to reshape and restructure economies, in addition to the normal investment in replacement and renewal needed to maintain efficiency. This investment can occur only in conditions of moderate and stable prices, costs and interest rates, and of stability in exchange rates, so that national and transnational investment on the scale required can be made with confidence and security.*

*9. Unless we are prepared to reshape and restructure our economy, we will lose out in the new competitive conditions being created by our trading partners. Overseas investment will pass us by and go where costs will be more competitive. We will be unable to produce and sell sufficient goods and services to absorb our growing labour force. This Plan outlines the measures we must take. The decision to take them or not is for all the people.*

*10. In considering what decision to make, it is salutary to remind ourselves of what other nations and Governments have done, or are proposing, in the face of the same adverse economic forces and factors which beset all our economies. The principal features of these measures are summarised in the Appendix to this Chapter.*

*11. In spite of the measures they have taken, or propose to take, most countries expect unemployment to continue to grow for some further period dependent on the success of the new measures. The European Commission expects unemployment to continue to rise throughout the Community in 1983. In Denmark, France and the Federal Republic of Germany, the countries where unemployment is lowest, it is expected that the rate of unemployment will rise to the 10% level. Unemployment in the United States has already exceeded the 10% level and is expected to increase further.*

*12. These are all countries with richer and stronger economies than ours. We face the same economic and financial realities which they face, but in our case, they are in many respects more severe. Our inflation, our unemployment, our internal and external deficits and our foreign borrowing are higher. But more important in the long-run than these and more fundamental to our decisions is the fact that our population and labour force are increasing much faster than in other EEC countries.*

*13. Our population is now increasing at a rate faster than it was in the period before the Great Famine of 1847. Unlike then, we are now a sovereign and independent people and, as such, we face the responsibility of providing ourselves for the economic and social welfare of a population increasing faster than it did in the first half of the nineteenth century. The Government are putting forward in this Plan, and shortly in the estimates and Budgetary proposals for 1983, a comprehensive series of decisions required to enable us to begin to construct an economy which can satisfactorily cater for the unprecedented population increase we will experience in this and coming decades. We cannot and must not fail the challenge. We cannot allow divisions and disunity to deflect us from the national measures we must take.*

*14. The decisions are not easy. They require moderation of income and welfare expectations. They require some sacrifice and acceptance of some new burdens. But the Government believe that all these are necessary and bearable. There is no other way in which we can hope to provide satisfactory economic and social future for our growing population.*

*15. We, more than any other people because of our tragic history, must be prepared to accept readily the responsibility of caring and providing for our young people who, thankfully, now crowd our cities, towns and countryside instead of being scattered throughout the world as were so many past generations of young Irish people. This Plan shows how we can build an economy to support this growing population if we have the will, courage and responsibility that is required. The decision is for the nation to take now.*

In the election a Fine Gael-Labour coalition took power and a little more than a year later put forth a plan entitled *Building on Reality 1985-1987*. Up to the point of publication of that plan, successive governments appeared to be able than to do no more than acknowledge the problems of government borrowing, unemployment, and inflation. Also by 1984 the government had abandoned in its plan the notable objective in *The Way Forward* of elimination of government borrowing to meet deficit spending by 1986. The means selected to achieve the stated goals included redirecting development grants along the lines suggested by *Industrial Policy* creating a National Development Corporation to set strategy for industrial development; halt the rise in taxes and reduce government borrowing.

*BUILDING ON REALITY 1985-1987*
*A SUMMARY*
*1984*

*SUMMARY OF MAIN POINTS*

*This summary is set out as a guide to key decisions and proposals in the document* Building on Reality. *It is not a definitive statement of Government policy. That is contained in the Plan itself.*

*JOBS*

*The first objective of the Plan is to increase employment.*

*In the past four years employment has dropped by 40,000. Helped by the recovery in exports and output that is already under way—manufacturing output is currently almost 13 per cent above last year's level—new Government policies will stimulate a recovery in employment in manufacturing and internationally traded services. (2.13-2.35)*

*The Government in their policies will now:*

* *Give grants selectively in order to build strong firms which can export, provide substitutes for imported goods, or supply the needs of exporters. (2.24)*
* *Channel more grants to assist export marketing and the acquisition of technological know-how, and less for fixed assets and machinery. (2.25)*
* *Develop the national linkage programme so that foreign industries will buy more of their sub-supplies in Ireland. (2.26)*
* *Obtain the maximum commercial value from our natural resource industries. (2.28)*
* *Improve access for industry to venture capital. (2.29)*

- * *Establish the National Development Corporation to give a new commercial and strategic thrust to public investment in industry. (93.68-3.71)*
- * *Improve efficiency in State enterprises, freeing them from socio-political pressures and improving management and board control. (3.62)*
- * *Concentrate on reducing industrial costs and getting inflation rates down (1.11-1.15)*

*To finance this new approach, the cash provision for industrial grants is being increased by one-third.*

*In addition, the Public Capital Programme, slimmed down as a result of completion of such major programmes as power station construction and development of the telecommunications infrastructure, will be re-directed towards areas involving a higher construction element. There will, by 1987, be:*

- * *An increase of over 52 per cent (£53 million) in capital for major road projects, raising the level of activity in this sector by 10 per cent above that provided for in respect of these years in the National Roads Plan where, up to now, activity has fallen below target. (3.24-3.38)*
- * *An increase of £32 million or over 38 per cent in educational investment, much of it in the 3rd level sector. (7.85)*
- * *An allocation of £30 million for a new runway at Dublin Airport. (7.64)*

*These projects will between them stimulate many additional jobs in the construction industry.*

*An additional £50m. contingency provision has been made for capital purposes in 1987 to enable projects not yet evaluated to be started within the Plan period. (Table 7-2)*

*Overall employment in public sector services will continue to decline, as the Government offset continuing increases in employment in sectors like education by increased efficiency in many areas. The recovery in output and employment in industry and construction will stimulate the growth of private services activity, in which employment rose by 6,000 a year, even during the recent recession. (1.21)*

*Employment growth in industry and private services, even without the help of special employment measures, will be of the order of 35,000 in three years. (Table 1-2) But this will be insufficient of itself to absorb the increase in the labour force during this period or to reduce unemployment, especially as there will be a continuing drop in the numbers in agriculture and in public sector services.*

*Special Action on Unemployment*

*In order to reduce unemployment, therefore, the Government are taking additional special action designed to encourage unemployed people to set up their own businesses, and to get long-term unemployed people back into the workforce, while improving the efficiency of the youth employment services.*

* *The Enterprise Allowance Scheme, started at the end of last year, has already put 3,500 unemployed into self-employment. Together with other employment schemes introduced recently, it is expected to reduce unemployment by about a further 11,000 over the three years. (4.6)*
* *A new scheme, for Social Employment, will provide part-time jobs for 10,000 long-term unemployed people within the next twelve months, at a gross cost of £57 million, almost two-thirds of which will come back to the Exchequer through savings in unemployment payments and additional tax revenue. (4.11-4.13)*
* *A new training and placement scheme for the long-term unemployed will give a new chance to 2,500 people per annum, each for a six month period. (4.14-4.17)*
* *The youth employment services are to be more effectively co-ordinated at national level, and in half-a-dozen areas COMTECs (Community Training and Employment Consortia) are to be established on a pilot basis to secure effective co-ordination at local level. (4.8)*

*The net effect of all these measures is to absorb the increase in the labour force to April 1987, and to reduce unemployment by an estimated 10,000 below the expected end-1984 level. (1.28)*

*Agriculture*

*A number of measures are being introduced to assist agricultural growth and efficiency. A new impetus will be given to the disease eradication programme with safeguards to ensure the full clearance of bovine TB. Additional funding is being provided here, and for restocking of affected herds. (2.51)*

*There is also to be an increase in headage payments from £32 to £70 for beef cows in the disadvantaged areas from 1986. The Western Drainage Programme is being revived in 1986. (2.39, 7.68)*

*Transport*

*The Government have decided to introduce a complete re-organisation of CIE. CIE will remain as the holding company, but subsidiary companies will be established to administer the Dublin city services, provincial bus services and the railway. Certain loss-making services will be eliminated unless they are shown to be profitable in 1984 and 1985, and there will be no new substantial investment in railways. (3.43)*

*A new Dublin Transport Authority is being established, with a key role in the planning and operation of Dublin's transport resources and with responsibility for traffic management in the Dublin area. (3.45)*

*Road haulage will be liberalised. (3.40)*

*Tourism*

*A liberalisation of alcohol licensing arrangements will be of particular benefit to the tourist trade. There will be more full licenses available to restaurants and licensing hours will be extended in the summer months. (2.59)*

*TAXATION*

*The second objective of the Plan is to halt the rise in taxation, both direct and indirect.*
*Government policies will:*

* *Prevent any further rise in the share of national output absorbed by taxation, vix. 36.5 per cent of GNP. (6.3)*
* *Increase the income tax bands and allowances each year so that the income tax burden on taxpayers will not rise. (6.3)*
* *Reform taxation of farmers by introducing from 1986 a Farm Tax, based on adjusted acres to be collected locally for local government purposes and to yield double the amount paid by farmers under the present Income Tax system. Amongst full-time farmers only those with over 80 adjusted acres viz. less than 10 per cent of all full-time farmers, will thereafter be required to make income returns, and Farm Tax payments — which will be at a rate of about £10 per adjusted acre — will in their cases be credited fully against their income tax liability, so there will be no question of double taxation. Farms of less than 20 adjusted acres will be exempt from the Farm Tax. (6.16-6.17)*

*Additional Measures*

*The 1 per cent special Income Levy will be phased out as soon as resources permit. (6.8)*

*The PAYE taxation and social welfare payments systems will be fully integrated and computerised by 1987 so as to enable short-term social welfare payments to be subject to taxation for those with a tax liability. (6.9)*

*The number of items subject to the higher VAT rates will be reduced on a selective basis, at the same time reducing as far as possible the number of VAT rates. (6.12)*

*VAT on newspaper sales will be reduced during the period of the Plan, starting with a reduction from 23 per cent to 18 percent next March. (6.13) The excise duty on spirits, which is at a level that is causing large-scale cross-border trade diversion, will be reduced shortly. (6.14)*

*Anti-evasion methods already introduced including publication of the names of tax evaders, will have increasing effect in the period immediately ahead, and the release of some of the staff resources now devoted to Farm Income Tax will speed up the collection of arrears. (6.18)*

*The new provisions introduced in the 1984 Budget for Capital Acquisitions Tax will start to yield significant additional sums during the Plan period. (6.15)*

*SOCIAL POLICY*

*The Government are introducing major initiatives in social policy: fundamental improvements in the structure of social welfare and housing policy and continued development in other main areas, notably the rapid growth in the education sector and in health.*

*Social Welfare*

*Overall exchequer provision for Social Welfare for 1987 is being increased by one-quarter over this year's figure.*

*A new Child Benefit Scheme in 1986 will rationalise the structure of child support payments and give particular help to the families of low-paid workers. (5.58)*

*The EEC Directive on equal treatment between men and women in matters of social security will be implemented in 1985. The additional cost of this improvement will be £17 million in 1985 and some £20 million in 1987. (5.59)*

*A framework for a national income-related pension plan dealing, in particular, with pensions for the self-employed will be published. (5.61)*

*Action to Combat Poverty*

*Provision has been made for the establishment of a permanent Combat Poverty Organisation to develop constructive community action against poverty (5.64)*

*Housing*

*There will be significant changes in housing policy. In order to maintain the availability of local authority housing while reducing the cost of providing it, the Government have decided to introduce a grant of £5,000 for a local authority tenant buying a private house and giving up a local authority dwelling. Combined with the building programme provided for, this scheme should mean that, as in recent years, 9,000 local authority dwellings per year will become available for new tenants. Joint venture housing will be further promoted as another means of encouraging people to buy private houses, and the provision of residential accommodation for private renting will be supported by an extension of tax incentives. The £1,000 grant and the £3,000 mortgage subsidy will be retained, as will tax relief on mortgage interest. (5.76, 5.78, 5.85)*

*The Government will act to reduce the high cost of conveyancing and of bridging finance. (5.81, 5.82)*

*Education*

*Additional provision is being made for disadvantaged areas, including increased provision for remedial and guidance teachers, and a provision of £1 million by 1987 for free courses in community education and in literacy, in such areas. (5.28)*

*Among the other improvement in education services will be a number of programmes to provide young people, particularly those without qualifications, with full time courses involving basic vocational training. Already in this new academic year, these courses will cater for 19,000 students — a five-fold increase. Increased funding from the European Social Fund has been secured for these courses as well as for the existing middle-level technician programme in the RTCs and colleges of technology. (5.24, 5.25)*

*The level of real resources for third-level education will be increased by 5 per cent during the period; third-level student grants are to be increased by 10 per cent in real terms next September and indexed thereafter. (5.22)*

*As mentioned above, a number of major new educational building projects will be started in the period of the Plan. (7.85)*

*Youth*

*The National Youth Policy Committee has just presented its report, which is being published. Even in advance of publication, the Government have decided to set aside money for the implementation of certain of its recommendations. (5.70)*

*Health*

*There have been improvements in the efficiency with which health services have been provided in the last few years, and further improvements in this area will be a priority. During the Plan period £177 million is being provided for the hospital development programme. The development of health policy will be based on moving more and more towards a preventive approach (e.g. a measles immunisation programme.) and to promoting community care. Special attention will be given to the health needs of the travelling people. Additional resources are being provided to combat drug abuse. (5.33-5.48)*

*Sport*

*The Government have decided that a National Lottery will be established. Part of the proceeds of this will go towards the promotion of sport. (5.32)*

*Children*

*It is intended to introduce three new Bills in relation to the care and protection of children, in order to bring our existing outdated legislation more in line with current concepts in regard to the well-being of the child. (5.41)*

*Development Aid*

*Aid for The Third World remains a priority for this country. While we remain well short of our long-term objectives in this area, the Government have decided to continue to increase the share of GNP devoted to this purpose by 0.015 per cent per annum, thus raising this provision by 47 per cent from £34 million to £50 million by 1987. (5.96)*

*REDUCING BORROWING*

*All these measures have to be undertaken within the framework of a Plan that will reduce the current budget deficit and borrowing, sufficiently to halt by 1987, the rise in National Debt and interest payments as a share of national output and taxation. (7.9)*

*To secure these public finance objectives:*

* *The current deficit as a proportion of national output will be reduced from 7 1/2 per cent to 5 per cent of GNP.*
* *Exchequer borrowing will be reduced from 12 3/4 per cent to 9 3/4 per cent of GNP.*

- *Public sector borrowing (which includes borrowing by State enterprises) will be reduced from 17 per cent to 11 1/4 per cent of GNP.*

*The need for recourse to foreign borrowing will be greatly reduced, as will pressure on the domestic financial market — freeing more resources from domestic savings for productive investment outside the Government sector. Achievement of the Government's public expenditure target requires the growth in the public service pay bill to be severely restricted. The Government have therefore decided on specific amounts to apply to the public service pay bill for each of the three years 1985, 1986 and 1987. These allow for little nominal change in the pay bill in 1985, followed by a moderate increase thereafter. If severe reductions in public service staffing are to be avoided, restraint in the pay bill must be achieved primarily by curtailing the growth in average pay per head. (7.21)*

*In order to achieve the relative reduction in current expenditure required, the Government also have had to limit existing programmes, and a number of services and subsidies have to be curtailed. Further reductions in food subsidies will, however, be postponed until the introduction of the Child Benefit Scheme. These further measures include: (7.25, 7.34)*

- *Curbs on recruitment to local authorities, health boards and grant-aided bodies, to complement the embargo on replacement of two out of three vacancies in the civil service, which will be maintained. Total public sector services employment already reduced by 3,000 in the past two years, will drop by a further 5,000 during the Plan period.*
- *Rationalisation of certain State bodies, in addition to the abolition of the Land Commission, already announced.*
- *Abolition of the malicious Injuries Scheme, already announced.*
- *Curtailment of rate support grants.*
- *Suspension of the coastal erosion service for the duration of the Plan period.*
- *Increases in Land Registry Fees.*
- *Increases in third level fees and school transport charges.*
- *Reductions in the cost of the health service by increases in charges for private and semi-private patients, and securing contributions from consultants for private use of public facilities.*

*CONCLUSION*

*The assumptions with respect to international economic conditions upon which this Plan is based are set out explicitly at the outset. The estimates of growth of GNP and employment based on these assumptions are those furnished by the relevant experts in the public service. The planned provisions for current Government spending by Departments for each of the next three years, and of public capital spending by programme, are based on specific Government decisions covering the three-year period.*

*Thus, subject always to any unpredictable major upset in the international economic environment, this Plan is firmly based on reality. It provides, for the first time, a stable environment within which all concerned can plan for the three years ahead — knowing what the Government's policies will be, knowing what the tax environment will be, and knowing how public capital investment will develop.*

*This stable policy environment provides the most favourable possible situation for enterprise to develop — and brings to an end the period of uncertainty which has persisted since this decade began.*

Both *The Way Forward* and *Building on Reality* project goals for the years 1985, 1986 and 1987. We can examine the success of the policies by comparing the projections of the two documents for those years with the actual performance in the four key areas as shown in Table 2 in the Appendix.

In the realm of employment the projections of both plans were under the real unemployment rate. The projections moreover did not take into account the degree to which emigration would lower the total workforce at an ever increasing rate. The emigration figures were:

| | |
|---|---|
| 1983 | 14,000 |
| 1984 | 11,000 |
| 1985 | 21,000 |
| 1986 | 29,000 |
| 1987 | 29,000 |

Thus the struggle to increase available jobs foundered on the decreasing rate of agricultural employment *and* a decrease in industrial employment.

The projections of inflation in the plans, unlike the period 1977-1982, overestimate the rate of inflation compared to that which actually prevailed, especially in 1987 when the actual rate dropped to 2.5 percent.

The growth in GNP estimates revealed the degree of undue optimism in the Irish economy on the part of the government and in the rate of recovery in the global recession. *The Way Forward* was more modest in its projections of 3.5 percent per year, while *Building on Reality* projected 10 percent per year for three years. In fact the Irish economy shrank three of the five years projected.

Government borrowing was most forthrightly addressed by *The Way Forward* which projected the elimination of borrowing to meet the current deficit by 1986. In 1986 T. K. Whitaker had warned that "the financial policy mistakes of the past were grevious and cannot easily be rectified. To borrow more would be to plunge deeper into the morass" (Whitaker 1986: 16). Despite program projections borrowing continued unabated throughout the five years and Ireland plunged deeper and deeper into the morass.

With respect to agricultural policy, *The Way Forward* in 1982 noted that agricultural prosperity could not depend on price increases alone but required control of inflation and "improved efficiency and increased output at the individual level" (*The Way Forward* 1982: 61). The plan called for the creation of a working group to help formulate policy. The plan also called for increased investment in the national herd, farm modernization, disease eradication, and an analysis of land ownership structures. The plan's projected increases in gross output for the years 1983 to 1987 and the actual output were:

| | 83 | 84 | 85 | 86 | 87 |
|---|---|---|---|---|---|
| Projected | 2 | 5 | 7 | 9 | 12 |
| Actual | 3.3 | 8.4 | -1.5 | 12.1 | 1.0 |

*Building on Reality* in 1984 was on target in diagnosing the problems of Irish agriculture: "the need for greater efficiency in the industry;" "diversify production;" "improve competitiveness;" "an adequately trained farm labor force;" "cost effective new technology;" "that ownership and management of land is in the hands of those best fitted to work it" (*Building on Reality* 1984: 44). While *Building on Reality* does not project agricultural growth rates, they were less than spectacular, as noted: -1.5 in 1985, -2.1 in 1986, and 1.0 in 1987.

The coalition government did not substantially alter the pattern of economic policy in place since 1977, if not since 1973. The elements of the picture were relentlessly negative save for the inflation rate. The absolute numbers were grim as unemployment went from a figure of 100,000 in 1980 to 242,000 in 1987. The ratio of the national debt to GNP went from 88 percent in 1980 to over 150 percent in 1987, reaching a sum of over £25 billion and requiring about £50 a week from each Irish worker for debt service. And, finally, the nation experienced an emigration rate of 30,000 per year.

By 1985 the National Economic and Social Council "had become extremely concerned at the scale of the economic and social problems facing the country and was worried about the consequences of continuing present policies." In November 1986 the Council produced a study which called for a concerted medium term program to bring the Irish economy out of its deadened state, *A Strategy for Development 1986-1990*. The report reprised the poor performance from 1980 to 1986 and called for

- correcting the imbalances in public finance
- strengthening export industries

- revising the tax system
- reallocating industrial incentives to develop Irish firms

As it happened the year 1987 brought an election and the Fianna Fail party under Charles Haughey took power in February 1987. Years earlier in January 1980 Haughey had stated in a television address:

> As a community we are living beyond our means we are living at a rate which is not justified by the amount of goods and services we are producing. To make up the difference we are borrowing enormous amounts of money, borrowing at a rate which just cannot continue....We have got to cut down government spending. (Lee 1989: 501)

Seven years later, facing the £25 billion debt, and attendant debt service, the government began to adopt policies which would bring the spending under control. Negotiating with unions, business, and agricultural groups (the social partners) the government produced the *Programme for National Recovery* in October 1987. Very similar to the NESC plan mentioned above, the *Programme* addressed the crisis and proposed sharp cuts in government spending, agreements on pay increases, tax reform, and increased employment opportunities.

*PROGRAMME FOR NATIONAL RECOVERY*
*1987*

*INTRODUCTION*

*1. The Government, the ICTU, the FUE, the CII, the CIF, the IFA, Macra na Feirme and the ICOS, conscious of the grave state of our economic and social life, have agreed on this Programme to seek to regenerate our economy and improve the social equity of our society through their combined efforts. The principles that should govern such efforts were set out in the National Economic and Social Council study* A Strategy for Development 1986-1990.

*2. The Programme will cover the period to end-1990. It envisages progress being made in that period in four broad areas:*

*(i) creation of a fiscal, exchange rate and monetary climate conducive to economic growth;*

*(ii) movement towards greater equity and fairness in the tax system;*

*(iii) diminishing or removing social inequities in our society; and*

*(iv) intensification of practical measures to generate increased job opportunities on a sectoral basis.*

*3. The new concerted efforts by all interests contained in the Programme will represent a major attempt to overcome the serious obstacles which at present exist to impede economic and social development.*

*4. The following factors give an indication of the extent of the difficulties which have to be confronted:*

- *(a) a Gross Domestic Product per capita which is only 64 per cent of the European Community average,*
- *(b) a National Debt of over £25 billion which is equivalent to more than one and one-half times of our Gross National Product and the servicing of which consumes annually one-third of Exchequer tax revenue,*
- *(c) an Exchequer borrowing requirement of 10.7 per cent of Gross National Product in 1987 to finance both current and capital expenditure. This is among the highest budgetary deficits in the European Community,*
- *(d) high nominal and real interest rates which are a barrier to investment,*
- *(e) an unemployment rate of 18.5 per cent of the work-force amounting to 242,000 persons, of whom 73,000 are under 25 years of age. This is one of the highest rates of unemployment in the European Community,*
- *(f) employment in agriculture which continues to decline steadily at a rate almost twice the European Community average,*
- *(g) net emigration estimated currently at close to 30,000 and which is equivalent to the natural increase in the population, and*
- *(h) no overall growth in the volume of investment in equipment over the past 5 years compared with an increase of 20 per cent in the European Community.*

*5. Central to our efforts to achieve our full economic and social potential will be better utilisation of our resources, human and natural, and the fullest application of science and technology.*

*SECTION II*

*MACROECONOMIC POLICIES*

*1. A fiscal policy which faces the financial realities is the key to putting the economy back on the path to long-term sustained economic growth. The situation has been developing in recent years in which the National Debt and its servicing have been growing out of proportion to our ability to sustain them will be ended. The National Debt/Gross National Product ratio will be stabilised in the course of the Programme.*

*2. This will involve reducing the Exchequer borrowing requirement to between 5 per cent and 7 per cent of GNP, depending on developments in economic growth and interest rates. To that end, the measures taken by the Government to control and curtail public expenditure will be continued. The Programme will also contribute to that objective in so far as it increases economic activity, reduces interest rates and stimulates new employment.*

*3. As part of public expenditure control, the measures already taken to improve management of the National Debt will be pursued.*

*4. Reduced Exchequer borrowing will have a beneficial effect on interest rates and help to stimulate new investment and economic growth.*

*5. A low inflation rate is also essential for increased competitiveness and economic viability during the Programme and all interests are concerned to ensure this.*

*6. The exchange rate will be firmly linked to the European Monetary System so as to bring about greater cohesion of our interest rates with the EMS average and to promote investor confidence and inhibit speculative capital movements.*

*7. Monetary policy will be determined by the need to bring about the lowest possible interest rates consistent with international developments and exchange rate policy.*

*8. An appropriate pattern of pay developments has an essential part to play in the success of this Programme. Lower income taxation and a low level of inflation can help to bring about more moderate pay expectations. It is for this reason that the Government as part of tax reform under the Programme intend to make the income tax reductions outlined in Section III.*

*9. Against this background it is agreed that pay increases can be provided at a level not exceeding 2.5 per cent in each of the years 1988, 1989 and 1990. It is also agreed that special consideration should be given within this overall increase to lower paid workers. It is further agreed that discussions will take place at national level between the Government, the FUE, the CIF and the ICTU on a general framework within which the issue of working hours can be dealt.*

*10. The nature and extent of the pay increase to apply in both the public and private sectors, together with the position on lower paid workers and on working hours, will be dealt with in separate documents on "Proposals for a Public Service Pay Agreement", applicable also to the broader public sector, and "Proposals for an Agreement between the ICTU, the FUE and the CIF".*

*11. In realising their budgetary targets, the Government are committed to the need for the achievement of a reduction in the number of public service employees. They are committed to achieving this reduction on a voluntary basis. They are confident that the comprehensive voluntary arrangements they have introduced will achieve the reductions sought. If in practice, however, the take-up of these voluntary arrangements does not enable the Government's budgetary and structural objectives to be met, the Government will review the position but, in doing so, they undertake to consult fully with the ICTU. Such prior consultations will take place under the review mechanism provided for in the Programme.*

*SECTION III*

*TAX REFORM*

*General*

*1. The Government are committed to reform of the tax system. The Programme of changes, initiated in the 1987 Budget, will be accelerated to increase equity in the system, radically improve collection and encourage economic development.*

*Income Tax*

*2. The Government will introduce income tax reductions to the cumulative value, over the next three years, of £225 million, including increases in the PAYE allowance costing £70 million. In the context of this provision, the Government will make significant progress towards having two-thirds of taxpayers on the standard rate by adjustment of the 35 per cent band.*

*3. The Government will continue to ensure that only necessary expenses will be allowed for tax purposes.*

*4. The deduction at source system on professional fees paid by the public sector bodies set out in the 1987 Finance Act is operating effectively.*

*5. Farmers are now taxed on income on the same basis as other self-employed income-tax payers and this will be fully and consistently implemented.*

*Corporation Tax*

*6. The Budget estimate for the yield from corporation tax in 1987 is £262 million or 4 per cent of total tax revenue. This percentage share is low by comparison with other EEC countries. The main reasons for the low yield are the relatively small business base here and the range of business incentives, including the specially favourable regime for manufacturing industry. In the Budget this year, the Minister for Finance announced a review of the Corporation Tax code. This review is well advanced.*

*Capital Taxation*

*7. Capital taxation will be reviewed and the scope for increasing the yield from capital taxes will be investigated in the context of the 1988 and subsequent Budgets.*

*8. The aggregation of benefits from all sources will increase the yield from Capital Acquisitions Tax.*

*Tax Evasion, Tax Collection and Enforcement*

*9. The Government are fully committed to improving collection and enforcement, stamping out arrears and ensuring prompt payment of tax liabilities as they arise. This will be given priority. Whatever changes are considered necessary, whether administrative or legislative, will be made. Greater equity in the collection effort must be achieved.*

*10. Staff levels in the Office of the Revenue Commissioners are already equivalent to about one head of staff for every 150 taxpayers. Additional resources will nevertheless be made available as necessary to achieve improved results.*

*11. The Revenue Commissioners are drawing up, as a matter of priority, a programme and timetable for reduction and elimination of arrears.*

*12. The Government are committed to the introduction of self-assessment for Corporation Tax and Income Tax for the self-employed. Effective auditing procedures and appropriate penalties must play a major part. The conditions must be such as to guarantee a significant improvement in compliance.*

*13. The range of enforcement powers available to the Revenue Commissioners and the Sheriffs is being considered by the Law Reform Commission. The Commission have been asked to make their report on improvements in debt collection generally as soon as possible.*

*14. The requirement to have a tax clearance certificate as a precondition for securing public contracts over £10,000 is being stringently applied. A similar system is being introduced for all grant payments.*

*15. The introduction of improved identification systems to allow better coordination and control is under detailed discussion by the Revenue Commissioners and the Department of Social Welfare.*

### *SECTION V*
### *EMPLOYMENT*

*General*

*1. Lower interest and mortgage rates, a stable exchange rate, low inflation, stabilisation of the National Debt/GNP ratio and its subsequent reduction to a sustainable level, halting and reversing the flow of capital out of the economy, lower and more equitable personal taxation constitute the fiscal and monetary policy of the Government under the Programme. Already significant results in these areas have been achieved. This fiscal and monetary climate will stimulate investment confidence and greater economic activity, maintain existing employment and create new employment. The objective of the employment strategy will be to create viable jobs in the legitimate economy and not in the "black economy". The Programme contains a series of specific measures to achieve this effect.*

*2. The indigenous manufacturing sector must be strengthened so that is achieves the size and vitality which other small economies have achieved. Proportionate to those small economies, we should have 100,000 more persons employed in manufacturing industry. The weakness of the indigenous manufacturing sector, partly reflected in our exceptionally high level of imports, is a contributory factor to our heavy unemployment. The overseas firms employing 80,000 persons show our capacity to staff and manage successful and advanced manufacturing processes. Indigenous manufacturing industry must similarly expand and diversify, must exploit better our natural resources, must export more and must recover its share of the home market if we are to increase employment.*

*3. We will continue, through the incentives provided, to attract overseas manufacturing companies. The sound fiscal and monetary climate being created will be an added inducement to overseas companies to locate here.*

*4. Irish liability insurance rates place many Irish firms at a cost disadvantage, particularly in comparison with U.K. competitors. The Government will move quickly to facilitate a reduction in costs by proceeding with legislation to abolish juries in personal injuries cases, by introducing legislation to give effect to the main recommendations of the Commission of Inquiry on Safety, Health and Welfare at Work (the Barrington Report) and by promoting the introduction of safety audit arrangements by insurance companies. The scope for promoting the publication of a Book of Quantum of Damages, for introducing a pre-trial procedure system and reducing the level of legal representation in the Superior Courts to help reduce legal costs will also be examined. Insurance industry representatives have given assurances that reductions in liability insurance premia will follow the introduction of an improved framework.*

*5. The services industry will grow both independently and through the multiplier effect of the development of manufacturing employment. Tourism, international services and, in particular, financial services will contribute significantly to this growth.*

*6. The State-sponsored Bodies will be actively encouraged and facilitated to develop and diversify their economic employment-creating activities. Where new legislation is required to achieve this, it will be brought forward.*

*7. The State-sponsored Bodies, which provide utilities and services must, through greater efficiency and cost-containment measures, bring down the high cost environment now affecting the competitiveness of our economy and the growth of employment.*

*8. The moderate pay increases under the Programme will contribute significantly to our ability to compete more effectively and thus create more jobs. This discipline must be matched by better marketing and management and greater technological development.*

*9. A sectoral development approach will be applied in the creation of new employment.*

*Manufacturing*

*10. Ireland's economic and social prospects depend ultimately on the further development of our industrial base to produce quality traded goods and services for world markets. The objectives of policy in manufacturing industry involve creating approximately 20,000 extra jobs on average per year over the next ten years, the actual provision accelerating as the Programme policies take effect. The offsetting trend in job losses cannot be foreseen accurately by the more competitive economic climate and the greater attention given to the indigenous sector will make existing jobs more secure.*

*11. The policy measures to achieve this will be:*

*(i)* *a radical re-organisation and simplification of the industrial promotion agencies will be undertaken to provide a combined approach to the growth of the indigenous manufacturing sector covering development, marketing at home and abroad and technological change and innovation. The promotion of overseas investment in Ireland will be intensified on a specialised basis;*

*(ii)* *the market-oriented and technological development of the indigenous sector will have, as a priority, the expansion and growth of selected Irish companies firmly rooted in the economy. Ministerial Offices for Trade and Marketing and for Science and Technology have been established to further this strategy;*

*(iii)* *greater emphasis on State aid to achieve a significant shift in resources from the support of fixed asset investment to the upgrading of marketing, product development, R & D and management expertise;*

*(iv)* *the new trading houses for which provision has been made in the 1987 Budget will provide a new effective export service to indigenous companies and help to increase the share of Irish manufactured products in specific overseas markets;*

*(v)* *training grant expenditure will give greater emphasis to equipping Irish companies with marketing, management, technological and commercial language skills;*

*(vi)* *linking State aid more directly to employment so that disbursements will depend on the achievement of specific employment targets;*

*(vii)* *a sector by sector development strategy based on*

*(a)* *market research at home and abroad which will identify development and employment potential,*
*(b)* *our natural resources,*
*(c)* *the new advanced skills in our work-force and*
*(d)* *the achievement of increased market share in selected sectors and markets; and*

*(viii) the promotion of investment from overseas will give greater emphasis to the integration of such investments into the Irish economy*

*12. The Minister of State for Trade and Marketing is at present preparing a National Marketing Plan which will identify how Irish firms can be supported in securing increased market shares on home and overseas markets and which will pay special attention to marketing education and recruitment.*

*13. As part of the sector by sector approach, specific and realistic job opportunities will be identified for each sector.*

*Food Industry*

*14. The Government will give major priority to the development of the food industry where there are significant opportunities in certain segments for the creation of employment and wealth. The State agencies active in the promotion of the food industry are being co-ordinated under a special Ministerial Office for Food in order to make their activities more effective. A development plan for the industry, currently being drawn up, will be published in the coming months. An aggressive international marketing strategy will be developed designed to maximise exports of food products.*

The plan sought to bring the level of government borrowing to approximately 6 percent of GNP by 1990. Fine Gael, the opposition party in this period did not oppose the economic decisions of the government creating in effect a national government on economic policy. The results in the years 1988 and 1989 were remarkable as indicated by the growth in GNP, 3.5 in 1988 and 5.7 in 1989, the rate of inflation, 2.1 in 1988 and 3.5 in 1989 and, finally, the sharp drop in government borrowing as a percentage of GNP to 3.3 in 1988 and 4.6 in 1989. The only area not to move in a favorable direction was unemployment which remained high at 16.7 for 1988 and 18.5 for 1989. The sharp cuts in government spending of course produced unemployment as the government not only cut services but also workers. The unemployment rate should also be seen in light of a net emigration from Ireland of 32,000 in 1988 and 30,000 in 1989. The balance of payments in 1987, 1988, and 1989 produced a surplus. To be sure the government was the beneficiary of falling interest rates, from 14 percent in 1987 to 8 percent in 1989, and surging consumer demand.

Frances Cairncross had noted in *The Economist* of the Irish tax code: "Some ingenuity would be needed to devise a tax system with more weaknesses than the one the Irish have acquired" (Cairncross 1988: 6). The government had revised the tax codes in 1988 and the average tax rates were to fall 1.5 to 2.0 percent in 1989, yet revenues were higher than expected due to economic growth. In 1988 the government offered a one time tax amnesty which was estimated to produce £30 million and in fact produced £500 million. The effect on the necessity of the government to borrow was notable as mentioned above. Overall economic activity picked up based upon strong consumer spending and wage increases held to 2.5 percent, near or below the level of inflation in 1988 and 1989.

The *Programme for National Recovery* outlined a series of measures in agriculture, some perennial, such as eradicating bovine TB and rural development plans, others structural, to improve services to farmers. Agriculture was most affected in this period by the drop in interest rates and control of inflation which had come about after 1987. In the event gross agricultural output increased 1.3 percent in 1988 and 1.2 percent in 1989.

In 1988 the member states of the European Community passed the Single European Act. In this act the member states agreed to create an EC wide internal market through the removal of physical, technical, and fiscal barriers by 1992. The Commission recognized that the open market in Europe could exaggerate regional disparities and diminish the economic growth of undeveloped regions. Thus the Structural Funds were augmented with the goal of promoting economic and social cohesion in the community.

Ireland submitted a request for EC structural funds to be allocated from 1989 to 1993 of £3.35 billion to be matched by £3.6 billion from the government and £2.1 billion from the private sector. Consistent with the plans cited above, the *National Development Plan 1989-1993* of March 1989 makes projections on unemployment, inflation, GNP, and government borrowing. Unlike some of plans cited the projections appear to be in line with what the government had achieved and likely could achieve. The objectives of the plan include the creation of a program to increase jobs from 29,000 in 1988 to 35,000 by 1993; a growth in GNP of 3 percent per year or higher; and a drop in the government borrowing requirement to 3 percent of GNP by 1993. With respect to agriculture the *National Development Plan 1989-1993* recognized the structural issue noting "the preservation of the family farm is a central objective of Government policy. However, the sector is characterized by some major structural problems" (*National Development* 1989: 19). In 1987, the plan notes, only 10 percent of farms had incomes of over £15,000. A call for structural change as well as new economic activities in rural areas, such as small industry and tourism, were stressed as low income and rural unemployment were anticipated. While no projections of growth were made in the plan, economists were not optimistic. The Dublin consulting firm of DKM in 1988 projected average growth in gross output in agriculture from 1988 to 1992 at 0.1 percent and a drop in the agricultural labor force of 16 percent from 164,000 to 148,000 (DKM 1988: 11,26).

What follows is the assessment of the Irish government with respect to the economy for 1989 to 1993. It will be the task of others to judge whether these goals are fulfilled.

*Ireland*

*National Development Plan*

*1989 - 1993*

*1989*

*ECONOMIC AND SOCIAL ANALYSIS*

*PART 1 — OVERALL ANALYSIS*

*Introduction*

*1.1.1 The main features of the Irish economy which are relevant to the Community's aim of furthering economic and social cohesion, and to Ireland's capacity to share fully in the benefits of the completion of the internal market, are:*

- *low income and output levels;*
- *a population structure resulting in rapid growth in labour supply and a high dependency ratio;*
- *persistently weak labour demand, leading to unemployment and emigration;*
- *constraints imposed by budgetary imbalances and public sector indebtedness;*
- *high access costs resulting from the country's peripheral location;*
- *poorly developed infrastructure hindering development and adding to costs;*
- *a heavy dependence on agriculture both for employment and output;*
- *weaknesses in the industrial structure;*
- *low investment levels by Community standards and dependence on capital imports.*

*1.1.2 The features identified stem in a real, though not exclusive, way from Ireland's position on the periphery of Europe. The impact, in particular, of developments in the Community in trade, scale of production and innovation could produce structural consequences leading to an increase rather than a decrease in the disparities between central and peripheral regions in a Single Market context. On a theoretical basis, it is possible that the benefits of the Single Market could accrue predominantly to the central regions.*

*The Programme for National Recovery*

*1.1.31 While the analysis set out above is necessary to an understanding of the magnitude of the problems of the Irish economy, it must be seen in the light of recent experience, which demonstrates how decisive action based on a national consensus can achieve significant improvements.*

*1.1.32 A widespread recognition of the serious economic and social situation facing the country gave rise, in October 1987, to agreement between the Government and the Social Partners on a Programme for National Recovery covering the period up to the end of 1990.*

*1.1.33 The Programme provides for progress to be made in four broad areas;*

- *Creation of a fiscal, exchange-rate and monetary climate conducive to economic growth;*
- *movement towards greater equity and fairness in the tax system;*
- *diminishing or removing social inequities in our society; and*
- *intensification of practical measures to generate increased job opportunities on a sectoral basis.*

*1.1.34 The Programme has already created very favourable conditions for further recovery:*

- *inflation in 1988, at 2.1%, was below the Community average for the first time in many years;*
- *pay increases agreed throughout the economy at 2.5% annually for 1988 to 1990 underpin cost-competitiveness and provide a stable environment for planning by firms; there has been a marked improvement in industrial relations;*
- *domestic interest rates have fallen from 14% in early 1987 to 8% and are now less sensitive to upward movements abroad: this is a major boost to investment confidence;*
- *after stagnation or decline in recent years the economy has begun to grow again: over 1987 and 1988 an average growth in GNP of 3% was achieved in spite of action taken to redress the public finances;*
- *a balance of payments surplus was attained in 1987 and increased in 1988 to 3% of GNP;*
- *manufacturing output grew by 11 1/2% by volume and exports by about 10% in 1988.*

*DEVELOPMENT OBJECTIVES*

*PART 1 — ECONOMIC DEVELOPMENT STRATEGY*

*Introduction*

*2.1.1 The fundamental aim of this Plan is to advance the national and Community aspiration towards greater economic and social cohesion. To this end, the Plan seeks to:*

- *Prepare the economy to compete successfully in the internal market when it is completed in 1992;*
- *stimulate the growth needed to reduce unemployment, to raise productivity and to begin to increase per capita income towards average Community levels:*
- *improve further the state of the public finances; and accompany economic growth by a greater social dimension in our society.*

*2.1.2 To further these goals, the measures proposed in the Plan aim both to enhance the economy's output potential and to stimulate balanced and sustainable growth. The Plan deals in a meaningful and coherent way with the consequences of Ireland's position as a peripheral region in Europe and especially its implications in the context of an integrated European market.*

*2.1.3 Sustained progress in an open economy (or in a region of a larger economic unit) depends on the successful exploitation of comparative advantage, on expanding the capacity of the internationally-exposed sectors and on strengthening the competitiveness of the economy on all fronts.*

*2.1.4 A major policy effort will be needed if Ireland is to share fully in the benefits to the Community flowing from completion of the internal market, to turn to advantage the new opportunities it presents, to confront successfully the dangers it poses and to accomplish smoothly the adjustments in production structures which it will inevitably bring. In a Single Market context, an essential requirement for a peripheral and under-developed region is the development and intensification of competitive advantages. This involves not only the effective utilisation of the increased Structural Fund assistance — which is the primary focus of this Plan — but also, and even more fundamentally, the pursuit of supportive domestic policies on a broad front.*

*2.1.5 A concerted effort from national and Community policies will be needed to raise the economy onto a longer-term growth-path of convergence with the more prosperous European economies. This process, moreover, requires the active participation of the various social and economic interests. The objective of convergence relates both to employment opportunities and to income levels. In view of the onerous job-creation requirements over the period ahead, maximising the employment intensity of growth must receive equal priority with the acceleration of economic growth. The progress made thus far, both in creating the conditions for sustained economic growth and in ensuring that this reflected in job creation, shows that the consensus approach adopted in the Programme for National Recovery can greatly facilitate this task.*

*2.1.6 Underlying this Plan is a coherent approach to the development of the economy and the achievement of sustained growth in employment. It is recognised that the furtherance of wider national goals in ultimately dependent on the successful implementation of a sound economic strategy. Macroeconomic policy is addressing the fundamental requirements for expansion of the internationally-trading sectors, for investment in the economy generally and for the creation of self-sustaining jobs. By correcting the economic imbalances and maintaining a stable financial and cost environment, it is creating a basis for sound decisions. The thrust of microeconomic and sectoral policies is to facilitate and encourage exploitation of the economy's comparative advantages. A specific element of the strategy is to foster efficient working of markets, within accepted social conditions, in order that resources may be used to best effect and impediments to economic growth and job creation minimised. The Government's economic policy intentions for the coming years are developed in paragraphs 2.1.10 to 2.1.24.*

*2.1.7 The Government remain firmly committed to the broad economic strategy set out in the Programme for National Recovery, which has been progressively implemented over the past two years. This strategy will be developed and enlarged, in consultation with the parties to the Programme, in the light of evolving circumstances and emerging challenges.*

*2.1.8 The economic policy strategy of the Programme comprises the following inter-related elements:*

- *the pursuit of disciplined financial policies, directed at liberating the economy from the constraints of debt and debt-servicing and, thereby, at regenerating economic confidence;*
- *the firm linking of the exchange rate to the European Monetary System;*
- *the agreement to a level of pay settlements compatible with low inflation, improved cost-competitiveness and the need to underpin employment-creation;*
- *the reform of the taxation system, in pursuance of the objectives of stimulating economic growth, promoting employment and achieving greater equity; and*
- *the reorientation of sectoral development policies, with the aim of increasing their effectiveness and enhancing their contribution to the creation of viable jobs.*

*2.1.9 The implementation of this strategy has already registered major successes. The National Debt has been stabilised relative to GNP and interest rates have been reduced. Cost and price trends have moderated and there have been realistic improvements in take-home pay. Business confidence and investment have strengthened. Most significantly, there has been a recovery in activity and employment.*

*Domestic Policy Framework*

*2.1.10 At the macroeconomic level, the Government reaffirm their commitment to the maintenance of a fiscal, exchange-rate and cost climate conducive to sustained economic growth. This is of paramount importance in underpinning a better employment performance, in preparing the economy for the challenges of the enlarged internal market, and in ensuring the success of the sectoral development policies.*

*2.1.11 The thrust of medium-term fiscal policy will be determined, in the first instance, by the need to bring about a progressive decline in the ratio of debt, and the associated interest charges, to GNP. This is a key requirement for consolidating the improvement in interest rates and confidence. It is essential also in order to free resources for investment and development policies generally. It is indispensable if there is to be scope for further relief of taxation.*

*2.1.12 Accordingly, the Government intend to pursue a further reduction in Exchequer borrowing over the medium term. Specifically, fiscal policy will be conducted with a view to securing an Exchequer Borrowing requirement of the order of 3% of GNP in 1993. This would represent close to a halving of the overall rate of borrowing compared with the Budget target for 1989. Achievement of this fiscal objective will ensure a significant reduction in the ratio of National Debt to GNP over the coming years. Though the evolution of debt is influenced by factors other than the level of borrowing, a realistic expectation would be that, by the end of 1993, the National Debt might be reduced to about 120% of GNP, from 133% at end-1988. Realisation of this position should, given stable interest rates, reduce by about one-tenth the share of national resources absorbed by debt interest. In view of the investment needs of the economy, and of the requirement that domestic policies should be consistent with the economic objectives of the Plan, the curtailment of overall borrowing will be sought primarily on the current budget. This will require a strict discipline on public expenditure.*

*2.1.13 The Government consider that the level of personal and certain other forms of taxation, by adversely affecting the cost-competitiveness of the economy, is a major impediment to the achievement of sustained economic and employment growth. High personal taxes are a disincentive to enterprise, undermine work incentive and directly inhibit job creation. The reliefs in income tax introduced in recent years have played an important role in underpinning the moderation in pay settlements agreed under the Programme for National Recovery. The further easing of personal taxation will, therefore, be an important objective of fiscal policy over the medium term.*

*2.1.14 Any relief of taxation can only be sought, however, within the overriding requirement to reduce borrowing. While the resumption of economic growth will facilitate this task, the Government recognise that the simultaneous pursuit of continuing improvement in the budgetary position and reductions in personal taxation will require a strict discipline on public expenditure. Given the prior claim of debt-servicing costs and the need to give priority to programmes which contribute to the on-going development of the economy and the creation of self-sustaining employment, other expenditure will have to be rigorously contained, while ensuring that particular social and socio-economic needs continue to be met.*

*2.1.15 The income tax reduction introduced in recent years have been made possible not only by reductions in public expenditure but also by some broadening of the tax base. This has been brought about by some restriction of special reliefs and deductions and by more rigorous enforcement and improved collection including the introduction of self-assessment arrangements for the self-employed. In 1988 and 1989, the Government have made important changes in the taxation of corporate income with similar intent and they have indicated their intention to review the position in the 1990 Budget. The reforms introduced, both in relation to the tax base and the reduction of marginal rates, represent a significant movement towards a tax structure more neutral in its economic impact. The intention is to press forward with their approach, including widening the tax base, in the years ahead. As part of this it will be necessary to place a continuing emphasis on critically examining the role of various reliefs, exemptions and incentives.*

*2.1.16 In approaching the reform of the tax structure, the Government must take into account constraints on their freedom of maneuver in certain areas of taxation. While final decisions in regard to fiscal harmonisation in the Community have yet to be taken, the proposals tabled would entail major revenue losses. Moreover, if Ireland is to be able to compete effectively for internationally-mobile investment, which has made an important contribution to developing and strengthening the economy's productive base, it is necessary to retain a fiscal advantage over the more-favoured regions.*

*2.1.17 The Government recognise that, in addition to the pursuit of responsible and consistent macroeconomic policies, it is necessary at the microeconomic level to ensure that:*

- *public policies across the spectrum are consistent with allocative efficiency and, in particular, with the requirement of a more labour-intensive pattern of economic growth; and*
- *the economic system's capacity to function efficiently and to adapt to changing requirements is not inhibited by inappropriate regulatory frame-works or administrative structures.*

*2.1.18 The changes in the structure of taxation effected over recent years and the evolution to be pursued over the medium term (subject to broad budgetary requirements and other constraints) are consistent with the need to improve the competitiveness of the economy and to secure a more appropriate balance between labour and capital in the productive process.*

*2.1.19 A fundamental reorientation of industrial development strategy and policies has been set in train, with a greater emphasis on overcoming the crucial obstacles to industrial progress, on developing businesses' capacity for self-sustaining growth and on strengthening linkages between foreign investment projects and the domestic economy. The Government will critically examine the progress of this strategy with particular reference to the increased value-added and sustained employment achieved relative to the public resources committed.*

*2.1.20 The Government are also concerned to extend and develop competition in the economy, insofar as the freer play of competitive forces offers the prospect of efficiency gains and consequent cost benefits, and is not incompatible with wider social and economic objectives. A significant liberalisation of the exchange control regime has already been effected and it is the Government's intention to eliminate by end-1992 all controls on capital movements vis-à-vis other Member States. In relation to the financial services sector, legislative proposals which will have the effect of intensifying competition among the various institutions are either under consideration by the legislature or are in preparation. The progressive liberalisation of air access routes in the past few years has produced significant benefits to travellers, stimulated tourism and reduced business costs. The Government propose to update the legislation relating to internal transport services, with a view to liberalising access to road passenger transport.*

*2.1.21 The Government recognise that the State enterprises have an important role to play in the future development of the economy. It has, nevertheless, made clear that these enterprises will increasingly have to operate in a more competitive context and according to commercial criteria. Major restructuring of the enterprises is taking place, leading to improvements in efficiency and, in general, to better financial performance.*

*2.1.22 If the rate of job creation is to be accelerated significantly, a key requirement is the availability of a workforce equipped with the skills and aptitudes needed by enterprises. Chapter 3, Part 2, below outlines the Government's strategy for meeting the manpower requirements of economic development and of structural adjustment.*

*2.1.23 If the employment intensity of output is to be maximised, so that economic growth may lead to a commensurate increase in job opportunities, the market for labour must function efficiently. The long-term persistence of high unemployment in Ireland is largely attributable to inadequate output growth and to structural characteristics of the economy. The rapidity of structural change in the period since accession to the Community has tended to increase pressures in this regard. In common with other Member States, employment in Ireland has not been sufficiently responsive to economic growth. This could point to a need for some greater flexibility in the labour market, having regard to the pressing need to maximise the job-creating potential of output growth in all sectors of the economy. Relative to other Member States, the labour market in Ireland is not particularly encumbered by regulation. Yet care must be taken to maintain an appropriate balance in future developments between safeguarding the legitimate concerns of employees and ensuring that such measures do not create inflexibility in the labour market and hamper the creation of new jobs.*

*2.1.24 The Government have been conscious of the existence of areas of interaction between the social security and taxation systems which might bend to create "poverty traps" and inhibit the smooth operation of the labour market. Recent developments in regard to compensation of the unemployed particularly the concentration of welfare improvements on those in greatest need, and the alleviation of taxation on low incomes are mitigating the possibility of such overlaps. This trend can be reinforced by the targeting of welfare provision according to need and the reduction of personal taxation both of which are priority objectives of Government.*

*Community Policy Dimension*

*2.1.25 As regards the role of the Community and its policies, there are certain broad requirements:*

- *the pursuit of a common macroeconomic strategy which ensures that the European economy expands at a rate in line with potential and that the benefits of completion of the Single Market are fully realised; and*

— *the implementation of the internal market programme, and the development of the common policies generally, in a manner which accords with the spirit of the Single European Act and in particular with its commitment to furthering economic and social cohesion.*

*2.1.26 The fulfillment of the objectives of this Plan is crucially dependent on these conditions. The possibility of accelerated growth in the Irish economy, on a balanced and sustainable basis, could be seriously circumscribed if activity in the EC economy were to lose momentum, given that three-quarters of Ireland's exports find a market in partner countries.*

*2.1.27 The deployment of the additional resources made available through the increase in the Community's Structural Funds will, of course, make a major contribution to sustained economic growth. The measures put forward in this Plan will help to modernise and enhance economic infrastructure and to strengthen the overall competitiveness of the economy, as well as supporting the active sectoral development strategies being pursued by the Government.*

The history of the record of government policy to develop the economy of Ireland is certainly mixed. Some believe that the economic potential of Ireland has remained unrealized due to the government's proclivity to misread conditions, offer maladroit solutions, and to display a lack of political will (Lee 1989: 511-40). Others point out that Ireland has done about the best that it could under the circumstances and better than one might expect given the size of the country, lack of natural resources, and the persistent political turmoil (Kennedy, Giblin, and McHugh 1988). Does an analysis of the documents provide evidence to support one view or the other?

Three themes recur throughout that can illuminate the question. They include:

- The vulnerability of the Irish economy to external economic conditions
- The strategy of using agriculture as the key to growth
- The role of government in generating economic growth

There is, of course, no independent Irish economic policy from 1800 to 1922. In this respect the union of Great Britain and Ireland puts the development of Ireland in the hands of laissez-faire British liberals who are managing a British industrial economy. The British were groping for a policy that would trigger Irish development. Yet, however well intentioned, theoretically consistent, effectual or ineffectual their policies were, they were not made by the Irish.

The Commonwealth linkage with Britain after the creation of the Free State, and the political confrontation among the Irish over accepting the treaty, led to the 1932-1938 "Economic War." As a war it was no contest and the Irish economy suffered because Britain was so critical a trading partner. Though the "Economic War" may have been a self-inflicted wound, it occurred as a result of the nonpayment of the annuities owed to the U. K. for land that the Irish had purchased at the end of the nineteenth century.

The advent of World War II in 1939 stopped the development of the Irish economy. Despite Ireland's neutrality, the Irish could no more escape the effects of the war than they could influence its outcome. The postwar link to Britain as the trading partner and as a member of the Sterling Group tied Ireland's fate to the British pound despite the Republic of Ireland Act of 1949 which severed all Commonwealth ties to the U. K.

In considering entry into the European community Ireland was not free to enter without Great Britain for Ireland could not risk imposing a 17 percent tariff wall between the two countries. Due to the rejection of Britain's application by France, Irish entry was postponed until the U. K. was accepted in 1973. The Irish economy's vulnerability to the oil shocks of 1973 and 1979 indicates the degree to which planning in Dublin could be toppled not only by decisions in London but also in Riyadh or Baghdad.

Finally, periods of growth and recession in Europe are magnified in their impact on Ireland with its small market and dependence upon external demand for its products. EC institutional change also reveals the degree to which within the European Community Ireland's economy was vulnerable to decisions in Brussels. The 1973 and 1978 changes in the Fonds Europeen d'Orientation et Garantie Agricoles (FEOGA) supports significantly changed the income of Irish farmers, first up, and then down. The 1992 Single European market opens up "threats wherever manufacturing in Ireland is vulnerable to competition based upon scale economies, or to intensified competition based upon innovation" (NESC #88,1989: 528). Domestic macroeconomic policy in Ireland did not from 1922 to 1959 have a great degree of latitude in light of the dependence on the U. K. and from 1973 to 1989 "did not take sufficient account of the greatly increased interdependence of Ireland and other EC economies" (NESC #88,1989: 525).

Secondly, the central role of agriculture cannot be denied. The search for the key to agricultural productivity, the productions of crops for export, and the accumulation of capital for investment, preoccupies decision makers. The British policy in the nineteenth century emphasized the clearing of land, the draining of bogs, and the improvement of agricultural education. The search for a policy that would open up land for cultivation was misguided to the degree that a market to sell and distribute agricultural surplus was absent. Yet the echoes of the British policies are seen in the Irish documents of 1982, 1984, and even 1989 in the area of land reclamation and agricultural education.

The free market would generate the capital investment to develop Irish agriculture, concluded the British liberals. A protected market was necessary to guarantee the sale of products at set prices, concluded the Irish nationalists after 1932. The effects in either case were stymied by the structural arrangements of Irish land ownership though the particular arrangements were different. The protection of agriculture was preserved after the World War II and it was agricultural exports, to Britain of course, that were seen as the stimulus to production. Agricultural growth proved unable to undergird the economic development of Ireland, was unable to substantially increase production, was unable to employ sufficient numbers, and was unable to provide sufficient capital accumulation.

By 1964 the Irish government had ceased to see agriculture as the engine of development and were turning to industry. The surge in foreign investment in manufacturing seemed to be taking over as the stimulus to job creation and wealth creation. From the mid-sixties forward the documents shift their focus to agricultural efficiency and competitiveness as it was clear, from at least 1955, that it was not a sector of increasing employment. In fact the repetition of concerns; drainage, animal disease, agricultural expertise, increased capital investment in technology, and improved marketing, mark all the documents until the 1980s when the structural issue is more visibly addressed.

The rise of foreign investment in industry during the 1960s and 1970s was booming, the economy was growing, and the answer to triggering growth seemed clear. When the Telesis Report (published as NESC #64) challenged not only the success in creating jobs through foreign investment but questioned the very strategy itself the Irish government took heed. In 1984 the recommendation that indigenous industry was the stimulus to growth was adopted and there was a shift in resource allocation. It has been a mere twenty-five years since the Irish abandoned agriculture as the center of Irish economic growth. The reliance on foreign investment industries, and now indigenous industries, is a challenge in light of the deficiencies in Irish entrepreneurial innovation, managerial and marketing skills, lack of research and development, and the increasing competition from EC firms after 1992.

The role of the government in generating economic growth reveals several different approaches as governments have come to reject the classic laissez- faire approach and accept the Keynesian demand management approach. In the era of the classical laissez-faire approach, the nineteenth-century British policy makers were trying to create the conditions, as they saw them, for British capital to flow into Ireland. The lack of political turmoil was one goal, the others were increasing arable land and improving infrastructure. Though committed to laissez-faire the various commissions noted that in the case of Ireland perhaps direct government action to provide the conditions for growth was necessary. Industrial development took place in Belfast, the land issue in the rest of Ireland was solved by emigration after the famine and the sale of the land to the tenant farmers.

When the Free State took power they were neither capable of extensive government action in the economy nor disposed to do so ideologically. The question of stability was predominant after the years of the Anglo-Irish War and the Civil War. Moreover, they were in favor of free trade and private enterprise as the mainspring of growth.

When in 1932 the new government came to power it was in the context of seeing the period 1922-1932 as a failure. Thus the government adopted protectionism to develop Irish industry and employment in a drive for self-sufficiency. The increasing role of government in the economy might be termed statist as it certainly was not socialist. The rise of the semi-state bodies to fulfill the role that private enterprise either could not or would not, produced an extensive government participation in the economy and some industrial growth. Moreover the extension of the semi-state bodies was accompanied by an increase in regulation and controls. At the same time an "anti-materialist" ideology was advanced as appropriate to the Irish character and nation. This mixture of government activity, protectionism, and anti-materialism, as noted in the IBEC report, put the government in an extended economic role not as a manager of development but rather as a partial substitute for the private sector. This situation continued more or less the same after the war.

In the 1950s the government bewitched by the balance of payments ledger adopted policies that constricted growth. It is only in 1959 in *Economic Development* that the Irish government accepts the idea that protectionism no longer fostered growth in either industry or agriculture, that the government's capital programme must be a prod to productive enterprise, and that foreign investment could provide industrial growth and employment. While taking responsibility for incentive planning the government did not choose privatization and diminish its role in the semi-state bodies. In fact more government organizations were created to stimulate and guide economic growth. This reached a level that prompted the Telesis Report to note that economic development efforts "must be reorganized to emphasize the building of structurally strong Irish companies rather than strong agencies to assist weak companies" (NESC #64, 1982: 232).

The documents reveal an increasing role by government in planning, assessment, and policy directed at economic development. The policies adopted were not always appropriate and were frequently too often based on the short term. Moreover macroeconomic development policy did not adequately deal with structural constraints on Irish economic growth.

But whether the policies produced the growth aspirations or not, the government has become a major player in setting the agenda, providing the capital and organizational means, and assessing the results. As the NESC noted of Ireland's role in the EC: "membership in the community does not reduce the need for clear Irish policy aims and methods" (NESC #88,1989: 526).

In urging that Ireland be concerned about the pattern of economic development as well as its rate, Kennedy, Giblin, and McHugh note "there can be no certainty that Ireland will take hold of its future in the manner suggested" (Kennedy, Giblin, and McHugh 1988: 268). But we can conclude with their assessment of the Irish government's pursuit of its economic aspirations:

> The disappointments as well as the achievements of the past have produced a greater awareness of economic realities. Provided Ireland can recognize its past failings, and begin to learn to overcome them, then its potential for future development is considerable. (Kennedy, Giblin, and McHugh 1988: 268)

# Statistical Appendix

Tables 1 and 2 relate to pages 154 and 184 in Chapter 5. Tables 3 to 7 provide data on selected demographic and economic variables. Many of the secondary works listed in the Bibliography contain more detailed tables. In addition, the Central Statistical Office publishes the annual *Statistical Abstract*.

See Kirwan & McGilvray's *Irish Economic Statistics* for a "guide to the sources of Irish economic statistics and their methods of presentation and analysis."

Table 1
Projected and Actual Economic Indicators, 1979-1981

| | 1979 | | 1980 | | 1981 | |
|---|---|---|---|---|---|---|
| | Projected | Actual | Projected | Actual | Projected | Actual |
| Percent of Workforce Unemployed | 7.5 | 8.7 | 7 | 7 | 5 | 10 |
| Inflation | 5 | 13.8 | 5 | 18.2 | 5 | 20.4 |
| Growth in GNP | 7 | 3.5 | 7 | 2.2 | 5 | 0.6 |
| Government Borrowing as a % of GNP | 10.5 | 13.2 | 8 | 13.5 | 7 | 15.9 |

Source: adapted from data in the three white papers noted in the text and *OECD Economic Survey: Ireland 1988/89*, *Ireland in the European Community*, NESC, 1989.

Table 2
Projected and Actual Economic Indicators, 1983-1987

| | 1983 | | | 1984 | | | 1985 | | | 1986 | | | 1987 | | |
|---|---|---|---|---|---|---|---|---|---|---|---|---|---|---|---|
| | TWF | BOR | Actual | TWF | BOR | Actual | TWF | BOR | Actual | TWF | BOR | Actual | TWF | BOR | Actual |
| Unemployment % | 13.9 | | 14.0 | 14.7 | | 15.6 | 15.7 | 16.2 | 17.3 | 15.4 | 15.9 | 17.4 | 15.0 | 15.9 | 17.7 |
| Inflation | 10.11 | | 11.0 | 8.9 | | 7.0 | 8.9 | 7.2 | 5.6 | 8.9 | 6.9 | 7.3 | 7.0 | 6.1 | 2.5 |
| GNP growth | 3.5 | | -1.6 | 3.5 | | 2.0 | 3.5 | 10.0 | -0.1 | 3.5 | 10.0 | -1.3 | 3.5 | 10.0 | 4.8 |
| Government Borrowing % of GNP | 1.3 | | 13.7 | 10.5 | | 12.3 | 8.5 | 12 | 12.9 | 6 | 11 | 12.9 | 5 | 6 | 10 |

Source: TWF *(The Way Forward)*, BOR *(Building on Reality)*, *Ireland OECD Survey 1988/89* and *Ireland in the European Community*, (NESC, 1989).

Table 3
Population of Ireland
1926-1989

| Year | Total Persons (Millions) |
| --- | --- |
| 1926 | 2.97 |
| 1936 | 2.97 |
| 1946 | 2.96 |
| 1951 | 2.96 |
| 1961 | 2.82 |
| 1966 | 2.89 |
| 1971 | 2.98 |
| 1979 | 3.37 |
| 1981 | 3.44 |
| 1986 | 3.54 |
| 1989 (est.) | 3.52 |
| 1990 (est.) | 3.50 |

Source: *Statistical Abstract, 1990*, pp. 3 and 26.

Table 4
Average Annual Growth Rates of Real Product,
Various Periods, 1960-1986

| | 1960-73 | 1973-9 | 1979-86 |
| --- | --- | --- | --- |
| | % | % | % |
| Gross Domestic Product (GDP) | 4.4 | 4.1 | 1.5 |
| Gross National Product (GNP) | 4.3 | 3.4 | -0.3 |

Source: Kennedy, Giblin and McHugh, *The Economic Development of Ireland in the Twentieth Century*, p. 82.

Table 5
The Irish Labor Force, 1961-1989

| Year | Labor Force | Numbers at Work | Unemployed | Unemployment Rate |
|---|---|---|---|---|
| 1961 | 1,076 | 1,017 | 59 | 5.5 |
| 1971 | 1,110 | 1,049 | 61 | 5.5 |
| 1972 | 1,121 | 1,052 | 69 | 6.2 |
| 1973 | 1,131 | 1,067 | 64 | 5.7 |
| 1974 | 1,143 | 1,082 | 61 | 5.3 |
| 1975 | 1,157 | 1,073 | 84 | 7.3 |
| 1976 | 1,169 | 1,064 | 105 | 9.0 |
| 1977 | 1,188 | 1,083 | 105 | 8.8 |
| 1978 | 1,209 | 1,110 | 99 | 8.2 |
| 1979 | 1,233 | 1,145 | 88 | 7.1 |
| 1980 | 1,247 | 1,156 | 91 | 7.3 |
| 1981 | 1,272 | 1,146 | 126 | 9.9 |
| 1982 | 1,296 | 1,148 | 148 | 11.4 |
| 1983 | 1,309 | 1,125 | 184 | 14.1 |
| 1984 | 1,314 | 1,110 | 204 | 15.5 |
| 1985 | 1,305 | 1,079 | 226 | 17.3 |
| 1986 | 1,308 | 1,081 | 227 | 17.4 |
| 1987 | 1,312 | 1,080 | 232 | 17.7 |
| 1988 | 1,310 | 1,091 | 219 | 16.7 |
| 1989 | 1,292 | 1,090 | 202 | 15.6 |

Source: Central Statistics Office, *Statistical Abstracts.*

Table 6
Composition of Employment in Ireland, 1946-1989

Percentage of Total, by Sector

| Year | Agriculture | Industry | Service |
|---|---|---|---|
| 1946 | 45.7 | 15.0 | 39.3 |
| 1951 | 40.3 | 19.3 | 40.4 |
| 1956 | 36.7 | 28.3 | 35.0 |
| 1966 | 30.9 | 35.3 | 33.8 |
| 1971 | 25.8 | 29.0 | 45.2 |
| 1981 | 16.6 | 32.2 | 51.2 |
| 1986 | 15.5 | 28.4 | 56.1 |
| 1989 | 15.0 | 28.1 | 56.9 |

Source: Compiled from *Statistical Abstracts*.

Table 7
Consumer Price Index (All Items), 1969-1989
(Mid-November 1968=100)

| Year | Index | Computed Percentage Changes |
|---|---|---|
| 1969 | 105.7 | --- |
| 1970 | 114.4 | 8.3 |
| 1971 | 124.6 | 9.0 |
| 1972 | 135.4 | 8.7 |
| 1973 | 150.8 | 11.4 |
| 1974 | 176.4 | 17.0 |
| 1975 | 213.2 | 20.9 |
| 1976 | 251.6 | 18.1 |
| 1977 | 285.9 | 13.7 |
| 1978 | 307.7 | 7.7 |
| 1979 | 348.8 | 13.3 |
| 1980 | 411.9 | 18.3 |
| 1981 | 496.0 | 20.5 |
| 1982 | 580.9 | 17.2 |
| 1983 | 641.8 | 10.5 |
| 1984 | 696.9 | 8.6 |
| 1985 | 734.8 | 5.5 |
| 1986 | 762.8 | 3.9 |
| 1987 | 786.8 | 3.2 |
| 1988 | 803.6 | 2.2 |
| 1989 | 836.4 | 4.1 |

Source: *Statistical Bulletin*, March 1990, p.28

# Bibliography

## BOOKS AND ARTICLES


Bew, P., and H. Patterson. *Sean Lemass and the Making of Modern Ireland*. Dublin: Gill and Macmillan, 1982.

Black, R. D. Collison. *Economic Thought and the Irish Question: 1817-1870*. Cambridge: Cambridge University Press, 1960.

Blackwell, John. "Government, Economy, Society." In *Unequal Achievement*, edited by Frank Litton, 43-57. Dublin: Institute of Public Administration, 1982.

Bolton, Geoffrey C. "Some British Reactions to the Irish Act of Union." *Economic History Review* (August 1965): 367-375.

______. *The Passing of the Irish Act of Union: A Study in Parliamentary Politics*. London: Oxford University Press, 1966.

Boylan, Tom A., and Tadgh P. Foley. "John Elliot Cairnes, John Stuart Mill and Ireland: Some Problems for Political Economy." In *Economists and the Irish Economy from the Eighteenth Century to the Present Day*, edited by Antoin E. Murphy, 96-119. Dublin: Irish Academy Press, 1984.

Bristow, J. A., and A. A. Tait, eds. *Economic Policy in Ireland*. Dublin: Institute of Public Administration. 1968.

Butler, H.D. *The Irish Free State: An Economic Survey*. Washington, D.C.: Government Printing Office, 1928.

Cairncross, Frances. "Ireland Survey." *The Economist* (January 16 1988): 1-26.

Chubb, Basil, and Patrick Lynch, eds. *Economic Development and Planning*. Dublin: Institute of Public Administration, 1969.

Connell, K. H. *The Population of Ireland 1750-1845*. Oxford: Oxford University Press, 1950.

Crotty, Raymond. *Irish Agricultural Production*. Cork: Cork University Press, 1966.

______. *Ireland in Crisis: A Study in Capitalist Colonial Underdevelopment*. Dingle: Brandon, 1986.

Cullen, Louis M. *The Formation of the Irish Economy*. Cork: Mercier Press 1968.

______,(ed). *An Economic History of Ireland Since 1660*. London: Batsford, 1972.

Cullen, Louis M., and T. C. Smout, eds. *Comparative Aspects of Scottish and Irish Economic and Social History 1600-1900*. Edinburgh: John Donald, 1978.

Daly, Mary E. *Social and Economic History of Ireland Since 1800*. Dublin: The Educational Company, 1981.

______. *The Famine in Ireland.* Dublin: Dublin Historical Association, 1986.

Dickson, David. "Aspects of the Rise and Decline of the Irish Cotton Industry." In *Comparative Aspects of Scottish and Irish Economic and Social History 1600-1900*, edited by L. M. Cullen and T. C. Smout, 100-115. Edinburgh: John Donald, 1978.

Dinan, Desmond. "After the 'Emergency.' Ireland in the Post-War World 1945-1950." *Eire-Ireland* (Fall 1989): 85-103.

DKM. *The Irish Economy: Medium Term Forecast 1988-1992.* Dublin, 1988.

Donaldson, L. *Development and Planning in Ireland.* New York and London: Fredrick A. Praeger, 1966.

Dowling, B. R., and J. Durkin, eds. *Irish Economic Policy: A Review of Major Issues.* Dublin: Economic and Social Research Institute, 1978.

Fanning, Ronan. "Economists and Governments: Ireland 1922-52." In *Economists and the Irish Economy from the Eighteenth Century to the Present Day*, edited by Antoin E. Murphy, 138-156. Dublin: Irish Academic Press, 1984.

______. "The Genesis of *Economic Development.*" In *Planning Ireland's Future: the Legacy of T.K. Whitaker*, edited by John F. McCarthy, 74-111. Dublin: Glendale Press, 1990.

______. *The Irish Department of Finance 1922-58.* Dublin: Institute of Public Relations, 1978.

Finnegan, Richard B. *Ireland: The Challenge of Conflict and Change.* Boulder: Westview, 1983.

FitzGerald, Garret. *Planning in Ireland.* Dublin and London: Institutue of Public Administration, and Political and Economic Planning, 1968.

Glass, D. V., and Taylor, P. A. M. *Population and Emigration.* Dublin: Irish University Press, 1976.

Johnson, D. *The Interwar Economy in Ireland.* Dublin: Economic and Social History Society of Ireland, 1985.

Kennedy, D., and A. Pender, eds. *Prosperity and Policy: Ireland in the 1990s.* Dublin: Institute of Public Administration, 1990.

Kennedy, K. A. *Ireland in Transition: Economic and Social Change Since 1960.* Cork and Dublin: Mercier Press, 1986.

Kennedy, K. A. *Productivity and Industrial Growth: The Irish Experience.* Oxford: Claredndon Press, 1971.

Kennedy, Kieran A., and Brendan R. Dowling. *Economic Growth in Ireland: the Experience Since 1947.* Dublin: Gill and Macmillan, 1975.

Kennedy, Kieran A., Thomas Giblin, and Deirdre McHugh. *The Economic Development of Ireland in the Twentieth Century.* London and New York: Routledge, 1988.

Kennedy, L., and P. Ollerenshaw, eds. *An Economic History of Ulster 1820-1939.* Manchester University Press, 1985.

Kennedy, Liam. *The Modern Industrialization of Ireland, 1940-1988.* Dublin: Economic and Social History Society of Ireland, 1989.

Kennedy, R. E. *The Irish: Emigration, Marriage and Fertility.* Berkeley: University of California Press, 1973.

Lee, J. J. *Ireland 1912-1985: Politics and Society.* Cambridge: Cambridge University Press, 1989.

Lyons, F. S. L. *Ireland Since the Famine.* Dublin: Fontana, 1972.

Lyons, P. M. "The Distribution of Personal Wealth in Ireland." In *Ireland: Some Problems of a Developing Economy*, edited by A. A. Tate and J. A. Bristow, 159-185. Dublin: Gill and Macmillan; New York: Barnes and Noble, 1972.

McAleese, Dermot. "Ireland in the World Economy." In *Ireland in Transition*, edited by Kieran A. Kennedy, 19-30. Cork and Dublin: Mercier, 1986.

McCarthy, John F. "Ireland's Turnabout: Whitaker and the 1958 Plan for Economic Development." In *Planning Ireland's Future*, edited by John F. McCarthy, 11-73. Dublin: Glendale Press, 1990.

Malcomson, A. P. W. *John Foster: The Politics of the Anglo-Irish Ascendancy*. Oxford: Oxford University Press, 1978.

Meenan, James. *The Irish Economy Since 1922*. Liverpool: Liverpool University Press, 1970.

Mokyr, Joel. "Malthusian Models and Irish History." *Journal of Economic History* (March 1980): 159-166.

______. *Why Ireland Starved: A Quantitative and Analytical History of the Irish Economy, 1800-1850*. London: Allen and Unwin, 1983.

O'Grada, Cormac. *Ireland Before and After the Famine*. Manchester: Manchester University Press, 1988.

O'Hagan, John, ed. *The Economy of Ireland: Policy and Performance*, 5th edition. Dublin: Irish Management Institute, 1987.

O'Malley, E. J. *Industrial Policy and Development: A Survey of Literature from the Early 1960s*. Dublin: National Economic and Social Council Report no. 56, Stationery Office, 1980.

______. *Industry and Economic Development: The Challenge for the Latecomer*. Dublin: Gill and Macmillan, 1989.

Robson, John M., ed. *Essays on England, Ireland and the Empire by John Stuart Mill*. Toronto: University of Toronto Press, 1982.

Sexton, J. J. "Employment, Unemployment and Emigration." In *Ireland in Transition*, edited by Kieran A. Kennedy, 31-39. Cork and Dublin: Mercier, 1986.

Solow, Barbara. *The Land Question and the Irish Economy, 1870-1903*. Cambridge: Harvard University Press, 1971.

Vaughan, W. E. *Landlords and Tenants in Ireland, 1848-1904*. Dublin: The Economic and Social History Society of Ireland, 1984.

Walsh, Brendan M. "Economic Growth and Development, 1945-1970." In *Ireland 1945-1970*, edited by J. J. Lee, 27-37. Dublin: Gill and Macmillan, 1979.

Whelan, Bernadette. "The European Recovery Program (the Marshall Plan) and Ireland: Summary and Assessment." *Eire-Ireland* (Fall 1989): 78-84.

Whitaker, T. K. "Economic Development 1958-1985." In *Ireland in Transition*, edited by Kieran A. Kennedy, 10-18. Cork and Dublin: Mercier, 1986.

______. *Interests*. Dublin: Institute of Public Administration, 1983.

## SELECTED NATIONAL ECONOMIC AND SOCIAL COUNCIL PUBLICATIONS

*Comments on Economic and Social Development 1976-1980*, 1977.

*Policies to Accelerate Agricultural Development*, 1978.

*Comments on Development for Full Employment*, 1978.

*Tourism Policy*, 1980.

*Economic and Social Policy 1980-83: Aims and Recommendations*, 1980.

*Industrial Policy and Development: A Survey of Literature from the Early 1960s to Present*, 1981.

*Economic and Social Policy 1981: Aims and Recommendations*, 1981.

*A Review of Industrial Policy*, 1982.

*Policies for Industrial Development: Conclusions and Recommendations*, 1982.

*Economic and Social Policy 1982: Aims and Recommendations*, 1983.

*Irish Energy Policy*, 1984.

*Economic and Social Policy Assessment*, 1985.

*Manpower Policy in Ireland*, 1986.

*A Strategy for Development 1986-1990*, 1987.

*Ireland in the European Community: Performance, Prospects and Strategies*, 1989.

*A Strategy for the Nineties*, 1990.

## SELECTED DOCUMENTS: BRITISH PARLIAMENTARY PAPERS

*A Bill for the Union of Great Britain and Ireland*, 1800.

*Report from the Select Committee on the Employment of the Poor in Ireland*, 1823.

*Reports and Minutes of Evidence from the Select Committee on Emigration from the United Kingdom*, 1826-1827.

*First Report of the Commissioners of Public Works, Ireland*, 1832.

*Second Report of the Commissioners of Public Works, Ireland*, 1835.

*First Annual Report of the Commission on Drainage of Land, and Improvement of Navigation and Water Power*, 1843.

*Commissioners Report on the Working of the Landlord and Tenant (Ireland) Act, 1870*, 1881.

*Report from the Select Committee on Industries (Ireland)*, 1884-1885.

*Reports of the Royal Commission on the Financial Relations between Great Britain and Ireland*, 1896.

## IRISH OFFICIAL PUBLICATIONS EXCERPTED

*Final Report of the Commission on Agriculture*, 1922.

*Final Report of the Fiscal Inquiry Committee*, 1923.

*Shannon Scheme*, 1924.

*Final Reports of the Banking Commission*, 1926.

*Reports on Agricultural Policy*, 1945.

*The European Recovery Programme: Ireland's Long Term Programme (1949-1953)*, 1948.

*Industrial Potentials of Ireland: An Appraisal*, 1952.

*Committee of Inquiry into Taxation on Industry Report*, 1953.

*Commission on Emigration and Other Population Problems 1948-1954 Reports*, 1954.

*Capital Investment Advisory Committee Third Report*, 1958.

*Economic Development*, 1958.

*Programme for Economic Expansion*, 1958.

*Second Programme for Economic Expansion Part I*, 1963.

*Second Programme for Economic Expansion Part II*, 1964.

*Committee on Industrial Organization: A Synthesis of Reports*, 1964.

*Committee on Industrial Organization: Final Report*, 1965.

*Third Programme: Economic and Social Development*, 1969-72.

*Membership of the European Communities*, 1970.

*A National Partnership*, 1974.

*National Development 1977-1980*, 1978.

*The Way Forward*, 1982.

*Building on Reality: A Summary*, 1984.

*Industrial Policy*, 1984.

*Programme for National Recovery*, 1987.

*National Development Plan 1989-1993*, 1989.

## OTHER SELECTED IRISH OFFICIAL PUBLICATIONS

*Report of a Committee of Inquiry*, 1938. (The effects of banking and state credit on industry and agriculture.)

*Report of the Committee on Vocational Organization*, 1944.

*On the Present State and Methods of Improvement of Irish Land*, 1948.

*Report of the Committee on Youth Employment*, 1952.

*Report of a Commmittee of Inquiry*, 1956. (The effects of taxes on industrial production.)

*Report of the Capital Investment Advisory Committee*, 1957.

*Second Report of the Capital Investment Advisory Committee*, 1957.

*Closing the Gap*, 1964. (The differences between incomes and productivity.)

*White Paper on Manpower Policy*, 1965.

*Arrangements for Planning at Industry Level*, 1966.

*Review of Incentives for Industry in Ireland*, 1967. (A report for the Industrial Development Authority by Arthur D. Little Inc.)

*Second Programme for Economic Expansion: Review of Progress 1964-67*, 1968.

*Survey of Grant Aided Industry*, 1968.

*Industrial Incentives*, 1974.

*Development for Full Employment*, 1978.

*IDA Industrial Plan 1977-80*, 1978.

*IDA Industrial Plan 1978-82*, 1979.

*Programme for National Development 1978-81*, 1980.

*Investment and National Development 1979-1983*, 1980.

*Four Year Plan for Agriculture*, 1984.

*White Paper on Manpower Policy*, 1986.

*Programme for Economic and Social Progress*, 1991.

# Index

Act of Union, 4-5
Adaptation Councils, 98
Adaptation to free trade, 75, 98, 108, 124
Agricultural Credit Corporation, 39, 41, 42, 71, 100, 136
Agriculture, 16, 45-52; Commission on Agriculture (1922), 17, 18-22; credit, 19, 21, 34, 39, 71, 92, 93; Department of, 49; education, 18, 20, 46, 205; employment, 42, 68, 94, 109-10, 140, 177, 184, 187, 196, 206; exports, 19, 20, 46, 89, 117, 123, 125, 130; exports to the United Kingdom, 12, 35, 41, 53, 206; marketing, 46, 73; output, 4, 21, 50, 56, 57, 65, 73, 95, 104; 1920s, 17, 39; 1930s, 41; 1940s, 42, 45, 51, 85; 1960s, 109; 1970s, 136, 141, 148, 155, 156; 1980s, 156, 185, 195, 196; performance, 3, 5, 8, 10, 11, 12, 47; policy, 46-48, 49, 94, 136, 141, 185, 205-7; prices, 10, 16, 19, 40, 47, 117, 123, 135, 136; productivity, 8, 46, 53, 178, 206; *Report of the Commission on Agriculture* (1922), 17, 18-22; *Reports on Agricultural Policy* (1945), 46-48; role in economy, 1, 11, 19, 30, 31, 40, 42, 89, 125; State assistance to, 20, 21, 22, 24, 38, 118; structure, 9; unemployment, 65, 68, 177
Anglo-Irish Free Trade Area Agreement (1965), 119, 121, 122

Balance of payments, 77, 84-85, 92, 115, 127-30, 141, 149, 154, 167, 197
Bank of Ireland, 94
Banking Commission of 1926, 17, 34-39
Banks, 15, 31; central, 37; credit supply, 28, 38, 71, 92, 133-35
Belfast, 206
Borrowing, 48, 85, 107, 127, 130; international, 92; percent of GNP, 155, 170, 182, 183, 187, 188, 194; requirement, 170, 187, 188, 200; targets, 151, 184, 188, 194, 200
Budget, 17, 74, 86, 201; deficit, 69, 85, 127, 165, 170-73, 182, 200; and jobs, 143, 189; and public service pay, 139; and social welfare, 137-38
*Building on Reality 1985-1987* (1984) 176-84, 185
Business: capital needs, 37, 38, 39, 133; confidence, 36, 59, 142, 200; government assistance, 38, 163, 190; management, 29, 61; methods, 20
Butter, 25, 30, 46, 49, 85, 155

Capital: availability, 38, 39, 92; expenditure, 93, 106, 107 (*see also* Public expenditure); flows to Ireland, 4, 6; foreign, 28, 31, 37, 130, 196; formation, 47, 57, 63, 84, 152, 166, 172, 183, 206; grants, 100, 157, 163; market, 37, 57, 161; private, 8, 20 21, 25; shortage, 5, 23, 28, 30, 34, 91, 93
Capital Investment Advisory Committee, 69-73, 81
Cattle, 73, 77; exports, 41, 51, 60, 117, 123, 130, 132, 138, 141. *See also* Livestock
Coal, 5, 26, 32
Commerce: credit facilities for, 34; Department of Industry and, 32, 33, 40, 41, 53, 55, 159, 164, 165
Commission on Agriculture (1922), 17, 18-22
Commission on Emigration (1954), 65-68
Committee on the Employment of the Poor in Ireland (1823), 5, 7
Committee on Industrial Organization (CIO) (1961), 98, 108, 109
Committee of Inquiry into Taxation on Industry (1953), 63-64
Common Agricultural Policy (CAP), 127, 136, 141, 155, 156, 205
Communication, 3, 8, 11
Congested Districts Board (1891), 12
Consumer prices, 117, 145, 149
Control of Manufactures Acts (1932, 1934), 69, 100, 108
Cosgrave Cabinet, 17
Cosgrave, Liam, 128
Cosgrave, William, 128
Cotton, 4
Cumann na nGaedheal, 16, 17, 40

Dail, 17, 24, 33, 40, 49, 109
Dairying, 16, 18, 28
Davitt, Michael, 10
Debt: government, 4, 37, 147, 155, 172, 182, 183-85, 186; service burden, 76, 84, 93, 141, 165, 199
Demand: foreign, 38, 42, 45, 53, 94, 120; internal, 76, 86, 129, 134, 147, 149, 154, 167, 169, 194, 206; labor, 7, 196
Demand management, 72, 84, 85, 90, 104, 106-7, 115, 206
deValera, Eamon, 40, 93
Devaluation, 154
Dublin, 52, 71, 140, 154, 177
Duties, protective, 18, 20, 23, 24, 25, 41, 59, 119, 120. *See also* Protection, Tariffs

EC. *See* European Community
*Economic Development* (1958), 54, 74-84, 86, 89, 90
Economic growth, 15, 141, 157, 167, 196-204; costs, 113, 130, 188, 201; European Community and, 124, 195, 198, 204; exports and, 57, 123, 135; government role, 69, 70-73, 137, 147, 149, 206-8; fiscal policy, 186, 187, 197, 200; need for, 71, 80, 112; nineteenth-century, 1, 2, 3, 4, 6, 9; policy, 31, 40, 91, 92, 122; rate, 85, 94, 111
Economic policy, 16, 17, 39, 41, 91, 109, 110, 185, 194, 199; external forces and, 128; nineteenth-century, 3-10; 1940s, 48; 1950s, 60, 61, 70, 74, 77
Economic War, 41, 205
Economies of scale, 5, 11
*Economist*, 194
Education, 80, 169, 173, 174, 177, 181, 194, 205; agricultural, 18, 20, 46, 205; commercial, 29; investment in, 97, 102, 104, 113, 114; technical, 11, 73, 92
EEC. *See* European Community
Efficiency: fiscal incentives and, 100; industrial, 52, 59, 67, 75, 98, 99, 185; labor, 27, 28, 203; management, 29; in public expenditure, 93, 173, 177, 182, 192

Elections: 1918, 17; 1932, 39; 1969, 110; 1977, 141, 142; 1981-82, 165, 176; 1987, 186
Emigration: Commission on Emigration (1954), 65-68; employment opportunities and, 31, 41, 57, 78, 90, 94, 100, 114, 123; before independence, 3, 7; 1920s, 39; 1930s, 51, 52; 1940s, 42, 45; 1950s, 86; 1960s, 96, 97, 125; 1970s, 114, 144-45; 1980s, 184, 185, 187, 194
Employment, 3, 5, 7, 21; agriculture, 42, 68, 94, 109-10, 140, 177, 184, 187, 196, 206; exports and, 98, 118, 122; goals, 66, 93, 96; government policy, 77, 107, 129-30, 191-94; growth, 100, 111, 112, 114; industry, 68, 94, 96, 132-35, 140, 147, 151-52, 158, 176, 192; 1920s, 39, 51; 1930s, 42, 51; 1940s, 45, 51-52; 1950s, 86; 1960s, 94, 125, 109-10; 1970s, 144-45, 149-50; protective duties and, 25, 41; public service, 143, 166, 172, 177, 183
EMS. *See* European Monetary System
Energy, 127, 130-32
Enterprise Allowance Scheme, 178
Enterprise Development Programme, 154
Entrepreneur, 4, 23, 30, 80, 93, 152, 153-54, 206; foreign, 31
European Community: comparison to Ireland, 148, 187; inflation in, 146, 170; Irish membership in, 95, 109, 110, 116-24; markets, 96, 98, 127, 136, 140, 168, 204, 207; population, 169, 175; productivity, 148, 150, 156, 158; underdeveloped regions, 137, 195
European Free Trade Area (EFTA), 90, 120
European Monetary System (EMS), 154, 155, 188, 199
European Recovery Program, 49, 50, 53, 54, 55, 85
European Recovery Programme: Ireland's Long Term Programme (1948), 50-52
Expectations of progress, 5, 15, 30, 39, 100, 111, 140
Export Board, 55
Exports: agricultural, 12, 19, 20, 35, 41, 46, 53, 89, 117, 123, 125, 130; competitiveness, 31, 63, 94, 98, 102, 105, 118, 130, 206; composition, 19, 30; European Community and, 120, 121, 123, 124-25, 204; incentives, 69, 100; industrial, 69, 85, 99, 120, 122, 151; markets, 35, 51, 53, 60, 128, 154, 167, 206; 1930s, 41; 1940s, 45; 1950s, 50, 51, 85; significance, 20, 95, 104, 122, 134, 167, 172, 197
External reserves, 83, 92, 107

Famine (1845-51), 2, 5, 6, 8-9, 10, 175, 206
Fanning, Ronan, 89
Farmers, 8, 10, 11, 16, 21, 24, 31, 40, 45-48, 73, 155-56
Farming, 9, 11, 20, 22, 31, 48, 50, 70
Fianna Fáil, 41, 62, 65, 93, 186
Finance, Department of, 81
Financial institutions, 92
Fine Gael, 41, 48, 65, 69, 93, 165, 194
Fiscal Inquiry Committee (1923), 17, 18, 22, 23-30, 31, 32, 108
Fiscal policy, 24, 92, 94, 97, 115, 117, 187-88, 200, 201
Flour industry, 4, 24, 26, 29
Foreign investment, 41, 63, 69, 73, 89, 92, 93, 108, 157
Free market, 3, 4, 8, 86, 206

Gold standard, 16, 35, 39
Government: borrowing, 48, 85, 127-30; debt, 4, 37, 185, 187, 188, 200; grants, 20, 49, 65, 69, 70, 98, 99-100, 108, 109, 117; role in economy, 43
Great Depression, 39, 40
Griffith, Arthur, 30, 40

Gross National Product (GNP), 42, 46, 85, 86, 87, 106; growth and decline, 153, 155, 184, 194, 195, 197; in Second Programme, 94, 96, 97, 104, 109, 111;

Haughey, Charles, 186
Home Rule, 6, 12, 15; League, 10
Health and hospitals, 75, 76, 90, 91, 114
Housing, 69, 77, 80, 91, 114
Human capital, 8, 110

Imports: capital, 196; domestic demand and, 49, 52, 84, 107, 115, 116, 167, 191; energy, 127, 131; European Community membership and, 119, 121; substitution, 152; World War II, 42, 45-46, 51
Incentives: domestic firms, 153, 159, 161, 164, 186; to foreign investors, 191; government, 65, 69, 100, 147
Incomes policy, 101, 102, 104, 105
Industrial Credit Company (ICC), 59, 93, 164
Industrial Development Authority (IDA), 55, 65, 69, 81, 100, 108, 109, 118, 133, 157, 164
Industrial Organization, Committee on (CIO) (1961), 98, 108, 109
Industrial Policy (1984), 157-65
Industry, 23, 30, 31, 41, 42, 47, 51-52, 54-55, 68; adaptation, 108; capital, 124, 132-33; competitiveness, 98, 99, 100, 101, 109, 118, 124, 138; credit requirements, 34, 92; Department of Industry and Commerce, 32, 33, 40, 41, 53, 55, 159, 164, 165; development, 18, 24, 30, 31, 41, 60, 133-34, 152-53; disadvantages, 26, 27, 28, 29; economic growth and, 123, 125, 135; efficiency, 52, 59, 67, 75, 98, 99, 185; employment, 68, 94, 97, 132-35, 140, 147, 151-52, 158, 176, 192; European Community membership and, 117, 119, 120, 121, 122, 125; exports, 69, 85, 99, 120, 122; foreign investment in, 147, 161, 176, 206; nineteenth-century, 3, 4, 5, 11, 12; 1950s, 93; Northern, 18; output, 41, 42, 45, 56, 100, 176, 177, 197; policy, 52, 55, 66, 157-65, 206; protection, 22, 25, 207; in Second Programme, 94, 95, 97-98, 104, 110; structure, 100
Inflation, 57, 58, 112, 146, 170
Infrastructure, 7, 11, 91
Ireland National Development Plan, 1989-1993 (1989), 196-204
Irish Congress of Trade Unions (ICTU), 108, 161, 186, 188, 189
Irish Free State, 33
Irish Tourist Board, 53, 54

Labor, 16, 28, 57, 58, 59; costs, 4, 27-28, 101, 121, 168; force, 82, 94, 100, 101, 125, 145, 149; management relations, 106; productivity, 23, 56, 92, 94, 105, 107, 146, 169, 185, 203; supply, 3, 6, 7, 26, 96, 120
Labour Party, 17, 48, 110
Laissez-faire, 6, 13, 204, 206
Land: annuities, 16, 41, 205; cost, 4, 155; demand, 5, 6; drainage and reclamation, 3, 7, 8, 11, 21, 48, 49, 50, 178, 206; labor ratio, 6-7, 9; ownership, 185; policy, 42; purchase, 10; question, 9; rents, 6, 10; supply, 7, 8; tenure, 3, 6, 7, 156
Land Acts: 1870, 9, 12; 1881, 10; 1949, 50
Land League, 10
Landlords, 9, 10
Lemass, Sean, 40, 41, 55, 69, 93, 109, 110
Linen industry, 11
Linkage, 120
Literacy, 181
Livestock, 50-51. *See also* Cattle; Sheep

Living standards, 41, 42, 56, 68, 78, 90, 92, 93, 96, 101, 107, 115, 166, 186; in the United Kingdom, 27, 112, 146
Lynch, Jack, 108, 110
Lynch, Patrick, 89

McEntee, Sean, 41
Malthus, T.R., 6, 7, 8
Management, 28-29, 80, 82, 98, 99, 123
Marketing, 19, 20, 23, 28, 29, 35, 46, 73, 98, 108, 120, 176, 194
*Membership of the European Communities: Implications for Ireland* (1970), 116-24

A *National Partnership* (1974), 128-40, 141
Natural resources, 6, 62, 67, 79, 80

Organization for Economic Cooperation and Development (OECD), 95
Output, 143, 147, 151, 166, 167, 171; export related, 91, 92, 95, 97, 98, 107; national, 1, 3, 18, 85, 90, 93, 100, 105, 112, 114, 115, 125. *See also* Agriculture; Industry

Planning, 74, 103, 110; difficulties of, 156, 205; Minister for Economic Development and Planning, 142; policy, 165, 207; targets, 91, 185, 195
Population: age, 169; decline, 3, 39, 86, 96; and domestic demand, 90, 95; growth, 94, 114, 125, 140, 149, 167, 173, 175; and labor force, 100, 145, 149; migration, 145, 187; problems, 5, 6, 65-68; World War II, 42
Price control, 59
Prices, 117, 129, 139, 145, 149, 158; agricultural, 10, 16, 19, 40, 47, 117, 123, 135, 136; competitive export, 41, 67, 106-7, 138, 146; import, 31, 41; oil crisis and, 127, 130, 132, 141, 154, 155; rising, 105, 116
Private enterprise, 8, 16, 42, 58, 64, 91, 93, 190; incentives, 58, 60
Productivity, 97, 99, 100, 101, 102, 147, 148, 150, 156, 158; agricultural, 8, 46, 53, 156, 178, 206; labor, 23, 56, 92, 94, 105, 107, 169, 198
Profits, 129, 137, 157
Profit incentives, 58-59, 153, 161
*Programme for Economic Expansion* (1958), 73, 89, 90-93, 94, 95, 101, 107
*Programme for National Recovery* (1987), 186-94
Protection, 22, 23, 25, 27, 30, 31, 41, 42, 49, 52, 54, 59, 66-68, 89; removal, 73, 75, 89, 99, 108, 119, 121, 123, 207. *See also* Duties; Tariffs
Public Capital Programme, 70, 91, 177
Public expenditure, 72, 76, 84, 85, 90, 128, 140, 141, 153, 177, 184, 187; borrowing for, 168, 188, 200; increases, 146, 149, 153; taxes and, 166, 170, 173, 201

Railways, 11, 30, 179
Real income, 5, 42, 75, 95, 97, 102, 141
Remittances, 36
*(Final) Report of the Banking Commission* (1926), 34-39
*Report of the Capital Investment Advisory Committee* (1958), 69-73
*Report of the Commission on Agriculture* (1922), 18-22
*Report of the Commission on Emigration* (1954), 65-68
*Report of the Committee of Inquiry into Taxation on Industry* (1953), 63-64
*Report of the Fiscal Inquiry Committee* (1923), 23-30
*Reports on Agricultural Policy* (1945), 46-48

Research and development, 99, 154, 157
Resources: material, 6, 11, 33-34, 115, 160, 169, 193; utilization, 90-91, 92, 107, 112, 114
*A Review of Irish Industrial Policy* (Telesis Report, 1982), 157-65
Roads, 7, 30, 177
Royal Commission on the Financial Relations between Great Britain and Ireland (1896), 12
Royal Commission on Irish Public Works (1888), 11
Royal Dublin Society, 22

Saving, 36, 84, 92, 97, 112, 114
*Second Programme for Economic Expansion, Part I* (1963), 93, 95-104
*Second Programme for Economic Expansion, Part II* (1964), 104-8, 109, 110
Select Committee on Emigration from the United Kingdom (1826, 1827), 7
Semi-state bodies, 32, 40, 42, 207
Services: development, 96, 100, 103, 134, 152, 177; export, 95, 97, 104, 105, 106, 159, 161, 162, 176
Shannon (River), 32, 33
Shannon Custom Free Zone, 119, 120
Shannon electrification scheme, 31, 33, 34
Sheep, 117
Sinn Fein, 16, 17, 40
Social investment, 84, 91
Social services, 40, 75-77, 84, 93, 118, 171-72, 181-82
Socialism, 110

Tariffs: European Community, 127, 140, 205; reduction or removal, 5, 99, 108, 119, 121, 132, 158; support for, 23, 24, 25, 41, 66, 67, 85, 86. *See also* Protection
Taxes: and development, 4, 40, 59, 63, 159, 160; new, 129, 139, 155, 166, 167; Pay as You Earn (PAYE), 171, 180, 189; policy, 40, 71, 84, 92, 117, 156, 179, 180, 188, 189-91, 200-1; Value Added Tax, 180
Technology, 4, 33, 187, 193, 206
Telesis Report (*A Review of Irish Industrial Policy*, 1982), 157-65, 206-7
Tenants, 9, 10, 91, 156, 181
Terms of trade, 41, 42, 53, 94, 154
Textile industry, 4, 61, 132, 140
*Third Programme for Economic and Social Development* (1969), 109, 110, 111-16, 121, 125
Three Fs, 10
Tillage, 18, 47
Tourism, 32, 49, 53-54, 85, 97, 102, 103, 179, 202
Trade: European Community, 119, 120, 121, 136, 196; free, 16, 17, 23, 31, 39, 89, 93, 98, 127, 152, 207; international, 20, 35, 51, 91, 159, 164, 168, 193, 194; restrictions, 4, 18, 41, 59
Trade unions, 15, 29, 103, 104, 105
Training, 53, 65, 80, 97, 98, 99, 104, 134, 178, 181
Transport, 26, 179
Turf, 32, 42, 55, 66, 131

Ulster, 3, 9, 17; custom, 11
Unemployment, 83, 93, 94, 125, 153, 155, 178, 191, 192; agricultural, 65, 68, 177; 1950s, 85, 86; 1970s, 140, 144, 145, 149, 151; 1980s, 158, 167, 171, 175, 184, 185, 187, 194
United Kingdom, 43, 148, 170; economic dependence on, 57, 60, 61, 122; economic relations with Ireland, 1, 12, 31, 41, 42, 45, 204; exports to, 50, 51, 53, 85, 136, 154, 167, 206; living standards, 27, 112, 146; monetary system, 34, 35, 36, 39; political relations with Ireland, 15, 16
United States, 43, 175; aid program, 48, 50, 85; migration to, 7, 39; tourism to Ireland, 53

Value Added Tax (VAT), 180

Wages: costs, 104, 170; level, 24, 27, 28, 40, 82, 101, 105, 155
*The Way Forward* (1982), 165-75, 176, 184, 185
Wheat, 23, 26, 117
Whitaker, T. K., 73, 74, 89, 90, 141, 185
Women, 115-16, 145, 180
Woolen industry, 25, 52
World War I, 15, 23
World War II, 39, 41, 42-43, 56, 205, 206

**About the Authors**

JAMES L. WILES is Professor of Economics at Stonehill College. He is the author of several articles that have appeared in scholarly and professional journals.

RICHARD B. FINNEGAN is Director of Irish Studies at Stonehill College. He is the author of *Ireland: The Challenge of Conflict and Change* (1983) and *Law and Politics in the International System* (1979).